TOXIC COWORKERS

How to Deal with Dysfunctional People on the Job

Alan A. Cavaiola, Ph.D.
Neil J. Lavender, Ph.D.

NEW HARBINGER PUBLICATIONS, INC.

Publisher's Note

This publication is designed to provide accurate and authoritative information in regard to the subject matter covered. It is sold with the understanding that the publisher is not engaged in rendering psychological, financial, legal, or other professional services. If expert assistance or counseling is needed, the services of a competent professional should be sought.

Distributed in Canada by Raincoast Books

Copyright © 2000 by Alan A. Cavaiola and Neil J. Lavender
New Harbinger Publications, Inc.
5674 Shattuck Avenue
Oakland, CA 94609

Cover design by Poulson/Gluck Design
Cover image from Comstock, Inc.
Edited by Carole Honeychurch
Text design by Michele Waters

MIX

Paper from
responsible sources

FSC® C011935

Library of Congress number: 00-134870

ISBN-10 1-57224-219-1
ISBN-13 978-1-57224-219-7

Printed in the United States of America

New Harbinger Publications' website address: www.newharbinger.com

15   14   13

20   19   18   17   16   15   14   13

Contents

CHAPTER 1

The Problem with Personality Disorders

When we told our friends and family that we were entertaining the idea of writing a book on personality disorder in the workplace, we had a very intriguing reaction. A smile of recognition would come to their faces and they would say something like "Oh, why don't you come to where I work? There's enough there to give you material for *three* books! I'm working for this guy who . . ." They would then go on to tell their stories about some individual at work who was continuously making them crazy. The following is not untypical:

> Here's something to put in your book. I work with this guy who's driving me nuts. He is the most inconsiderate bastard I've ever met. We share an office together, and we're both supposed to answer the phone, but he never does. It could be two feet away, but he just lets it ring until I pick it up. And, when I'm on the phone, he talks to me and asks me questions, getting upset if I don't interrupt my call and answer him right away. We're supposed to alternate Friday afternoons off, but he's taken the last four; each time he says he's got some kind of family emergency. Yesterday, he tossed some papers on my desk and told me to take them to Janice (the secretary) while he went for a cup of coffee! When I refused, he got right up to my face and screamed, "Just do it!" I go to the boss to complain, but she gets annoyed with me and tells me we all have to get along here. She wants me to try to "understand" him because he's a good sales rep. The boss sat down with the both of us to discuss our "personality differences" but she missed the whole point. I think I'm going to start looking for another job.

Often the stories that people told us were quite amazing, describing behavior that was next to unbelievable. What struck us even more was that, with rare exception, everyone seemed to have a horror story, no matter who we talked to: our family, our students, and our patients (even our coworkers and book editors we submitted this manuscript to!). It seemed like everyone had somebody who was driving them crazy at work.

The reader must understand that we're not talking about the normal types of spats or the occasional head butting that arises from time to time at work. The type of stories that we heard were far more destructive and damaging. These disturbing individuals had a way of getting under their coworker's skin, to the point where they obsessed about them night and day, even to the point of dreaming about them. Often, the people we talked to identified interactions with these people as the most stressful part of their jobs. One hospital employee complained so much about one of his coworkers that his wife threatened to leave him if he continued to complain about the guy or to take one more day off! Another man spent almost every minute of his psychotherapy session talking about an inefficient and obstructionistic subordinate who he could not get to do even a small portion of his assigned duties. We discovered that it is not unusual for people to take medications before they go to work for the sole purpose of helping them cope with some disturbing person at work.

When we began to look into this phenomenon more deeply, we were struck by the dearth of literature dealing with these issues. Most of the research dealt with the understanding of how "normal" individuals relate in a corporate setting. However, it's not the psychologically healthy coworker or boss who keeps people up worrying all night; it's the psychologically unsound boss or coworker who one worries about, talks about, and obsesses over. It is those situations in which one feels trapped, abused, demeaned, and powerless that keep one exhausted, angry, and frustrated. There are bosses who harass and treat individuals unfairly, often picking as their "favorites" some poor, hardworking employee whose life becomes a wreck as a result. And yes, there is also the employee who is stifled by a difficult administrator who will not allow a new idea to generate without either stifling it or somehow taking credit that is undeserved, and this can be just as frustrating. And it is not just our bosses who drive us crazy. There are also those administrators who spend countless hours dealing with troubled employees who refuse work assignments, who undermine the overall well-being of the organization, or who sabotage anything productive. Human resources staff spend countless hours trying to come up with strategies to deal with personality conflicts between coworkers or between management and staff. We're certain that there are work sites that do function as one big happy family; however, it has been our experience that what may appear to be a happy family to the outside world is often filled with turmoil once one looks beneath the veneer.

These problems caused by difficult people at work can create enormous disturbances and disruptions in our lives. Some are really amazing in their cruelty, self-centeredness, and lack of compassion. For example, one man in his early twenties and just out of college found that he was drinking every day, just to face his boss. He worked for a small company that designed custom software. The boss was also the owner. It was a very small company with only five or so employees. Consequently, the patient was forced to have almost constant contact with the boss. The boss was a very angry man who expressed his anger in extremely passive aggressive ways. For example, one day the patient could not immediately locate one of his computer disks. The boss waited impatiently while he searched for it and eventually found it. About two days later, the young man discovered that other disks were missing. The man was terrified because the project was due shortly and the disks were needed to complete the project. He was baffled because he had put the disks in a safe place. The poor guy worked late several evenings to redo the work on the missing disks. When he was through, his boss approached him with the original disks in his hand—he had had them all along! "This will teach you a valuable lesson," he said in his most preachy tone, "to always organize your work efficiently." The fact that the boss was highly inefficient himself made this statement even more bizarre.

This story represents only one example of many similar stories we've heard from our patients, friends, and coworkers over the years. Our own study of personality factors and stress in the workplace showed that over 80 percent of our sample worked with at least one individual whose behavior was a significant source of stress for them (Cavaiola & Lavender 1999). Moreover, when asked what types of problems these coworkers, bosses, and subordinates caused, the type of characteristics people found most troublesome were similar to or identical to may of the personality disorders described in this book.

Personality disorders are a special group of psychological disorders of which the general public and most workplaces are unaware. They are distinctly different and potentially more malignant than other types of disorders, such as depression or anxiety. Personality disorders present a vital challenge to the workplace, because working with an individual with a personality disorder can be one of the most stressful things a worker will encounter on the job. This book will teach you how to deal with them.

What Are Personality Disorders?

Although we will be discussing specific personality disorders in greater detail throughout this book, a general introduction is useful here. Personality disorders are long-standing disturbances in personality that usually begin in late adolescence and continue throughout adulthood. They reveal themselves when an individual engages in repetitive patterns of nonproductive interactions with others, which is a manifestation of the impaired aspects of their personality. Personality disorders cause a person to consistently act in disturbing patterns of behavior in both occupational and social relationships. Almost always, people afflicted with personality disorders are unaware of the impact that their behavior can have on those around them—often they are unaware of having a problem at all. There are many different types of personality disorder all of which we will be addressing in the book. The following are some short descriptions. Keep in mind that an individual can have traits of several different types of personality disorders; there really is no one "pure" type. Also, personality-disordered people can have different intensities or severity of their disorder. Some mild cases can be quite productive and function "normally." More detailed descriptions of each personality disorder will be found in subsequent chapters.

- *Paranoid*: Highly suspicious, distrusting, cold.

- *Schizoid*: No desire for human closeness. No close friends. Doesn't understand people and their needs.

- *Schizotypal*: Really odd, even bizarre. Likely to say something like, "The boss yelled at me, but I didn't care. My body kind of left the room." One schizotypal we knew lived in his car.

- *Antisocial*: No or little sense of morals. Motto is "Do unto others. Then leave." Mostly male.

- *Narcissistic*: Self-centered and grandiose to the point where he or she can't consider another's point of view. If narcissism is not too bad, they can be highly effective, usually attracted to leadership positions. Their motto is "What have you done for me lately?"

- *Histrionic*: Dramatic, flamboyant, overemotional, and shallow. Mostly female.

- *Borderline*: Moody, angry, with highly intense and stormy relationships. Probably the most likely to litigate. Hold on for one wild roller coaster ride!

- *Obsessive Compulsive:* Overconscientious, picky, obsessed with details and timeliness. Very perfectionistic. Like narcissists, likely to be successful if disorder is not too bad.

- *Avoidant:* Afraid of taking risks to have a relationship. Corporate wallflowers.

- *Dependent:* Can't make individual decisions; needs constant reassurance. Good but insecure team player, often loyal to company. These individuals are often referred to as codependent.

- *Passive Aggressive:* Angry, but won't show it overtly. Covert expressions of anger include inefficiency, blaming management and other authority figures, tardiness, and other quietly obstructionistic behavior.

Each of the various personality types described above have certain traits or characteristics that make them unique and, in some ways, predictable. In certain instances, these traits can be very functional and self-promoting. In other instances, such as when personality disorders are too strong, the affected person's behavior becomes dysfunctional, self-defeating, and highly disruptive to the social fabric of the workplace. For example, if you go to an internist for an ache or a pain, you expect the doctor to be thorough in their investigation of whatever is bothering you. You would want every possible cause investigated. In this instance, an internist with obsessive-compulsive traits would not be entirely self-defeating. The traits may even be self-enhancing, in that he or she is likely to be perceived as being thorough, competent, and professional. However, if this internist's demeanor is perceived as cold, scientific, uncaring, or uncompassionate (which are traits often ascribed to the obsessive compulsive), then these obsessive-compulsive traits become self-defeating. It is often difficult for such an individual to modify or change such behavior, because personality traits, and hence personality disorders, are so enduring and because these behaviors may be perceived by the individual as having several payoffs or benefits—being able to picture themselves as perfect, for example. This would be the case with the internist described above, who would tend to see him or herself as someone who makes sound, well-considered clinical decisions and judgments.

In the chapters that follow, we will provide other illustrations of the functionality, or the useful aspects, of various symptoms of personality disorders. This is very much like the old joke that goes: A woman walks into a psychiatrist's office and says, "Doc, my husband thinks he's a hen." The psychiatrist replies, "Well, bring him in, and I'll treat him" to which the wife replies, "I can't—we need the eggs." For many, the reluctance to give up symptoms that have certain perceived payoffs becomes their way of saying, "I don't want to change—I need the eggs!"

Although we would like to say that the personality types we will be discussing are discrete and mutually exclusive, this is not the case. In each of the chapters to follow, for example, we will outline a particular personality or character type. However, as you begin to identify individuals whom you may work with, you may observe that they fit under several of the descriptors' not just one. Take, for example, an individual with Attention Deficit Disorder (which is not a personality disorder), who also has Avoidant Personality Disorder. This individual may have difficulty focusing on tasks or working on projects for a sustained period of time. In addition when they fall behind in their work, they may avoid dealing directly about the problem with their supervisor or manager. Another problem is that people with personality disorders often are unaware that they possess problematic personalities; in fact, they may be quite proud of the very traits that are disturbing! For example, a person with Obsessive Compulsive Personality Disorder will often pride themselves on being meticulous. An individual with Antisocial Personality Disorder might see his lack of morality as a sign that he is more intelligent than others, able to "get over on stupid people" and take advantage of others before they take advantage of him. As a result, individuals with personality disorders are unlikely to see themselves as the source of their problem. More importantly, they are highly resistant to any change process that involves correcting their own behavior. It's not difficult to see why these individuals wreak havoc in the workplace.

The need for social interaction is a part of being human. It's not surprising, therefore, that problems occuring in the business environment are so often "people problems." As much as we wish to see corporations as holistic entities, they are simply collections of individual people. And, in spite of sophisticated office equipment, dazzling websites, and e-mail-driven days, businesses are run by *individuals*, who come to the job with personality patterns that are unique, intricate, subtle, and that may contain traits threatening to the organization. When those people's abilities are hampered by the dysfunctional personality traits, the goals of the organization are not met efficiently. Although it's true that not all "people problems" in an organizational setting are caused by personality disorders, we believe that these problems are more frequent than most organizations are aware of. Moreover, we've seen how this problem can function like a hidden cancer, slowly and persistently sucking the life out of productive and viable organizations by creating inefficient management, sexual harassment, excessive litigation, escalating expenses, and job-related stress. The magnitude of the problems that these people cause for their organizational settings are of such astounding proportions that they may be immeasurable. Organizations are forced to waste hours of time resolving disputes, fielding and responding to countless memos, refereeing endless battles, or, when the problems get worse, going to court. Many corporations have been crippled as a result of an individual with a personality disorder.

Types of Problems

Below are some specific ways people with personality disorders cause significant problems in the workplace. These problems are not confined to just corporate leaders but to all employees of an organization. As we will see later, the impact of personality disorders is not just confined to the afflicted individual but also affects those who work with that person.

Stress

Individuals with personality disorders often heighten job stress for their coworkers. Most workplaces are considered to be highly stressful. Many people consider their jobs to be the greatest sources of stress in their lives, especially given that most of us spend at least 50 to 75 percent of our waking hours at work. With this amount of stress, even small imperfections in an individual's personality structure can crack under the unbearable pressures of today's workplace. Perhaps with the exception of a few work settings, work-related stress appears to be an unavoidable fact of life. Stress research has identified several sources of work stress including low pay, long hours, high demands for productivity, ambiguous job roles, and poor working conditions. While positive relationships with coworkers can help buffer this stress, it appears that, when there are negative interactions, personality conflicts, or problems, this can often be a major source of work stress. Work stress can often bring out the worst in people. Individuals with personality disorders often will crack under the stress and end up taking out their stress on others. Such would be the case with a narcissistic administrator who, under fire and criticism from the company president, might turn on a subordinate, criticizing them for being lazy or incompetent. In doing so, the administrator deflects or displaces their stress on to their subordinate, thereby making their life into a living hell. It is estimated that approximately 25 percent of the nation's workforce suffers from an anxiety disorder or a stress-related illness which causes the worker to miss approximately sixteen to twenty-two days per year and also results in poor morale. About one in five employees suffers from some type of mental disorder and mental disorders are exacerbated by increased levels of stress (Dauer 1989; Moffie et al. 1985). Moreover, it is stressful to deal with stressed individuals! And as the stress of the workplace grows ever greater, personality disordered individuals find themselves becoming more distressed and will often cause even more stress for those around them. Many corporations are presently addressing stress management through workshops, in-house fitness centers, and educational sessions on wellness. Some companies even offer a nap room for their employees. However, most organizations usually neglect to deal with the interpersonal aspects of stress. There are in some cases Employee Assistance Counselors who are called in to troubleshoot these types of work group problems, but in our experience, there are few corporations that go to these lengths.

Power Abuses

One of the primary ways that workers with personality disorders disrupt a work environment is by abusing power. This is one way they increase stress for coworkers, as we mentioned before, and this abuse can cause myriad other problems in the workplace. There are many different types of power that each individual may have. It is obvious that certain administrative or managerial positions give one the authority to make decisions involving others. We are all aware of horror stories in which bosses or managers abuse this power. Sexual harassment is probably at the top of the list of such abuses. However, consider also the person who works in the repair shop of his company, a shop that's crucial to the maintenance of company machinery. By deliberately slowing down his repair of needed instruments, this employee can, in effect, grind the operations of the company down to a halt. This is an abuse of power that may very well go unnoticed but has substantial consequences.

What are some other abuses of power? It's not uncommon for supervisors or administrators to demand more work for less pay. When the worker tries to rectify such a situation he may be confronted with the attitude that they should feel lucky to even have a job. This is abusive. When someone's job responsibilities are not clearly defined, delineated, and agreed upon, it can result in abuse. When a worker is subjected to demeaning comments, is excluded from decisions that directly effect their ability to do their job, or their expertise is diminished in some way, they are in an abusive situation. When an administrator makes decisions arbitrarily, promotes arbitrarily, or gives raises or bonuses out arbitrarily, it can constitute abuse. We have also witnessed several instances where companies have merged and many managers were given increased responsibilities for other departments within the newly merged company, with no pay, no recognition, no promotion. This, too, is abusive. These types of abuses can often be a function of corporate politics or even the politics of downsizing. However, this is not always the case. In some instances there may be an antisocial personality, one who has no compassion or guilt when it comes to manipulating people for their own ends. The narcissistic personality will protect their pay and title, even if it ends up costing more crucial jobs. For example, a Midwestern medical center recently laid off several of their nursing staff, thus jeopardizing direct patient care, while retaining about a dozen vice presidents and two interior designers. Our guess is that this kind of absurd situation is often the work of narcissistic decision makers concerned more with protecting their interests than in doing the right thing.

Keep in mind that abuse can run both ways. One doesn't have to be the boss to misuse power. For example, the employee who refuses to complete a needed work assignment on time may be using passive-aggressiveness to wield power. An employee who is continually negative about every idea for change uses their negativity to wield power. People's expressed attitudes toward others can be very abusive. The employee who goes after an administrator by running them into the ground at every turn, or who goes behind that administrator's back with a problem to another administrator is being abusive with their power. While an undergraduate, one of the authors worked as an aide in a state psychiatric hospital. Assigned to the graveyard shift were two male aides. One, in particular, was a horrendous employee. He would often not show up for work, or report to his shift late. He frequently had alcohol on his breath, and whenever the head nurse would confront him on his absenteeism or tardiness, he would tell her off, exasperating her with his confrontational behavior. He would then usually find a cozy place to sleep the rest of the shift away. Although he had disciplinary actions filed against him constantly, he would usually shape up long enough to get the administrators off his back. Then he would go right back to his old behaviors. His coworkers would joke that the only way Ed would ever get fired was if he killed a patient—and admitted it. Ed was a classic example of Narcissistic Personality Disorder in that he felt rules did not apply to him. He felt that he was above having to do menial tasks or having to function like his coworkers. In Ed's narcissistic view, reporting to work on time or calling in if he were taking off from work were inconveniences.

Sexual harassment and sexual abuse often constitute yet another form of an abuse of power. All too often, people in positions of power use that power to take sexual advantage of another. Most workplaces have become highly sensitized to issues of sexual abuse and are adopting stringent and highly detailed policies regarding sexual harassment and attending sexual harassment seminars has become a staple in corporate life.

We often see cases of sexual harassment and sexual abuse being committed by people with either Antisocial, Borderline, or Narcissistic Personality Disorders. These disorders share an egocenticity or self-centeredness, which often results in rule and boundary violations. So, when one of these individuals makes an inappropriate sexual advance or comment, they often see nothing wrong with their behavior and often will justify it with a host of rationalizations or excuses, such as, "She was coming on to me," or "I thought she would be flattered by my advances."

A female retail-store clerk named Susan had begun to have problems with her boss about a month into the job. The boss knew that this young woman was a single parent who desperately needed this job in order to support herself and her six-month-old child. She described that her boss would often make lewd remarks about what she was wearing or about her figure. This progressed to where he would grope her when she was working in the back room. One evening, Susan found herself the only employee left in the store with her boss. His advances became more aggressive and, if it were not for the security guard who happened to be making rounds early that evening, Susan would have surely been raped. Susan was clearly traumatized and resigned from the job. She did seek legal counsel but was told that it would be difficult to prove her case unless other workers came forward on her behalf.

It's very possible that Susan fell victim to a boss with Antisocial Personality Disorder. It was later discovered that he had sexually harassed several other female workers in this and a prior position he held, at another retail store. He also had been let go from a prior job for embezzling funds. As with many individuals with Antisocial Personality Disorder, he had not the slightest bit of remorse for his actions.

Violence in the workplace, an extreme type of power abuse, is an area where personality disordered individuals may have a huge impact. In this case, knowing how to recognize and deal with personality disorders could save lives. According to the Bureau of Justice Statistics of the U.S. Department of Justice, workplace violence represented 15 percent of all violent acts committed in 1994. Over one million people were victims. Besides crimes of homicide, battery, and rape, a work environment that is high tech becomes a breeding ground for crimes such as computer sabotage and e-mail harassment. Violence in the workplace is also the leading cause of deaths in the workplace for working women. In 1992, 750 lives were lost.

These types of crimes are often committed by individuals with personality disorders (Dykeman 1995). Again we often find that individuals with Paranoid, Antisocial, or Borderline Personality Disorders are often at highest risk for workplace violence. These personality disorders are often the most volatile or erratic and, therefore, may be the most prone to resorting to violence in order to achieve their aim.

What Personality Disorders Cost

Workplace disruptions brought on by personality disorders, including increased stress, the abuse of power, and comorbid conditions, cause corporations to lose money. Individuals with personality disorders often cause their organizations to run in a highly inefficient manner, potentially costing the corporation millions. One highly visible and growing problem has been one of prolonged and costly litigation. For example, the median compensatory award in wrongful termination cases topped $200,000 in 1995, up 45 percent from the year before. Workers with personality disorders often cause corporations to pay millions in damages to victims of their behavior. But, bear in mind that this problem is two pronged. Not only do corporations often have to pay for the damage PD (personality disordered) people have wrought against others, but they must often pay for the damage that workers with PDs believe has been done *to them*. Up until this point, we have only talked about perpetrators of harassment and violence as being afflicted with a personality disorder. However, people's perception of themselves as victims can often stem from personality disorders as well. As the number of cases litigated increases, it is becoming more and more clear that individuals with personality disorders are often those involved in harassment and discrimination suits in the workplace as either the victim or the persecutor. But, either as victim or perpetrator many individuals with personality disorders have personality traits that are in some ways harmful to those around them (e.g., suspiciousness, manipulativeness, anger, etc.) often resulting in litigation. Presently, our legal system is beginning to recognize the fact that harassment and discrimination cases often involve individuals with personality disorders who are either the plaintiffs or defendants in these cases. Individuals with personality disorders can often misinterpret the actions of others and act unreasonably, yet rationalize their own dysfunctional behavior. "To the personality-disordered individual, 'believing is seeing'"(McDonald & Lees-Haley 1996, p.76).

Another costly legal consideration involving individuals with personality disorders is whether or not a personality disorder can be considered a disability and therefore be "accommodated for" under the Americans with Disabilities Act (ADA). An understanding of personality disorders may indeed be the key to coping with the high levels of litigation and the often astronomical costs they bring. Although personality-disordered individuals can cost their companies millions, the real issues that motivate these individuals have only recently been identified.

The direct and observable costs, however, are just the tip of the iceberg. Most of the costs that these personality-disordered individuals incur to an organization are astronomical but difficult to measure, because the costs are not as conspicuous as other, more obvious, employee-related costs. For example, if Mrs. Jones, a middle manager for a financial institution, becomes depressed, she is referred to the Employee Assistance Counselor, who does an initial assessment and then usually refers her for treatment. This treatment would be covered, at least partially, under her health insurance plan. If Mr. Smith, a union worker at a automotive assembly plant, comes to work under the influence of alcohol, he will also be assessed by the Employee Assistance Counselor and most likely referred to an alcohol rehab program. These are obvious cases with palpable costs and outcomes. If, however, Mr. Allen, a narcissistic middle manager for a large medical laboratory, verbally abuses his staff, ignores cost-saving ideas, or continuously makes administrative decisions that only benefit him, then he will incur enormous hidden costs. What are some of these costs? Higher rates of absenteeism; undermining loyal employees' commitment to the organization; reduction in employee self-esteem, creating a sense of malaise, high turnover and retraining costs; higher levels of stress accompanied by increases in stress-related accidents; resistance to new managerial directives; counsel fees; litigation including high settlement fees and jury awards; just to name a few. And the number of hours spent discussing the problems will increase until Mr. Allen is eventually identified as the problem. And, in the case of a well-paid, high-profile administrator, it could often take years before workers are willing to come forward to address the adminstrator's problems. Unfortunately, the "real" problem, the underlying personality disorder of the administrator, is never identified. After all, how many people know that self-centeredness, an inability to see another's perspective, and a lack of empathy constitute a legitimate psychiatric disorder?

Furthermore, what management has historically seen as damaging behaviors, such as disobedience, job-related accidents, wasted supervisory time, procrastination, and chronic absenteeism may indeed have at their foundation a personality-disordered individual. Even more psychologically rooted problems, such as anxiety, depression, and substance abuse, may be a direct consequence of a personality disorder. Addressing these problems without treating the underlying personality disorder can only be fruitless. And because problems caused by personality disorders work in a type of slow, erosive manner, their impact is often hard to detect. But their cumulative effects can often cause tremendous eruptions that can bring day-to-day business operations to an abrupt halt. We believe that in some of the more dramatic cases, the downfall of many corporations can be traced back to one or more key players who had a personality disorder.

Like a hidden cancer, personality disorders gradually infect the entire body of the orgainization, undetected and proliferating. We believe that at the root of the stickiest personnel problems there lies an undetected, insidious personality disorder. We realize that this is a strong statement to make. But we believe it is all too true. The financial costs of this problem are enormous but the personal damage to those employees who must interact with a personality-disordered coworker are incalculable. While the broader problem remains unaddressed, it becomes essential that workers learn how to best cope with their coworkers afflicted with a PD.

Who Should Read This Book?

As you know, work occupies at least half of the waking hours of most Americans. This does not even include those times spent commuting to and from the workplace; the time spent performing work-related tasks outside of the workplace; or talking about work-related issues, problems, and plans. Having worked as clinical psychologists for the past twenty-two years, we've found that it's not unusual for the issue of work to come up as a source of grist for the therapeutic mill. After all, there are very few jobs in which people work in isolation from others. Therefore, our work lives become a series of social interactions in which we are performing tasks with others, for others, and to others. It's obvious that work is, by and large, a social phenomenon and we are social creatures. We like our relationships at work to run smoothly. We want to enjoy the pleasant company of our coworkers. We *like* our jobs if we get along with those we work with. Therefore, we could say that this book is written for anyone who works and has some type of relationship with another person on the job. However, it would be more reasonable to recommend it to anyone who finds themselves troubled by the social interactions in their work, anyone who is plagued by inefficiency of their workgroup, anyone who finds themselves in an abusive work situation, or anyone who finds their work or productivity thwarted or inhibited by the interactions within their workplace. Please keep in mind that we did not write this book solely for executives, administrators, or managers. It wasn't written just for line staff or employees, either, but is really meant to cover a wide range of problems and situations that make your workplace difficult. We wrote this book to share the information we have gleaned through our training and experience with you so that you can better cope with the problems that corrupt your workplace.

How to Read This Book

There are two ways to approach this book. First, you will readily be able to identify many of the problem characters or personality types that you work with. This may help provide some validation of what you're experiencing and some recommendations for how to best deal with those difficult personalities and situations. The second way to read this book is with the idea of self-exploration. As with even the most dysfunctional family, even the sanest member gets affected, even the sanest member plays a role. It is often the same in a dysfunctional workplace. Therefore, it's important to look upon these writings with some introspectiveness. Remember, if you're not part of the solution, you may be part of the problem. You might want to look at changes that you need to make, first, in order to bring about change within the organization.

The next chapter gives an overview of personality disorders. It will give you a much better understanding of the problems you may be dealing with. Subsequent chapters will explore each type of personality disorder in greater detail. These chapters will provide useful information on how to deal with personality-disordered individuals whether they be your supervisors, subordinates, or coworkers. We will guide you in identifying what type(s) of personality disorders you may be dealing with.

You might have a toxic coworker whom you wish to deal with *immediately*. In that case, you can jump to the chapters appropriate to that coworker. If the toxic person seems odd, strange, and distant, begin with chapters 11 and 12 first. If they appear dramatic, domineering, stormy, or manipulative, read chapters 3, 4, 5, and 6 first. If the coworker appears anxious, picky, or perfectionistic, you may wish to begin by reading chapters 7, 8, 9, and 10.

We believe that people affected by personality-disordered individuals should not wait for management to act; rather, they should arm themselves with effective tactics to protect themselves and their families. Up until now, there hasn't been a whole lot of information out there on how to do that. Both the business and therapeutic communities need to meet the challenge to learn how to effectively help workers with personality disorders and how to handle the problems the disorders cause. This book is an effort in that direction. But these problems are affecting you now, so you can begin by arming yourself with the information and tactics in this book.

Our hope is that reading this book will make you, in a sense, a more informed coworker, capable of making a pretty accurate diagnosis and formulating and executing a "treatment plan." But the treatment plan is for yourself rather than the treatment of another individual (getting a license to practice psychology and "treat" these individuals is considerably harder than reading a book!). In some cases, you will be gaining knowledge that heretofore has been reserved for clinically trained professionals, and your ability and effectiveness in dealing with these individuals should increase dramatically. You will be able to identify the problems caused by your personality-disordered coworkers and be more sensitive in the detection of their symptoms. It is our hope that, as a result of reading this book, the workplace—and you—will function better. Heck, you might even enjoy going to work!

CHAPTER 2

Introduction to Personality Disorders: Our Cast of Characters

Human relationships are, by far, the most complex and intriguing experiences that we will have during our lifetimes. They are of tremendous import to our self-esteem and well-being. Our lives are vibrant and full when we have successful and loving relationships with our families, when we can have trusted friends and be with good coworkers, or when we fall in love. Conversely, we are forlorn when divorce, loneliness, arguments with loved ones, and interpersonal conflicts in the workplace frequent our days. We're significantly diminished when good relationships leave our lives. Most of the energy we expend during our typical day is in the pursuit, maintenance, and the enjoyment of good relationships. However, try as they might, some people just can't seem to "get it right": they argue incessantly with others, they can't seem to fall in love and stay in love, they always seem to have hidden agendas, and they seem to be overly sensitive. It seems that they don't appear to understand the subtleties and complexities of human interaction, and yet they don't recognize this deficit in themselves (although they can be quite vocal about it in others!). We are certain that you've met such people in your life.

This lack of ability to interact with others in a productive manner is so corrosive and detrimental to the person's being that it can actually be a form of mental disorder when it becomes too intense. Mental-health professionals call this type of disorder a personality disorder, a term you were introduced to in chapter 1. Personality disorders are separate and distinct from other types of mental disorders in a number of ways that we will address shortly.

Identifying, defining, and diagnosing personality disorders can be a tricky business. Mental-health professionals often conceptualize mental disorders from different theoretical perspectives, using different technical vocabularies. This can often be very confusing to professionals, let alone the lay person. Consequently, there is a reference guide that we use to eliminate a lot of the confusion. *The Diagnostic and Statistical Manual of Mental Disorders, Fourth Edition* (DSM-IV) is a book that sets the guidelines for diagnosing mental disorders. It is "The Bible" of all abnormal psychology texts in that it provides what are considered the standard and universally accepted definitions of mental disorders. It allows mental health professionals to communicate with each other about various disorders without resorting to pet theories or faddish terminologies. In short, if it isn't in DSM-IV, it probably isn't a legitimate disorder.

DSM-IV defines a personality disorder as "an enduring pattern of inner experience and behavior that deviates markedly from the expectation of the individual's culture, is pervasive and inflexible, has an onset in adolescence or early adulthood, is stable over time, and leads to distress or impairment (American Psychiatric Association 1994, 633)." Additionally, DSM-IV states that, in order to be diagnosed as having a personality disorder, one has to have ". . . impairment in social, occupational, or other important areas of functioning." It is precisely the area of occupational functioning that this book addresses. In the chapters that follow, we'll attempt to describe the symptoms of each specific personality disorder. This chapter will deal with symptoms that are common to all or most personality disorders.

We should point out that there are some differences in the way psychologists conceptualize personality disorders. On the one hand, there are psychologists that see personality disorders as discrete categories or distinct clinical syndromes. Like the measles, either a person has it, or they don't. Others believe, however, that personality disorders represent "maladaptive variants of personality traits that merge imperceptibly into normality and into one another" (American Psychiatric Association 1994, 633) They see personality disorders as a sort of spectrum reflecting various types of personality traits. Experts in the field of mental health are still investigating this issue.

Types of Personality Disorders

DSM-IV describes ten different types of personality disorders. There is the possibility that additional ones exist, but there is not enough definitive research on these at this time. The personality disorders listed seem to form what psychologists call "clusters," or groups of disorders that are similar to each other. Presently, there are three clusters: The "A" cluster, which can be described as odd or eccentric; the "B" cluster, who are dramatic and manipulative; and the "C" cluster, which comprises a grouping of personality disorders that are all somewhat fearful or anxious. Although we will devote a chapter each to the most important ones, including ways to deal with each, we'll begin here with a short description of each cluster.

The A Cluster

The person with Paranoid Personality Disorder is overly suspicious and distrusting of the motives of others around him. The Schizoid Personality Disorder is aloof from others and really does not wish to have social interactions. The Schizotypal Personality Disorder is often bizarre and embodies the words "odd" and "weird." Some people say that this type of personality disorder is related to the more severe psychotic disorder of schizophrenia, but in a milder form.

The B Cluster

The person with Narcissistic Personality Disorder is characterized by a sense of overinflated self-esteem and entitlement. Their constant need to be admired often brings them into positions of leadership. The Histrionic Personality Disorder includes symptoms of being overly emotional, shallow in relationships, and in constant need of attention. The person with Antisocial Personality Disorder lacks a sense of morality and empathy for the well-being of others. It is found most commonly in men. People with Borderline Personality Disorder have intense and stormy relationships, are angry and moody (sometimes suicidal), and lack a sense of identity. Borderline Personality Disorder presents one of the most arduous of challenges for both mental health workers and people who come into contact with them in the workplace.

The C Cluster

This cluster contains people who are overly anxious. Perhaps the most recently popularized has been Dependent Personality Disorder, which has been colloquially referred to as "codependency." People with this disorder are overly reliant on others for security and self-esteem. They seem unable to make independent decisions and suffer deeply when an individual "abandons" them, as in divorce. The person with Obsessive Compulsive Personality Disorder is overly moralistic, perfectionistic, and critical. They can become so obsessed with details that they miss the main goal of the task. These people can often be excellent workers if the disorder is not too extreme. This personality disorder is not to be confused with Obsessive Compulsive Disorder, which is characterized by ritualistic obsessions and compulsions such as worrying about dirt and washing their hands constantly. It's possible, even fairly common, for a person to have both of these disorders (see, we told you it can be confusing!). But this book will deal only with the *personality disorder* and not the *disorder* which are two separate things. Finally, the person with Avoidant Personality Disorder will not engage in social relationships unless they are guaranteed acceptance by the other person. The risk of embarrassment in social situations is so great that they avoid social interactions, hence the name Avoidant Personality Disorder.

Mixing It Up

It is quite rare for a person to have a pure form of a personality disorder. Most people with personality disorders actually have traits of other personality disorders as well, especially traits from other disorders in their cluster. Thus, a person with Narcissistic Personality Disorder will often have some of the traits of Histrionic or Borderline. One way of looking at personality disorders is that they are like colors. Most colors in our world are not of pure hue but rather are a mixture of different shades that comprise various colors. Colors also vary in brightness, and the same is true of personality disorder. Some people have a more intense form of a personality disorders than do others. One Avoidant man might be much more intense in his symptomology than another with the same disorder. In fact, all of us have at least some mild form of personality disorder, but it's not usually severe enough to cause major difficulties in our lives. So, you probably have seen yourself in some of these descriptions. But before you race off to contract for sessions with your local psychotherapist you should read on. Keep in mind while your reading that it is useful to conceptualize all personality disorders as having both positive *and* negative traits. For example, one can be altruistic and empathic to the needs of others. But the person with Dependent Personality Disorder will take these very positive traits to extreme lengths, perhaps neglecting their own needs to the point of endangering their health. Furthermore as we will see later on, mild forms of personality disorders may also produce certain strengths in people. Who would want to go to a physician who was not somewhat obsessive compulsive, meaning perfectionist, dedicated to details, and concerned with cleanliness? Simply getting through the insane rigors of medical school requires a certain amount of obsessive perfectionistic behavior.

A special type of mental disorder that we have included here is Attentional Deficit Hyperactivity Disorder (ADHD). Although it is not considered a personality disorder per se, ADHD and personality disorders can be functionally quite similar. Both are present by adolescence (ADHD is usually diagnosed before the age of six), and both disorders present interpersonal challenges in the workplace. Symptoms of ADHD are impulsivity, inattention, and hyperactivity. People affected with ADHD are highly distractible, tend to procrastinate, can often be moody, and are known for their tendencies not to finish what they start. These traits cause them to wreak havoc when they are on the job. We will address this disorder in chapter 13.

Qualities of Personality Disorders

It is often difficult enough for the trained clinician to diagnose a personality disorder, so you may wonder how you, a lay person, can try to do it. But trust us, it's not impossible and, with a little training and effort, even someone who is not formally trained in psychology can learn to recognize a personality disorder. You only really have to know what to look for. Following is a list of symptoms that are common to most, if not all, personality disorders. Knowing these will give you a good start. Perhaps in your interactions with personality disordered people, you have felt many of these things intuitively—many people do. Because one of the main symptoms of personality disorders is the inability to interact effectively with others, the very fact that you are having repeated problems with an individual is probably a good first clue.

Difficulties in Interpersonal Relationships

Perhaps one of the most frustrating experiences a person can have is to come in close contact with an individual who makes ordinary social interactions difficult. Somehow, things just don't seem to go right with these people: reasonable requests are ignored, deadlines are not adhered to, simple differences of opinions become major arguments, a simple faux pas becomes a corporate lawsuit. If you watch carefully, you can see that when there are problems in the organization, it's probably these same individuals who will be in the center of the fray. They are the ones who fire off memos, who hold the grudges, who are so picayune with details that they infuriate others. They are the ones who have been "wronged by management" or who've been suspended for making their fourth off-color remark. They seem to be the ones who take more than their share of sick days, are the rumor mongers, the malcontents, the ones who retaliate when passed over for promotion, and the ones who aren't on "speaking terms" with someone else. They are only interested in making themselves look good, ignoring the needs of the organization and their coworkers. They are too intense, or they might be too aloof. They are overly suspicious. What makes them even more difficult to deal with is that they can also be some of the most gifted and productive employees when they are not engaged in some type of dysfunctional human relationship.

One way to conceptualize these people is to see them as "relationship impaired"; they just don't respond to human interaction in the same ways as others do. They misinterpret people's intentions, they respond to others with inappropriate levels of intensity, they personalize events, often incorrectly believing that a certain organizational decision was made "just to get back at them." They believe that if a coworker "barks" at them because she's having a bad day, or if someone neglects to respond to one of their suggestions with the appropriate level of enthusiasm, those people must not like them. Their subordinates "deliberately" didn't make quota, just to make them look bad.

Ego-Syntonic

What makes personality disorders so problematic is the fact that the person with the personality disorder actually sees their symptoms as virtues and strengths. In psychological jargon, we say these traits are *ego-syntonic*. This means that people who have these traits see them as consistent and normal parts of their personality structures and not alien to who they want to be. Moreover, people with personality disorders *will often see their symptoms as virtues* that they are quite proud of and don't wish to change. The fact that personality disorders are ego-syntonic makes people with personality disorders particularly exhausting to deal with, because they have no particular desire to transform themselves—they don't believe there's anything to change.

These are people who could benefit from psychological help, but who are usually unwilling participants in the psychotherapeutic process because they do not see themselves as having a problem. Exasperatingly enough, they usually see others as the source of their problems, blaming *them* for all their troubles and not seeing that bad relationships are a recurring pattern in their lives. When we do see these people as patients, it's because they have been coerced into coming by a spouse, the legal system or, in some cases, because they have another co-existing disorder, like depression. Sometimes these people will want to come for marriage or family counseling, but only because they wish for the other people in their lives to change so that they can better accommodate the personality-disordered person's needs.

It is, therefore, usually ineffective to point out what they are doing wrong. If you tell a coworker, for example, that she is getting bogged down in minutiae to the point where she is not achieving the goal of a project, she will most likely reply that these are essential matters and that she is just being thorough. Moreover, she will most likely think that it is you who are being too careless, and that you probably don't take your job very seriously. As she probably is also a dedicated and hard-working employee (if her personality disorder is not too severe) who will often work long hours of overtime, you will probably decide not to pursue the discussion and attend to your own part of the project. This won't help your frustration at her slow rate of work or your bafflement at her attitude, though.

The fact that personality disorders are ego-syntonic has made them a most difficult challenge for mental-health professionals and the community of business organizations alike. After all, how can you ask a person to change deficient behaviors when he is *proud* of them? Mental health professionals have been able to make inroads into this area, and we will be discussing them later.

Lack of Empathy

From the time we are infants, we learn to "vibrate" with the feelings of others. We feel sad when others feel sad, are angered by the injustices that have been done to our coworkers, and share in the excitement of our friend's new promotion. Most adult human beings can be described as emotionally responsive to those around us, which is one sign of maturity.

People with personality disorders do not seem to have this quality, at least not to the depths that people without personality disorders do. This lack of empathy could be due to a number of reasons. One is the fact that the person with the personality disorder is so caught up and consumed in her own agenda that she does not focus on what those around her are experiencing. For example, a person with strong approval needs might be so involved in getting her coworkers to reassure her of her capabilities that she doesn't see that people are becoming annoyed with her insecurities.

Another reason for the apparent lack of empathy might be due to the fact that many of these people didn't have an "emotional education" when they were growing up. Most people learn to be empathetic because they themselves have been shown empathy while they were children. Those of us who are fortunate enough to have had the experiences of being shown empathy on a routine basis by our parents, relatives, and other significant individuals in our lives will ourselves learn to be empathetic. If, on the other hand, a person is not shown empathy or, worse yet, is only ignored and treated with cruelty, the whole concept of empathy will not be formed and the person may not know that such a thing even exists. It's easy to see how this lack of empathic experience can lead a person to act in such a way that he appears to be totally uncaring about the needs of others.

Difficulties Maintaining Boundaries

Boundaries are a natural part of our lives. Some boundaries are physical, like your house and yard. It would be unimaginable, for example, for you to return home from work to find your neighbors using your barbecue and picnic tables to entertain their friends and relatives. Or for people to come in off of the street, let themselves into your house, and use your phone. Other boundaries are more psychological in nature. Most of us wouldn't think of telling strangers intimate details about ourselves or of telling our children about our sex lives. Healthy people can maintain and respect boundaries.

Boundaries can be varied and complex in nature. A twenty-foot brick wall presents itself as quite a different type of boundary than, let's say, a picket fence with a gate. There are walls with doors and some with open windows. Psychological boundaries can be even more complex. Knowing under what conditions it's okay to tell a bawdy joke (as well as knowing which coworkers would appreciate it) requires a type of knowledge that psychologists call social or emotional intelligence.

In the delightful movie *What About Bob?*, Bill Murray takes boundary violations to new heights as he shows up at his psychotherapist's house, dates his daughter, and shows up for the cameras when his therapist is being interviewed on television. Interestingly enough, many of the real therapists I spoke to about the movie told me that it made them nervous, and that they had a hard time enjoying the movie. The problem seems to be that they've had to deal with people with personality disorders on a daily basis who are constantly testing boundaries. *What About Bob?* is a therapist's worst, albeit common, nightmare.

In the workplace, boundaries are particularly important, as they are essential for the organization to run smoothly. Some of the most important boundaries are laid out in the organizational chart. Organizational hierarchies are constructed so as to achieve maximum efficiency in accomplishing workplace goals while minimizing the squandering of time and resources. Organizations have available an endless number of hierarchical structures to draw upon, depending on their needs and goals. Management must be sensitive enough to the surrounding business environment and organizational problems so that they may change the structure of the organization to adapt. In other words, organizations must be flexible and their employees must be compliant to these changes. The roles that employees must carry out contain implicit behavioral boundaries. Individuals with personality disorders will often overstep these boundaries.

Other boundaries in the organization might not be as clearly laid out, and there is often an alternative organizational structure just below the surface of the official one. The astute employee is aware of this "covert" organizational structure with its own implicit boundaries and uses them to her advantage. Charlotte, who is the branch manager at a bank, recognizes that whenever she makes a change in office procedures that she not only tells her head teller, but also Sherry, who is one of the secretaries. She tells Sherry personally, because she knows that Sherry is a popular secretary who is well-liked and well-respected by her coworkers. She therefore carries more clout than her job title suggests. Successful employees know how to utilize these types of relationships, while people with personality disorders most often do not.

Rigid, Irrational Belief Patterns

Human beings are interpretive creatures. Although it may seem at times that we give knee-jerk responses to situations, most of the time we evaluate situations according to our patterns of belief. We filter our experiences through our belief systems. In other words, we first perceive a situation, evaluate it according to our belief system, and then we respond. Interestingly, we all have different belief systems and interpret situations differently. Our belief systems do not have to be perfect—they almost never are—but just good enough to navigate our way through the many situations that we encounter during the day. Most people's belief systems are good enough to do this. Mary, for example, ususally interprets a reprimand as instructive. She almost welcomes them, as she believes (and here is her belief system working) that criticism makes one a better person. Ralph, on the other hand, is angered by criticism, because he believes that it must mean that he is defective in some way. Larry sees a reprimand as a challenge, and when he receives one, he'll go out of his way to show that he is a better person than the person issuing the reprimand. It's important to recognize that, although these people's beliefs regarding reprimands are different, all their belief systems are good enough to get them through life without causing major hassles.

Our understanding of belief systems and how they affect behavior comes originally from the pioneering work of George Kelly (Kelly 1955) and has been further developed by A. T. Beck and A. Freeman and Albert Ellis (Beck & Freeman 1990; Ellis 1962). These psychologists assert that human beings have belief systems that function like "hypotheses" about the world and the people in it. As we go through life, we acquire data that will either contradict or support our hypotheses (belief systems). In that sense, we are always revising our hypotheses according to the supporting or nonsupporting data. It is almost as if we are scientists, constantly throwing out old hypotheses for new ones in the face of new "evidence."

It is different for people with personality disorders. These individuals have rigid, irrational "core" beliefs about the world and the people in it. Some of these irrational belief systems are: "If I follow orders, I am weak"; "I am worthless if my ideas are not accepted"; "To make a mistake means I am a failure"; "I must be the center of attention at all times"; "People are always picking on me"; and "Only truly gifted and talented people understand me." There are innumerable others as well, but they are all irrational, inflexible, and maladaptive, and lead the personality-disordered individual into patterns of dysfunctional behavior in the workplace.

Hidden Agendas

Organizations have goals on many levels. In order to achieve these goals, it is necessary for the individuals within to cooperate and pull toward these shared goals. What makes the behavior of the person with a personality disorder so dangerous to the productivity of the organization is that they have their own (often unconscious) goals that often sabotage the major goals of the organization. For example, when a new record-keeping system was introduced in the psychiatric wing of a medical hospital, one of the therapists was quiet vocal about how he did not like it because he felt it entailed too much paperwork. Infuriated that his protests went unheeded and that the record-keeping system was implemented anyway, the therapist deliberately kept faulty records, insisting that the system was too complicated to follow. His hidden agenda was to prove that he was right and that others should notice and take heed of his opinions. This ran, of course, counter to the productivity and well-being of the hospital.

You know you're dealing with a hidden agenda when simple things do not seem to go in the obvious direction that they should: Simple things become convoluted, obvious facts are ignored, and simple tasks become complicated. Later on in this book, we will show you specific techniques for dismantling hidden agendas and getting the individual with the personality disorder back on task.

A Lack of Emotional Intelligence

Emotional intelligence is a concept that was developed by New England psychologists Peter Salovey and John Mayer and popularized in a book by Daniel Goleman, a science writer for *The New York Times*. Emotional intelligence can best be described as understanding one's social surroundings and an ability to respond to others and solve interpersonal problems in an emotionally healthy manner (Goleman 1998). From the moment we're born, we are learning how to interact with others and to respond to them in appropriate ways. It's as if we are in a constant dance with others, instinctively modifying and gauging our behaviors in response to other people. This dance begins when the infant makes her first vocalizations and her mother comes over to the crib. The infant turns her head toward her mother and the mother, in turn, talks back in a high-pitched, overly simplified, almost musical kind of speech psychologists call "Motherese." Mother and infant smile at one another. The infant then turns her head the other way signaling that she is done with the interaction. Mom walks away. The dance has ended and both dancers have enjoyed the dance. This simple exchange sets the groundwork for future interactions: You talk, I listen; I talk, you listen; I wait for pauses in your speech to tell when I can talk. My whole tone of voice changes, and I break off eye contact with you when I am finished and wish to leave. You rise as I do, and we both escort the other to the door. Most human beings understand this complex pattern of interaction as well as many other patterns.

Although we are not clear on just why, the person with a personality disorder does not seem to have this understanding of emotional matters. Perhaps it is a result of poor parenting, biological deficits in the brain, or both. Contrariwise, there are certain types of emotional situations for which they show a high degree of emotional inteliigence. Individuals with Dependent Personality disorder are highly sensitive to the needs of others, for example.

"Long Term" and Inflexible.

People with personality disorders are often "one-trick ponies," as they seem to respond to life in a stereotypical type of pattern that does not vary from one situation to another. They often do one thing very well to the exclusion of others.

Kevin Scott was the head of his own construction company. He prided himself on being an excellent craftsman and a tough negotiator, and most people saw him as such. However, when things did not go his way, he would berate the person whom he saw as responsible, often going on for hours at a time. He prided himself on his excellent command of the English language and would spend days thinking of clever retorts and put-downs. Often, when he knew he was about to demean someone, he would call others in to watch the debacle. Although they would often laugh with him about it afterwards, his subordinates hated him and would deliberately do poor work to get back at him. When some of his key people quit, he rationalized that he was better off without them. His perpetual gloating over real and imagined victories blinded him to the fact that his business reputation was being damaged. Although there were many different and more productive ways that he could have dealt with many of these situations, his need to dominate others prevented him from doing so. Berating others was the one trick of this one-trick pony. An interesting truism about one-trick ponies is that often, if you can take away their one trick, they are left deflated and powerless, because they lack the resources and skills for dealing with problems any other way.

People should also avoid assuming that a person has a personality disorder if it is not long-standing. In other words, if a person is going through a depression or an anxiety disorder, they might temporarily show signs of a personality disorder but not necessarily have that personality disorder. Evidence of true personality disorders can be traced back to adolescence.

It is important to state here that no one in this world is perfect. None of us have perfect genes, perfect upbringings, or perfect life circumstances. In short, we are all "personality disordered" to a degree, and we can often function in a dysfunctional manner. No doubt, you will see many of your own behaviors here and reflections of yourself in the many case examples we have provided. Indeed, you may even have a personality disorder, but if you can see symptoms in yourself and have made attempts to modify your behavior in the past, the chances are that you don't actually have an actual personality disorder. The rest of this book is devoted to trying to help individuals who are troubled by personality-disordered individuals and who have tried just about everything to make things work. Your best designed plans for dealing with these individuals that should have worked, didn't. Here is Plan B.

CHAPTER 3

All Hail the Conquering Narcissist

Did you hear the one about the surgeon who consults with his patient?

Patient: Well, Doc, give it to me straight. What do the X-rays say?

Doctor: I have good news and bad news. Which would you like to hear first?

Patient: The bad news.

Doctor: Well, you only have about six weeks to live.

Patient: (*In obvious alarm*) Six weeks! My God! What could possibly be the good news?

Doctor: I had sex with my receptionist last week!

The uncaring and obviously self-centered nature of the doctor in this joke is a great illustration of the narcissist. Their lack of empathy and selfishness can be quite alarming at times. The narcissist's absorption with his own self-image precludes him from being concerned with the feelings of others. A kingly lion who expects special treatment and unceasing admiration from others, the narcissist is attracted to positions of status and leadership and are therefore frequently found in organizational settings.

The word "narcissist" is derived from the Greek myth of Narcissus. Narcissus was a handsome youth who spurned the love of a Nymph named Echo. This so angered Aphrodite, the goddess of love, that she cast a spell on Narcissus so that he would fall in love with his own reflection. He was to die of longing for the unattainable image, mistaking that image for reality. As we discuss the narcissist, we will see that he is indeed concerned primarily with image. Appearances are what matters most to the narcissist, more than other people's feelings or the world outside himself. He is notoriously self-centered.

What Is Narcissistic Personality Disorder?

Simply recognizing the symptoms of the narcissist can go a long way in reducing the level of stress that one experiences when dealing with this person. One cannot expect the narcissist to behave in a rational, giving, and cooperative manner, and if you do so, you will experience nothing but frustration in your interactions with them. Your first dealings with the narcissist will most likely be positive, as the narcissist will often distinguish herself by working hard. But the goal of the hard work is based more on the narcissist's own needs rather that the requirements of the task itself or any organizational goals. It's easy to hire a narcissist, because they can be attractive people who are very adept at making first impressions. Later on, however, they can be abrupt, rude, and lacking in gratitude toward others. Although they themselves expect special treatment, they rarely give it to others. They can be incredibly demanding of others. For example, one manager made his secretary come into work the day after she suffered a miscarriage (Beck & Freeman 1990, 224).

Narcissists usually sees themselves as leaders and are often drawn into leadership positions in organizational settings, sports, acting, and politics. They believe they have unusual or special talents and should be surrounded by others who are the same. Often, they do have a quality or talent that has distinguished them from others. They might be physically attractive or highly intelligent. Sometimes, they are successful athletes in college or high school. They are used to being the center of attention, often being one of the "popular kids" in high school. They are used to being admired as children and expect it in their adult life. Oddly enough, as they grow older and realize that the continuing admiration of others has not occurred, they will often become depressed. This can often be a good thing, as it often leads the narcissist into psychotherapy and coming to grips with her selfish behaviors. One such man came into psychotherapy when he realized that he was not the number one salesman in his office. He stated that he believed he would naturally be the best when he took the job. Fortunately, this led him into other discussions of how he was never good enough for his father when he played basketball and how he was tired of always trying to be something he was not. This led, eventually, to a gradual acceptance of the fact that he was one of us "mere mortals," as he put it.

Narcissists do not like routine or "ordinary" work, such as making reports, taking notes, attending routine meetings, and doing paperwork. They often believe that they have "special talents" that the organization should be utilizing. They believe that their ordinary ideas are brilliant when, in fact, they aren't. One narcissist told one of the authors that he would not wish to win the Nobel prize if it meant that he would only be an "average" Nobelist! Because narcissists feel that they are far above the norm, they will often violate boundaries of authority, making decisions they are not qualified to make or taking on tasks they really aren't trained to do. The narcissist expresses his feelings of superiority in a number of ways, such as the disrespect of authority, ethical violations, the abuse of others (such as sexual harassment), ignoring deadlines, overcharging clients, and generally expressing an attitude in almost everything they do that says, "It doesn't matter what I do, as long as I get my way."

In most of her interpersonal relations, the narcissist is abrasive and demanding. Her needs always come first. If she is sick, hungry, or sexually aroused, those needs must be satisfied by others around him. You are expected to be concerned about her hunger and help get her something to eat. Moreover, she believes that she is *entitled* to have these needs met by others. Therefore, when others do not respond appropriately, the narcissist will often have a temper tantrum, shouting and verbally abusing the poor individual unlucky enough to be involved in the interaction. Consequently, the narcissist has few stable and close relationships, although he usually boasts of having many "close" friends.

Let us now take a moment to look at a case history of a narcissist described by Millon and Davis (2000, 272). This will allow a more in-depth understanding of the narcissist. Million and Davis cite the case of Malcolm, who storms out of his supervisor's office after being told that he was going to be terminated: because of his poor relationship with both his supervisors and subordinates. His relationships had deteriorated in part because Malcolm would always invent new procedures that affected everyone around him. He lacked sympathy for those around him and expected everyone around him to follow his dictates. Even though many of his ideas didn't work, he insisted that his subordinates follow these ideas to the letter. He was certain that these misguided ideas would work if only his coworkers "could get their heads out of their asses long enough to see the big picture." He would refer to his colleagues as "cretins," going on to state that he didn't know why "the magnitude of my innovations is not obvious to everyone." When asked about his future, he stated, "I can only imagine that, in time, I will be fantastically successful. It is my destiny." He stated that he felt a bond with Einstein and Salk, people who "had suffered nobly for being ahead of their time, just like me." In spite of the fact that he had been forced to leave other companies for creating the same types of problems, he continues to blame others, accusing them of being envious or jealous. Now, facing termination from yet another job, he is resisting their suggestions that he seek counseling, and instead, continues to blame the company and not himself.

Like all personality-disordered individuals, the narcissist has parts of his or her personality that are overdeveloped and parts that are underdeveloped. You will find that the narcissist has overdeveloped behaviors that serve to make her look good in the eyes of others. They are often high achievers, hard workers, leaders, and can often be very good "idea people." Hence, the narcissist often has achieved a great deal for herself. Also, the narcissist has overdeveloped competitive behaviors. She'll work hard at skills that will help her to beat others and come out on top. Keep in mind, however, that these efforts are all in service of their own self-aggrandizement and not the needs of the organization.

The current concept of narcissism is best clarified in DSM-IV (American Psychiatric Association 1994, 658) which defines the Narcissistic Personality Disorder:

> "as a pervasive pattern of grandiosity (in fantasy or behavior), need for admiration, and lack of empathy, beginning in early adulthood and present in a variety of contexts, as indicated by five or more of the following:
>
> 1. has a grandiose sense of self-importance (e.g., exaggerates achievements and talents, expects to be recognized as superior without commensurate achievements).
>
> 2. is preoccupied with fantasies of unlimited success, power, brilliance, beauty, or ideal love.
>
> 3. believes that he or she is 'special' and unique and can only be understood by, or should associate with, other special or high-status people (or institutions).
>
> 4. requires excessive admiration.
>
> 5. has a sense of entitlement, i.e., unreasonable expectations of especially favorable treatment or automatic compliance with his or her expectations.
>
> 6. is interpersonally exploitative, i.e., takes advantage of others to achieve his or her own ends.

7. lacks empathy: is unwilling to recognize or identify with the feelings and needs of others.

8. is often envious of others or believes that others are envious of him or her.

9. shows arrogant, haughty behaviors or attitudes.*

The Narcissistic Organization

Levinson (1994) was the first to talk about "Executive Narcissism" and "Organizational Narcissism," in referring to both corporate and political executives and organizations who manifested this inflated sense of self-respect and self-confidence. Levinson points out that the higher one rises in an organizational structure, the higher one's self-esteem becomes and, concurrently, the less supervision one is likely to have. "The combination of these factors frequently gives rise to narcissistic inflation that becomes overconfidence and a sense of entitlement. That, in turn, leads to denial of those realities that threaten the inflated self-image and to contempt for other individuals and organizations" (432). This similar dynamic is found in the "groupthink" (Janis 1972) phenomena, in which both executives and their immediate subordinates, when working in groups, develop certain characteristic behaviors or attitudes, such as 1) an illusion of invulnerability, 2) a sense of superiority to those considered to be part of the outgroup or competition, 3) discarding or demeaning information that is contradictory to already held beliefs. There are several examples that Janus provides and several examples from the corporate world that support these notions. For example, Janus cites the example in which United States naval and military leaders at Pearl Harbor may have had prior information that the Japanese were mounting an attack. However, their perception of the United States invulnerability and righteousness resulted in this crucial information being diminished and discarded. Narcissism often permeates from the executive level on down, affecting policy in a kind of "domino effect." For instance, if the CEO is considered to be inaccessible even to their direct subordinates, then it's likely that these VPs will often be inaccessible to their department directors and middle managers. This is how a "narcissistic attitude" can pervade organizations, eventually affecting every single employee.

---

*   Reprinted with permission from the *Diagnostic and Statistical Manual of Mental Disorders*, Fourth Edition. Copyright 1994 American Psychiatric Association.

The Narcissistic Administrator

Now let's translate these behaviors into the work setting, for it is here where many problems are bound to occur, given the primacy of social interactions in most work settings. The NPD administrator is most likely to be one of the most difficult to work with or work for, because their attitudes or behaviors in the workplace are so often caustic or prone to misinterpretation. One might expect an administrator to have healthy self-esteem, to think well of themselves, to be gutsy enough to make tough decisions, and to be responsive to the needs of their subordinates. The narcissist, on the other hand, is far from this egalitarian type of administrator; the narcissist needs to be the "King" and will have little concern for the welfare and needs of those around them. In fact, narcissists are often drawn to leadership positions precisely because of their drive for perfectionism and admiration. Employees exist only to feed the narcissist's sense of power.

Working with the Narcissistic Administrator

Becoming familiar with the previously listed DSM-IV symptoms will help you immensely in your quest to recognize and subsequently manage your relationship with the narcissist. In addition to these symptoms, the administrator with narcissism will show additional distinctive symptoms as well, because they are in a unique situation where they can abuse their power. What are the traits or characteristics of such an individual? Here is a checklist of things you might expect to see in the workplace.

1. The narcissistic administrator will expect you to work unrealistic hours, with no recognition of your having a life outside of the work setting. This individual will avoid any discussion of anything beyond work, e.g., family, hobbies, interests, problems, and so on. In his mind, you don't exist other than as an employee.

2. The narcissistic administrator will expect you to have brilliant new ideas, concepts, or plans. You will often feel like he is expecting you to be brilliant, and if you fail to live up to this unrealistic expectation, you will often feel a pervasive sense of inadequacy as nothing is ever quite good enough. However, if your brilliant ideas do work, the narcissist will

take the credit. If they fail, you will be made to take the blame.

3. She will expect your undaunting admiration. The unspoken rule is, "If you don't have anything good to say about me, then don't say anything at all." These individuals do not want your feedback or critique, only for you to provide a positive reflection of them. Remember, this is not an egalitarian leader.

4. He will exploit you for his own ends and accomplishments, but will not return the favors or loyalty.

5. The narcissistic administrator will think nothing of canceling meetings with you at the last minute. But God forbid that you have to cancel a meeting with them for any reason, short of hospitalization or death—and you'd better have a valid death certificate to show them!

6. She may be committed to hard work, but the purpose is self-centered and the goal is self-recognition (Beck & Freeman 1990). Therefore, don't expect a lot of compliments for *your* hard work.

7. The narcissistic administrator is often one who uses power inappropriately, so sexual harassment, verbal abusiveness, and other abuses of their power are often common. Remember the TV interviews with Senator Bob Packwood after his resignation? You would think he was the one who was victimized. Although we are by no means diagnosing this individual, the behavior noted in those interviews is a great illustration of narcissism at its best.

8. The narcissistic administrator lacks empathy and feels that rules of propriety apply to others, not to them. They feel they operate under different rules because they are special. A great example of this feeling of being "above" the rules is found in the behavior of Marge Schott, ex-owner of the Cincinnati Reds baseball team. When you consider the Cincinnati Reds as a metaphor of a family, Marge is like the pre-senile grandmother or aunt who embarrasses everyone at family functions, but whom everyone tiptoes around because they don't want to lose their inheritance. So Auntie Marge goes along making vitriolic, caustic comments about anyone and everyone, needing to have the spotlight on her, needing the attention and admiration of others, while the rest of the family cringes in fear at what she may say next. When the baseball commissioner banned Ms. Schott from the Reds'

stadium, it was tantamount to sending Auntie Marge "to the home." (Naturally, we are not implying that Marge Schott has Narcissistic Personality Disorder, but some of her reported behaviors are similar to NPD.

Those who have the misfortune of working for this type of administrator often find themselves feeling totally frustrated, left alone to fend for themselves, and filled with either rage or self-doubt. Physical complaints are common, as the subordinate will often react to this type of emotional stress and tension by developing tension headaches, stomach upset, colitis, and the like. Some employees find some solace in being able to vent to coworkers, but this relief is necessarily short-lived, because the difficulties in getting along with this type of administrator will continue to crop up. Those in positions subordinate to this type of administrator sometimes feel that if they were just left alone to do their job, things would not be so bad. However, this remedy is unlikely to come about as the narcissist continues their never-ending demands for perfection. They insist that their subordinates be just as perfect as the narcissist perceives himself to be.

When working for a narcissistic administrator, our best advice for you is, "Don't take it personally." The fact that your boss does not appreciate you probably has nothing to do with your actual work performance. This becomes clear when you consider the fact that their lack of appreciation has remained constant regardless of your good or bad performance. The narcissist is simply incapable of being empathetic and fulfilling another's needs for recognition.

If you find yourself in a job where you have to deal with a narcissistic administrator, then you need to learn to cope with whatever emotional response is most predominant in this individual, e.g., rage, self-doubt, sadness, or frustration. Remember, you can't change this type of individual—it's taken years to make them that way, and it would take something short of a miracle to bring about lasting change. In Dicken's Scrooge, we are enthralled by the cataclysmic change that Scrooge undergoes as a result of his Christmas Eve nightmare. There are instances where individuals do undergo tremendous change as a result of "hitting bottom." We certainly see this with addictive diseases, such as alcohol, drugs, gambling, or sex addiction, where an earth-shattering event breaks the denial system of the individual. However, a narcissistic administrator will usually be pretty well insulated from such attacks on their psyche. That is part of their problem. This is not to say that it's impossible to intervene with such individuals. We were once approached by employees who worked for a tyrannical and unusually dysfunctional administrator who was becoming progressively more disruptive to the organization because of her extreme narcissism and unwillingness to see things from anyone else's point of view. Most staff, like family members in a dysfunctional home, learn to adapt to these tyrannical behaviors, living their lives around the problems and dysfunctional behavior. Some employees take pity and protect the person; some become the dutiful employee (like Bob Cratchett) and take the abuse; some suffer in silence, while others act out in anger. Eventually, the staff we talked with came up with a strategy for how they would confront the tyrannical boss. Similar to an "intervention" with an alcoholic, the staff decided to speak with their boss about their concerns but not in an attacking way. They decided to bring up specific issues that they wanted addressed, which ranged from how they were treated on a day-to-day basis to issues over vacation requests. They decided not to barrage their boss with all of their complaints. Surprisingly, the tyrant narcissist heard them out and did not fire even one of them. The approach worked, and it began a dialogue with this administrator toward better, less-stressful working conditions. Unfortunately, not all cases like these have a happy ending. What brought this staff to this point was that they figured they had nothing to lose. If things had continued as they were, they all would have quit or been fired anyway.

The Narcissistic Coworker

Although working with a narcissist is less intimidating and less anxiety-provoking than working for a narcissistic administrator, it is certainly not necessarily less frustrating. Of course, there are also more possibilities to intervene or to confront the narcissist without the threat of having one's livelihood taken away from you. How do you know if your working with a narcissistic? Again, referring back to the DSM-IV criteria, the narcissistic coworker may present with some of the following traits.

1. Since the narcissistic coworker sees themselves as "special" or "unique," they will expect the company rules or policies to apply to you—not to them.

2. The narcissistic coworker will think nothing of taking your office supplies, or removing things from your desk or locker, but God forbid you should touch any of their things.

3. The narcissistic coworker, in times of crisis or conflict, will expect you to "fight the dragon," while they sit back at a safe distance and watch you wage battle.

4. The narcissistic coworker will spend a lot of time maintaining their personal appearance, while you do the work.

5. The narcissistic coworker will be insensitive to your needs, feelings, or problems. After you pour your heart out about a problem at home or a fight you had with your spouse, they may respond with something like, "So what are we having for lunch? Don't you hate the meat loaf in the cafeteria?"

6. You may often find yourself saying about the narcissistic coworker, "Why do I even bother trying to be friends with that jerk?"

There are several frustrations inherent in working with the narcissist that go beyond the items discussed above. Because they lack any sense of humility, they are often great at selling themselves to others, especially to bosses, managers, and supervisors. In doing so, they are likely to gain promotions more quickly and have their talents recognized more quickly and frequently. Again, their sense of entitlement makes this appear right to them, but it can be extremely frustrating for you. Somehow, workers seem to adapt to having a narcissist in their midst, at least in a coworker role. People get used to taking up the extra slack, or the fact that their coworker will call in sick at the worst times, or will usually be involved in some earth-shattering crisis or in need of special attention. In some instances, however, you may have a narcissist whose identity is very much dependent on work accomplishments. Then you are in luck, as you will probably see more of a workaholic who is driven to get ahead, no matter what. Even though this individual is supposedly a peer, they don't see themselves in the same league as you, because they are just passing by on their way to the top. This is the individual who likes to sit in the boss's chair after everyone has left for the day, just to try it on for size.

Working with the Narcissistic Coworker

This coworker will ignore your concerns and has no real interest in your life or the things that you wish to talk about. If you have an issue with something on the job, he will be uninterested. He most likely will be thinking your concerns are petty. He might even chide you for wasting time on this unimportant concern when you could be taking up his cause. In the case of one narcissistic professor, when one of his coworkers asked if he would serve on the student health committee, the professor became indignant. He quickly launched into a tirade against this colleague, ranting and raving that she was shortsighted and not really concerned about the "real" problem on campus, which he claimed was the administration's negative attitude about their department, a fact he claimed was evidenced by their not buying him a computer.

The narcissist coworker will never give you credit for the good things you do. In a lot of cases, you will find yourself working harder and harder to gain their approval. (This is especially true of people who may have an obsessive compulsive or dependent personality style.) But all your work does not matter because the narcissist lacks the ability to empathize, to step inside your shoes for a while and experience life from your point of view and to "reverberate" with you. Furthermore, your good deeds will seem threatening to her, and she will be envious and jealous of your good work. It will be most difficult for her to acknowledge your achievements because, deep inside, she feels shame that she herself did not do those things. Recognizing that the problem lies in the *narcissist* and not *you* will save you a whole lot of agonizing and regrets about your own behavior.

The narcissistic coworker will make requests of you that are quite unreasonable and will become angry at you if you don't honor them. In one instance, a nurse asked her colleague to take her late shift because she wanted to go on a date with a new love interest. When her coworker refused, stating that she had to tend to her three sick children while her husband was on a business trip, the nurse was furious, saying that she would have to take it up with their supervisor and that she would have to seriously reconsider their friendship. The poor woman with three children ended up feeling guilty and actually considered hiring a baby-sitter so that her friend could have her "hot date."

It's difficult to accept the fact that the narcissist often believes that only "special" people can truly understand him because he, himself, is so special. Your good words and advice will often go unheeded by him, even though the advice and the guidance are excellent. Don't take it personally.

Finally, we would like to emphasize a crucial point in coping with a narcissist. Always try to keep in mind that your narcissist coworker will not change because of anything you may say or do. When you feel yourself getting frustrated and exhausted by trying to fight your coworker's selfish and suspicious traits, you might want to step back and ask yourself, "How many of the actions I have taken in dealing with this coworker have been designed *to try to change him*?" If you are like most people, you will most likely answer that a large number of your actions are, indeed, actually attempts to try to get the narcissist to change. And we can assure you that this approach is fruitless, because it is safe to say that the narcissist will probably never change. Avoid the traps of self-blame and feelings of inadequacy by always remembering that the problem lies with the narcissist—not you.

The Narcissistic Subordinate

If you are a supervisor, boss, manager, administrator, or CEO you have probably seen the double-edged sword of having a narcissistic employee under your direction. For at the same time that they appear to be helping you fly higher, they are also discreetly trying to clip your wings, as well. It's like the story of the snake and the frog. There was once a snake who was stranded on one side of a lake. One day a frog was hopping by, and the snake implored the frog, "Please take me to the other side of the lake. I can sit on your back while you swim across." "How do I know you're not going to bite me?" replied the frog. "Bite you? Of course, I won't bite you" said the snake. "If I bite you, I'd drown along with you." The frog agreed, and the snake climbed on the frog's back. When they were half way across the lake, the snake bit the frog. As they both sank under the water, the frog gasped, "Why did you bite me?" To which, the snake replied, "I couldn't help it—it's my nature." It is often the nature of the narcissist to use those above them for mentoring, for promotions, or to build their resume. But when push comes to shove, they will have no sense of loyalty, gratitude, or appreciation and will think nothing of "biting" those who help them. The narcissist may be a hard worker and may be goal oriented, but the goals they aspire to are theirs, not necessarily yours. I once had a recovering heroin addict, who was directing a program that I was supervising, say very openly to me, "In order to get ahead, I have to do two things: watch my back from those working for me and try to push you out, either by getting you promoted or fired." This is a fitting example of why it can be extremely uncomfortable having narcissist employees under you.

It's very common for the narcissistic employee to feel that rules, policies, and procedures apply to others within the organization—but not to them. For example, if you set a deadline for work that needs to be completed, the narcissistic employee will feel that the deadline applies to everyone else in the organization except them. The narcissistic subordinate may also demonstrate little or no loyalty. Therefore, if the ship is going down, they will be the first one to man the lifeboats, while you go down with the ship. They can often shift loyalties as easily as one changes clothes. So, while the narcissistic employee can be a hard worker and is often motivated and ambitious, always remember that it is you whom they will need to step on to get to the top. The narcissistic subordinate often has a poor sense of boundaries and, therefore, will think nothing of going around you or above you to get to the top, whether it's to bring new ideas to your superiors or to complain about you as a supervisor. They will usually treat others in the organization, especially those who are on their same or lower level, with little or no compassion, respect, or consideration. They do not contribute when a coworker's parent dies, and they don't pitch in when a group effort is needed, whether it be planning the office Christmas party or packing things to move. The message is, "I am better than you. You are not on the same level as I. I am superior."

The narcissistic subordinate may act arrogantly around others, but you will often see a sudden shift in attitude when a superior appears. All of a sudden, they may become obsequious or contrite. This is what we like to call the "Eddie Haskel effect." A helpful goal in dealing with someone like this in your employ is to keep them on track without allowing them to do too much damage. The narcissist, however, will usually go away once they learn that you are in charge, that you're not going anyplace, and that they would be better served to direct their ambitions elsewhere. Your most joyous moment will be on the day when the narcissistic employee announces (with deep regrets, of course) that they have taken a job with another company.

Working with the Narcissistic Subordinate

In order to protect yourself from the Machiavelli Junior in your midst, you need to be proactive. Let those above you know of the narcissist's hard work, but also let them know that this employee's ambitions and loyalties *may* not be as honorable as they appear. Keep your comments fair but succinct. Also, keep your superiors aware of any changes, problems, or potential problems within your area. It's much better for your superior to hear this from you, rather than from the narcissist. Remember, if there is a screw-up, the narcissist will be bursting at the seams to take the opportunity to make you look bad. Whenever you are reporting the accomplishments of your group, be certain to give credit where credit is due, but also make certain to let your superiors know that you have a strong handle in the work that needs to be done. It's important to make this point clearly, because the narcissist will often try to present that they are the ones holding down the fort, while you are off attending to other things, whether it be a personal or family crisis, playing golf, or just goofing off.

That raises another important point. Under no circumstances should you let the narcissist know your personal business. Any family problem or crisis should be kept private and any foible or past difficulties you may have had should also be under wraps with a narcissistic employee. They are certain to use this information against you. We aren't suggesting that you become paranoid or obsessed with "checking your back"—just be guarded and exercise caution.

In supervising the narcissistic employee, you can expect them to devalue your feedback or mentoring. After all, they can do your job better than you can or so they assume. When providing feedback or evaluations, you may need to couch your criticisms by offering positive statements first. By speaking to the side of the narcissist that thrives on compliments, you will be more likely to have the criticisms received. Although you may be angry or frustrated and want to be harshly critical, this tactic will only fuel their fire and justify their belief that you are the "enemy." Provide firm but fair critiques. Some organizations will have employees rate themselves first during performance evaluations. This is often a good tool to see if the individual, who you suspect of being a narcissist, fits the bill. If your assumptions are correct, you will get pages upon pages of their accomplishments and attributes. What you will find lacking, of course, is any mention of "areas needing improvement." If you suggest areas for them to work on, they may defend themselves, make excuses, or blame others. It is important, therefore, to keep the suggestions for improvement concrete, objective, and measurable, if possible.

Individuals with personality disorders are notorious for their rigidity and unwillingness to change. Nevertheless, there are things that you can do to make your experience with the narcissist far more tolerable than it is now. With some time, effort, and understanding, you can go a long way in turning around a relationship with a narcissist. It is critical in dealing with them that you recognize that it's the narcissist who has the problem, not you. Narcissism is perhaps one of the most challenging of all the personality disorders, and dealing with a narcissist can be stressful. He will often need to put others down as a way of regulating his own self-esteem. And although it's actually the narcissist who lacks self-esteem, it will be yours that is at risk. You will need to develop a very thick skin when dealing with him as you will, most likely, have to deal with some pretty strong negative interactions.

As a supervisor, you will constantly hear that you are not doing enough for them. Their insatiable sense of entitlement will drive them to nag you about where the perks are that they should have, especially if others in the organization have them. The secretary of a small real-estate office, for example, demanded a fully paid membership to a health spa as part of her employment package, simply because another employee had gotten one for winning a sales contest. Her sense of entitlement, as well as her hurt sense of pride, prevented her from recognizing the irrationality of her demands or discriminating between very different situations. (Perhaps even more ironic is the fact that the secretary had no wish to exercise!)

The narcissist will shake your sense of logic. You will, at times, seriously consider the idea that he might actually be right. After all, he does seem very sure of himself and so energetic in his arguments, especially when he believes he is in the pursuit of "justice." His long-winded, eloquent monologues will sound so convincing that you will find yourself saying, "You know, maybe this guy is right. I'm the one who is wrong here." You'll find, though, that when you think it through, these arguments are just rationalizations of his own self-serving behavior. It's difficult to imagine that this conceited, self-serving person who feels that she is "God's gift to the world" is actually a frightened child who is so insecure that she needs constant confirmation from those around her. Nevertheless, it's true. Keeping this fact in mind is a key factor in dealing with the narcissist. If you attempt to respond and react to the narcissist's grandiose self, you will easily become entangled in her problems. You will likely feel demeaned, inadequate, unappreciated, and angry to name just a few of the emotions commonly elicited by the narcissist. Moreover, typical responses to the narcissist's pretentious show of haughtiness usually result in the narcissist becoming more humiliated and this, in turn, leads to further displays of superiority to compensate for the humiliation. This vicious cycle is characteristic of the narcissist's relationships throughout his entire life. When, for example, a manager in a new car dealership confronted his narcissistic salesman with the fact he was driving customers away with his "know-it-all" attitude, the salesman responded by becoming even more self-aggrandizing. He claimed that he was losing sales not because of his grandiosity, but because he needed a bigger desk that would be more impressive to his customers.

The more effective means of dealing with the narcissist is by getting beneath the grandiose exterior to the feelings of inadequacy that are the driving force behind it. This is the real cause of the problem, and you will not get anywhere with him if you don't acknowledge the source. As strange as it may seem, you will get much further with the narcissist by helping him to build his self-esteem! This is not to say that you have to seriously entertain the idea that he is truly a superior person entitled to special treatment. Rather it's a suggestion for you to try to help the narcissist become less ashamed of their inadequacies by shoring up their *real strengths*. In other words, it is productive to deal with the narcissist by complimenting them on their realistic traits and behaviors. Remind them of their most recent successes. In doing so, be sure to use the language the narcissist understands best. He will really "hear" words like "admire," "star player," "the best," "outstanding," "superior," and all words that represent superiority. Language like this is his native tongue. For example, in the example of the car salesman, the manager would have gotten a better response if he were to remind his inflated salesman that his earnestness and enthusiasm were qualities that the manager *admired*, and that he would like the salesman to use these qualities more to achieve *superior* sales. If the salesman was in a slump, the manager could tell him that even Ken Griffey strikes out from time to time, and that he is still *a star player* around the dealership.

The following suggestions for dealing with the narcissistic employee or subordinate may help.

1. *Don't get caught on the roller coaster*. In the beginning, the narcissist will most likely overvalue your talents. He or she will most likely think that you're wonderful. She might even tell you that she admires you. Don't get caught up in this—even if it appeals to your own narcissism. If you allow yourself to get sucked in, you will feel even worse when the inevitable process of devaluation begins. The narcissist will soon become overtly or covertly very critical of you

2. *Stick to your agenda, not theirs*. When listening to his tirades or eloquent discourses on the ills of the organization, it will be tempting to try to respond to them. You will want to correct his errors of fact and logic or, worse yet, the extremes in his thinking caused by his tendencies toward overvaluation and devaluation. Responding really needs to be done in a tactful and supportive way, as it is very important to the narcissist that she be understood. Ignoring their concerns will get you nowhere, because they will continue trying to get you to see things their way, which they believe is the *only* way. The ability to stick to your agenda while not offending them requires a cool head and a great deal of practice

3. *Coach them to be a team player*. Showing a narcissist that there are personal rewards to being a team player might just entice

them into being more cooperative. You might be able to "bridge" this idea by having the narcissist put the group together.

4. *Put them in charge of feedback.* Direct the narcissist to obtain feedback from others. This could help override their lack of empathy by forcing them to be accountable for others' feelings.

5. *Be a coach to your star player.* When dealing with the narcissist, one should adopt an attitude that one is coaching one's star player. Acknowledge their successes and show them ways to become even greater. Avoid criticisms. For example, rather than saying to your top salesman, "You need to service your accounts better after the sale," say something like, "Your sales figures are terrific! Way to go! Once you get the servicing aspects on par with your sales, you'll be *untouchable.*"

6. *Resources, not competitors.* Show the narcissist that coworkers can be resources and not competitors. Show them that other people may have special talents that he might be able to use. If you are faced with a situation in which you have to correct a mistake the narcissist has made, do not criticize them. Rather point out that even the best employees have strengths and weaknesses

7. *Provide constructive but balanced feedback.* Be as specific as you can in providing constructive feedback of both their strengths and weaknesses. Avoid vague statements or global comments, which will only make them defensive.

8. *Build bridges.* Don't try to take on the narcissist head on. It's far more effective to try to find common ground. For example, it would be a good idea to "join" the narcissist and to appear to be on his side on an issue rather than to try to change his mind entirely (which would probably be a lifetime endeavor).

In the following exchange, Mr. White, an administrator, is listening to complaints made by his top salesman regarding one of his coworkers:

Salesman: I came to talk to you today about Tom. The way he dresses is just awful—I think that he must get his clothes from the homeless. I don't think he's bought a new suit in years.

Administrator: You know something, John? I believe that you might have made a very good point. Good

	grooming is important to our image. *(Notice that the administrator doesn't choose to put down the other salesman. He only acknowledges an area of common ground.)*
Salesman:	Sometimes a guy like that can hurt the image of the entire sales force. I don't know why you don't just fire him.
Administrator:	*(Again, finding a common ground or bridge.)* Believe me, I support the idea of firing an incompetent individual who is hurting the company.
Salesman:	Well, he sure is a guy who should be fired if only for the fact that he doesn't know that stripes and polka dots look awful together.
Administrator:	Maybe I'll have a talk with him about his effectiveness with the company.

Narcissist or Addict?

As we've said before we wish that we could tell you that each of these personality types were discrete entities. However, social sciences are not that exact and there are myriad individual differences that can complicate the matter. Therefore, while we can talk of Narcissistic Personality Disorder as having a set number of symptoms, often the ways these symptoms express themselves can yield a variety of patterns and variations on the theme. You will see later on, for example, when we talk about Antisocial Personality Disorder, that there are often overlaps with the narcissist in the fact that most antisocials will often demonstrate the same penchant for self-centeredness, a belief that the world should revolve around them, and a great sense of entitlement. The difference is that the antisocial will think nothing of breaking the rules and will do so without any sense of guilt or remorse. There is also an overlap between narcissists and those with substance related disorders and various addictions. There is a saying in Alcoholics Anonymous that the alcoholic is the "egomaniac with the inferiority complex." So, too, is the narcissist (Johnson 1994). Therefore, it is not unusual, depending on where they are in their addiction, for an alcoholic, drug addict, gambler, workaholic, or sex addict to demonstrate the same personality traits as the Narcissistic Personality Disorder. For example, if one is still actively addicted, their narcissism is usually at its most extreme. Even if the individual is fortunate enough to have gotten into recovery, the addictive behavior may have stopped, but the personality often remains the same. Therefore, you will often see an individual who still manifests the same characteristics as when they were actively using, e.g., low frustration tolerance, impulsiveness, self-centeredness, and so on. It is not usually until the addict is well into recovery that they begin to rebuild their lives and bring about some personality change. It is noteworthy that all twelve-step-based programs, e.g., AA, Narcotics Anonymous, Cocaine Anonymous, Sex and Love Addicts Anonymous, include in their fourth and fifth step the idea that the individual must take a "fearless moral inventory," in which they look at "character defects" and then go about sharing these with a sponsor or someone in the program who has made a solid recovery. These are important steps in being able to change the addict's narcissistic view of the world. In later steps (eighth and ninth steps), the alcoholic or addict will attempt to make amends to those whom they have injured through their addiction. All twelve-step programs emphasize "service," i.e., that the individual give back, in some way, what they have gotten from the program, whether making coffee before a meeting, helping to clean up after a meeting, or taking on a "speaking commitment" by telling one's story to other alcoholics or addicts. There are many other recommendations in twelve-step programs that are geared toward getting the addict or alcoholic to relinquish their narcissistic view of the world. In doing so, they can work toward bringing an end to the painful isolation of their addiction.

In closing, we wish to state that you'll find the narcissist one of the most challenging coworkers to deal with. But the effort can be well worth it. Narcissists, with their leadership qualities and charisma, can be excellent assets to the organization. With some effort in the right direction, the narcissist's strengths can be channeled to the advantage of the organization, while their toxic qualities can be minimized.

CHAPTER 4

Histrionic Personality Disorder: Lights . . . Camera . . . Action!

All the world's a stage,
And all the men and women merely players;
They have their exits and their entrances . . .

—William Shakespeare

If we were to sum up Histrionic Personality Disorder in one word, it would be *"dramatic."* In fact, in the DSM-IV, Histrionic Personality Disorder is grouped with a cluster of personality disorders that are referred to as "Dramatic, Erratic." Therefore, the types of character traits, behaviors, or moods one might expect to observe may vacillate from day to day, or from hour to hour, given the circumstances or events. Histrionics are very much attuned to the here and now of their immediate environment. They are adept at reading people and situations to see what is required of them. Why? Because, above all, the histrionic personality fears rejection and abandonment by significant others in their lives. In this regard, they are quite similar to the dependent personality. Where the histrionic and dependent differ is that the histrionic is much more active in their bid to seek reassurance and gain acceptance (Millon & Davis 1996). Histrionic personality types can become overwhelmed by anxiety if threatened with rejection. This is why they will often go to great lengths in order to impress others or to win their admiration or approval. As noted by Easser and Lesser (1965), histrionics will often gain tremendous pleasure in "entertaining others and assuming the role of hostess with graciousness, so long as they held the center of the stage, through integration and seductiveness as a rule, through temper tantrums when necessary."

Although our description of individuals with Histrionic Personality Disorder has been somewhat negative thus far, many people with this disorder do have positive qualities and traits. They can be quite outgoing, extroverted, and assertive. Many have a flair for art, music, and theatre. These are the "idea people," according to Oldham and Morris (1995), the ones who often thrive on creativity. Histrionic people are often described as being "the lives of the party," as their unbridled energy levels are often quite infectious in social situations. These characteristics will often be quite advantageous in various occupations where sociability and gregariousness are important commodities. Obviously, any entertainment-oriented occupation would be the perfect fit for those with HPD. Other occupations would include trial lawyer or any field involving advertising, marketing, or sales work, as these individuals are often quite skilled at selling ideas and generating enthusiasm. Just don't expect them to do the detailed, routine work. Also, jobs involving serving the people, such as hairdresser, tour guide, or certain types of teaching. In these occupations, where being "center stage" is a job requirement, the histrionic personality types will often thrive. This, of course, is providing that they can maintain the center of attention and, in doing so, gain the approval of others. In fact, Erich Fromm (1947) spoke of the histrionic personality as having a "marketing orientation." Fromm described how these individuals often are compelled to sell themselves or to present a "nice package" to the world. Yet, beneath this outer veneer of friendliness and sociability may be a person who can be shallow, deceitful, and demanding.

It appears, therefore, that problems can easily arise for and with the HPD person when the job or occupation involves a long-term or sustained relationship. Histrionic personality types are adept at creating a good impression and in impressing others with their "life of the party" antics. However, in the long run, they do not do well in relationships. In many instances, significant others in their lives either become a disappointment to the HPD person or they will "burn out" those people in their lives who just can't keep up with them or who become annoyed by their bids for constant attention. In essence, the histrionic personality type will often become bored with relationships once the initial "infatuation" wears off. This is true in both love and work relationships. Their extreme activity level, their outgoing style, and their flair for theatrics will often become grating to anyone who must deal with these individuals for any length of time. It's common that these significant others will often complain of the histrionic person's capricious moods, their inability to maintain emotional control, and their impulsiveness. This, naturally, can also become quite wearing for a boss, coworker, or friend.

What Is Histrionic Personality Disorder?

While many people can have histrionic traits or qualities, they may not manifest Histrionic Personality Disorder, per se. According to the DSM-IV criteria, Histrionic Personality Disorder is characterized as follows:

> A pervasive pattern of excessive emotionality and attention seeking beginning by early adulthood and present in a variety of contexts, as indicated by five or more of the following:
>
> 1. is uncomfortable in situations in which he or she is not the center of attention.
>
> 2. interaction with others is often characterized by inappropriate sexually seductive or provocative behavior.
>
> 3. displays rapidly shifting and shallow expression of emotion.
>
> 4. consistently uses physical appearance to draw attention to self.
>
> 5. has a style of speech that is excessively impressionistic and lacking in detail.
>
> 6. shows self-dramatization, theatricality, and exaggerated expression of emotion.
>
> 7. is suggestible, i.e., easily influenced by others or circumstances.
>
> 8. considers relationships to be more intimate than they actually are.*

As you consider the symptoms listed above, you will begin to get a picture of both the histrionic woman or man. Although HPD is thought to occur more frequently in women, there are also many men who suffer from the same disorder but in a different variation. For example, using the criteria listed above, the histrionic women is someone who can be quite flirtatious and seductive, which is evident in both her mannerism and her appearance (she would probably be wearing the shortest, most revealing dress and the most makeup and jewelry). Everything about her outer appearance shouts, "Hey everyone, look at me!" The histrionic male is often the hypermasculinized

---

* Reprinted with permission from the *Diagnostic and Statistical Manual of Mental Disorders*, Fourth Edition. Copyright 1994 American Psychiatric Association.

counterpart of the histrionic woman. He, too, is known for his flashy manner of dress, and for being quite "the lady's man." Think Dennis Rodman here. Histrionic men and women share many common features. For example, even a brief, chance encounter can make you their close friend and confidant. Emotionally, they are quite shallow and appear to others as phony. They have all the emotional warmth and genuineness of a nightclub or lounge singer. As can also be seen from the DSM-IV criteria, HPDs are often very difficult to "pin down," given their flare for impressionistic speech lacking in detail. A good example of a histrionic woman is Blanche DuBois in the play *A Streetcar Named Desire*. Blanche's overall style is quite typical of the histrionic, in terms of being seductive, and speaking with a wispy, ethereal quality.

Millon and Davis (1996) indicate that not all people with Histrionic Personality Disorder are alike, suggesting that there are six distinct subtypes. The *appeasing histrionic* is characterized by an overwhelming desire to please others, to seek their approval, and to prove to others that they are worthy. The *tempestuous histrionic* is known for their extreme emotional fluctuations and periods of impulsive acting out. These tempestuous periods will alternate with depressive periods, moodiness, and sulking. This subtype is also known for seeking excitement and needing a great deal of stimulation. An outer veneer of friendliness and sociability characterizes the *disingenuous histrionic*. They are adept at making good first impressions on others, but those who get to know people in this subtype are able to see their unreliability, moodiness, and frequent resentments. The behavior of the *theatrical histrionic* is more characteristic of what most mental-health professionals associate with Histrionic Personality Disorder. These individuals are known for their charm, and for their dramatic, romantic, and attention-seeking behavior. They're chameleon-like in their ability to read what others expect of them and, in this respect, are quite adaptable to most situations. The *infantile histrionic* is characterized by their childlike pouting, their clinging demands, their labile emotions, as well as their sexual provocativeness. The infantile histrionic fears rejection and abandonment, which accounts for their demanding and clinging behaviors. Finally, the *vivacious histrionic* is noted for their high level of energy, their flippant charm, and their optimistic worldview. They often act on impulse with little or no regard for the consequences of their behavior. There are both manic as well as narcissistic qualities to their personality makeup.

From the descriptions of the various subtypes noted in the section above, you may notice how HPD overlaps with the Borderline and Narcissistic Personality Disorders (which are described in chapters 3 and 6 respectively). Histrionic individuals share some of the impetuousness and mood fluctuations of the person with Borderline Personality Disorder, along with their fears of abandonment and rejection. Both usually have difficulty in sustaining long-term relationships, as their extreme behaviors will often result in tremendous relationship problems. Also, both the histrionic and borderline are not very good when left alone, at which point they often report feeling empty or, at the very least, bored.

The attention-seeking behavior and need to be center stage provide obvious overlaps between the narcissistic and histrionic personality. As mentioned earlier, however, while both may seek the attention and admiration of others, the narcissistic personality does so with a sense that this tribute is their due. The histrionic may feel that, no matter what they do, they will never really be appreciated, nor will they ever be able to fully gain the approval of others or prove their worth.

Histrionic Personality Disorders will also often overlap with depression. These depressions will often come about in the wake of major disappointments in relationships, rejections, or other disappointments in which the histrionic feels that they have lost the approval of others. In some instances, suicidal threats or suicidal gestures are common. This is evidence of the extreme emotional lability (the tendency toward mood fluctuation) of these individuals. It seems that when they are on a high, they are on top of the world. However when things "bottom out," they can crash terribly hard.

The Histrionic Administrator

On the surface, it may seem unlikely that someone with HPD could rise to a position of leadership, as it would seem that their lack of emotional control would probably make them a poor choice for most administrative positions. However, it is often by virtue of the HPDs outgoing, assertive personality style that they can sell themselves into leadership roles. There are many sales, marketing, or political jobs where the histrionic's energy level, gregariousness, and sociability make them rise to the top and win the confidence of those around them. But when this happens, it often spells disaster for those miserable souls who must work under them. Histrionic bosses can be quite demanding, and their fleeting emotional states often result in them yelling at you one minute while complimenting your new suit the next. They can often come up with a flurry of ideas and solutions to problems, but don't expect them to be the one to carry these solutions out. According to Oldham and Morris (1995), histrionic administrators do best when they have a conscientious secretary or administrative assistant who can help them organize their time and help them with implementing their ideas. Therefore, while histrionic bosses make good "front" men or women, they are rarely adept and organized enough to actually land deals or maintain accounts. So, if you're working for someone like this, expect to have a lot of the grunt work dumped on you, as they flit around the office and entertain the troops. Unfortunately, these character types often don't do much for morale, because most of the "troops" know that when the going gets rough the histrionic gets going—leaving their employees to clean up the mess.

Working with the Histrionic Administrator

In order to cope well with this type of boss, you'll need not only a great deal of patience and tolerance, but you'll also need to accept several basic facts. The first is that, even though you're probably more competent than they are, they will end up getting the credit for the work accomplished. That's what histrionics do best—they sell themselves. They are their own publicists and, given their extroverted character, they seem to get away with it quite well. If you were to adopt the same strategy, you would come across as self-serving. As indicated earlier, you may find yourself having work capriciously dumped on you without any particular rhyme or reason. You will need to accept, that at any given moment, you can become the hero or the goat, depending on the mood of your HPD boss. Therefore, it's best not to take your boss's tirades too seriously. If they are in a bad temper it's better to keep out of sight and lay low until the storm blows over. You might also find that you never really feel appreciated. After all, the star actor is really more interested in themselves than in acknowledging the stagehands. Watch any list of movie credits and you'll see that it is not the "detail people" who get the recognition. Finally, you will also need to accept that, above all, you cannot change this person. It's more productive to take a humorous approach to the situation. Try not to take their behavior (or, perhaps, yourself) quite so seriously One good thing you can count on with a histrionic boss is that your mistakes won't stay the focus of attention for too long, as the histrionic will quickly fly off to some other situation, problem, or crisis. At times, you may wonder to yourself, "How did I end up working in such a crazy situation?" You may begin to question if you can survive working for someone like this. In those instances, you'll basically know when you've had enough and when it's time for a change. It's not uncommon for those working for histrionic bosses to burn out rather quickly, as they find they just can't keep pace with the demands of the topsy-turvy work environment. There's nothing wrong with knowing when you've had enough and getting out.

The Histrionic Coworker

Working *with* someone with HPD can be just as draining as working *for* them. It can also be quite amusing. If you're working alongside a histrionic who has a flair for storytelling, drama, and gossip, it can actually be fun. However, if your coworker is a histrionic who is in crisis mode all the time, you may find yourself getting caught up in their crises. HPDs generally will have a very poor sense of boundaries. This means that they will often bring family or social problems to work with them, and you may find yourself exhausted listening to the seemingly endless litany of troubles that they'll bother you with. Everything seems to be an emotional crisis. There probably never seems to be a day where you can just work alongside this person assured that you'll be able to get a good chunk of work accomplished. Yet, their seductiveness makes it extremely easy to find yourself getting hooked into their behavior. Getting involved is a mistake, especially if you find yourself becoming their rescuer. Histrionics are similar to people with Dependent Personality and Borderline Personality Disorders, in that they are like "bottomless pits" when it comes to wanting their needs met. Once you get into the role of being the giving or forgiving coworker, you can be easily seduced into staying in that role. This can be especially true in the instance of a coworker of the opposite sex. One retail store clerk was quite skilled at getting his female coworker to cover for him, as he had gained her sympathy for the problems he was always having with his girlfriend. His attractiveness and seductiveness was quite flattering to this coworker, who truly felt that she was helping him out. It was only after months of such behavior that she finally realized that she was being used. At that point, she found she was able to detach from his histrionics and not get hooked into his constant states of crisis. She gradually became aware that he merely used these women to feed his own ego, just as he was doing with her.

Working with the Histrionic Coworker

If you find yourself working with a histrionic coworker who likes being the center of attention by way of their quick wit, their amusing stories, and being the office jokester, then you can sit back and enjoy the show. Just don't expect this person to do much in the way of real work or to help you out when the chips are down. Remember, these individuals usually have tremendous difficulty with details and organization, so you probably can't expect much in the way of real help. You may even need to distance yourself from this person, in the sense that you may not want to be identified with someone who is not seen as a hard worker. However, their needs for nurturance and reassurance may get them to do some work, so as not to alienate you totally.

If, on the other hand, you're working with the crisis-mode histrionic, one who's constantly distressed by one problem or another, it's important to learn to set boundaries. Sara, a bank teller, was a very responsible, conscientious worker who would often get stuck working with Jamie, who had many histrionic traits. Sara would find herself listening for hours to Jamie's tales of woe, only to find that she wasn't getting her own work done. Jamie would pick up and leave at the end of their shift, which then left Sara to count out the deposits and tally everything up. After weeks of this, Sara was fuming and felt that she was ready to explode at Jamie. Instead, her husband suggested that she take more of an assertive approach in order to set the boundary. "Gee Jamie, I'd like to help you out, but I'm really bogged down with work today. Maybe we can talk after work." Sara found that she could manage the situation better by being polite but very firm with Jamie. In many ways, histrionics are like adolescents, so Sara took a firm, motherly type of approach, as opposed to being her girlfriend. It worked.

The Histrionic Subordinate

The histrionic employee can either be your best, most devoted worker or can make a manager's life a living hell. Oldham and Morris (1995) suggest that, given the histrionic's need for approval and attention, it would be best to "Pamper your Dramatic employees, tell them how much you appreciate them, let them work the way they please, and they'll reward you with excellent work" (143). This recommendation is based on the supposition that you're dealing with a low-level type of histrionic personality or what Oldham and Morris term the "Dramatic Style" personality. In this case, where you have a more functional employee, it's probably true that you can get a lot of productivity by providing some praise, some loosening of structure, and encouragement. If your employee responds to these strategies, you're probably dealing with a more functional type of histrionic or someone with histrionic traits versus someone with Histrionic Personality Disorder.

Sometimes, though, a histrionic employee can try the patience of a saint. Although they may be good in some situations, especially where selling or dealing with the public may be concerned, don't expect them to be adept at organization or follow through. If, for some reason, they charm themselves into a job that requires emotional restraint, organization, regimentation, or a job where repetitious or technical tasks are involved, then you will see their enthusiasm fade rather quickly. Histrionics usually tend to function better in creative jobs that afford for greater flexibility. One histrionic office-equipment saleswoman would take days off on a whim, depending usually on how things were going with her boyfriend or what crisis she was trying to deal with. In any other job, she would have probably lasted only a couple of weeks, while in this job, she was the top producer. Why? On those occasions when she worked, she really put all of her energy into her job and was able to achieve great results. Many histrionic employees will often exhibit this kind of capricious attitude toward their job. After all, they are much more focused on their internal emotional world than on your external goals and objectives. "Practical" concerns are often irrelevant to the histrionic. So, they will think nothing of taking a day off and won't be bothered to consider the consequence or impact of this decision on you or their coworkers.

Working with the Histrionic Subordinate

As Oldham and Morris so aptly point out, "An essential rule is not to overreact to their overreactions" (151). It is better not to get hooked into their crises or their demands for special attention or favors. Most histrionics will often have a great "hard luck" story that is hard to resist, so it's best to set your limits and keep them to avoid being manipulated.

As college professors, we are often badgered by histrionic college students who always seem to be dealing with one crisis or another. In their minds, these crises serve as justification for why they should be given special treatment, such as being excused from an exam, or not having to turn in a written project on time. Obviously, there are times when a makeup exam is warranted, or where there is a bona-fide crisis. However, with histrionic students, *everything is a crisis*. The cardinal rule in situations like this is to treat everyone equally and not have some of the rules apply to some and not to others. The same holds true in the workplace. It's very important not to give in to demands or feed into the drama of the histrionic. This can be done in a reassuring way, by complimenting the histrionic on other aspects of their work that you wish to reinforce or increase.

Tiffany, a twenty-four-year-old single female, was working as an administrative assistant to a departmental manager at a marketing research company. She had been working there for the past six months, and was just past the probationary period, when erratic work performance began to emerge. She had been involved for the past month in an affair with a married coworker. It seems that when this coworker began to feel pangs of guilt and tried cooling the relationship with Tiffany, she began to have a total emotional meltdown. She would go into her boss's office and burst into tears, asking for time off and taking long breaks to try to meet with her ex-lover and resurrect the affair. Her boss, Dave, was becoming increasingly frustrated by her behavior. He had been initially hopeful that things would blow over as soon as the affair cooled down, and that Tiffany would then be back to more consistent work performance. Things seemed to get worse, however, rather than better. In addition, Dave now was having to hear complaints from Tiffany's coworkers that she was disrupting the office with her long, dramatic phone converstaions with her girlfriends and by constantly taking long breaks. Dave was in a bind and was feeling pressure from his boss and from other subordinates to "do something about Tiffany." So, Dave had a meeting with Tiffany and tried to console her. He praised her for the work performance during her probationary period and offered her reassurance that she could once again become part of the office team if she would begin to get her life together. He offered to set up an appointment with the Employee Assistance Counselor, an opportunity Tiffany declined. Dave then spelled out for her what was expected in regard to behavior changes she would need to make. He made it clear (both verbally and in writing) that he wanted her in on time, that he expected her to limit her personal calls to break time, and that he wanted her to limit her breaks to a reasonable period of time. Dave was also clear that if Tiffany deviated from the written agreement, Dave would need to write up a disciplinary action—although he was careful to reassure Tiffany that this is not what he wanted to do. Instead, he kept stressing that he wanted Tiffany to take charge of her situation and preserve her job. Unfortunately, although Tiffany agreed to the plan that Dave spelled out, she found that she was "just too emotional" to stay within the boundaries of the plan. Tiffany continued to come in late and continued to take long breaks. Eventually, after three more months of such behavior and three disciplinary actions, Tiffany was fired.

This case is illustrative of many aspects of the histrionic personality. First, there is an obvious boundary problem here. Office romances are generally frowned upon, under any circumstances. Tiffany's lack of appropriate boundaries led her into seeing nothing wrong with having an affair during her probationary period. She then fell apart when her married coworker tried to break things off. Rather than Tiffany accepting this rejection and moving on, she began to become clingy and demanding. She lacked the emotional control to separate her work behavior from her out-of-work behavior. Finally, when her boss made an attempt to get her to salvage her job, Tiffany lacked the ability to do so. This would have required a sense of self, a centeredness that most histrionics seem to lack.

Dave's only fault in this was that he may have acted sooner, or taken a more proactive approach before things got as bad as they did. The five months or so that it took to resolve this issue took its toll on the entire staff. It also put a strain on Dave and hurt his image of being an effective manager. Obviously, not all situations involving histrionics have an unhappy ending. As was alluded to earlier, histrionics tend to do well in work settings that can provide flexibility and offer that person the opportunity to express their creative talents. Histrionics tend to do poorly in self-employment situations, unless they have a conscientious person working with them or for them who can help organize the tedious details of life and work most histrionics abhor.

So, whether you're working for, with, or supervising a histrionic, remember it is important that you refrain from getting on the emotional roller coaster with them. Try to keep your sense of calm and composure and you will be able to avoid getting hooked into their crises.

CHAPTER 5

The Antisocial Personality: Rules Do Not Apply

*It is a wicked world, and when a clever man
turns his brains to crime, it is the worst of all*

—A. Conan Doyle, *The Adventures
of Sherlock Holmes*

The antisocial personality can be considered the most "dangerous" of all the personality types that have been discussed thus far. Yet, Antisocial Personality Disorders can encompass a wide range of behaviors. One of the common misconceptions of the term "antisocial" is that it refers to an individual who does not like to be around others, who is socially inept and certainly not gregarious. An individual possessing those traits would be considered "asocial," not antisocial. Individuals with Antisocial Personality Disorder (APD) are usually not asocial but are often gregarious, charming, and verbally skilled, which is why they make such good con artists.

What Is Antisocial Personality Disorder?

The range of behavior that individuals with APD display can best be viewed as existing on a continuum. At one end of the continuum, we have criminal psychopaths (e.g., monsters such as Adolf Hitler, Jeffrey Dahlmer, Ted Bundy, and Richard Speck), and on the other end would be people who are sometimes referred to as "successful psychopaths" or "subcriminal psychopaths." These are the individuals who most often do not act out in a criminal way, yet they can be just as manipulative and cunning as those psychopaths at the other end of the spectrum. On this end of the continuum would be people who swindle senior citizens out of their life savings, used-car salesman who knowingly sell a lemon with rolled-back mileage, and perhaps the boss who steals his employee's ideas and then fires the employee for coming in to work five minutes late. What is central to this personality disorder is that this boss would think nothing of their actions and would not even experience the slightest bit of remorse or guilt over them. Unfortunately, we run into people like this all the time, which is the theme of Robert Hare's landmark book, *Without Conscience: The Disturbing World of the Psychopaths Among Us* (1993). Hare devotes an entire chapter to "white collar psychopaths," and within this chapter is a section on the "subcriminal psychopath." It is this subtype of Antisocial Personality Disorder that we will be focusing on in this chapter.

There is obviously an overlap between the label "psychopaths" and the diagnostic term of Antisocial Personality Disorder. Beck and Freeman (1990), for example, point out that the terms "psychopath," "sociopath," and "antisocial personality disorder" have often been used interchangeably. Paul Babiak (1995) states that historically, psychopathy has been characterized as being "a mixture of *both* overt antisocial behaviours *and* personality attributes that typically include superficial charm; unreliability, untruthfulness, and insincerity; lack of guilt, remorse, or shame; a need to engage in thrill-seeking behaviour; failure to follow any life plan; impulsiveness; low frustration tolerance and the inability to delay gratification; pathological lying; lack of insight; failure to learn from experience or punishment; pathologic egocentricity and selfishness; inability to form meaningful relationships; antisocial or asocial behavior; rejection of authority and discipline; poor work and marital history; and an arrest record.

In its current form, the DSM-IV defines an Antisocial Personality Disorder as follows:

A. There is a pervasive pattern of disregard for and violation of the rights of others occurring since age 15 years, as indicated by three (or more) of the following:

1. failure to conform to social norms with respect to lawful behaviors as indicated by repeatedly performing acts that are grounds for arrest.

2. deceitfulness, as indicated by repeated lying, use of aliases, or conning others for personal profit or pleasure.

3. impulsivity or failure to plan ahead.

4. irritability and aggressiveness, as indicated by repeated physical fights and assaults.

5. reckless disregard for safety of self or others.

6. consistent irresponsibility, as indicated by repeated failure to sustain consistent work behavior or honor financial obligations.

7. lack of remorse, as indicated by being indifferent to or rationalizing having hurt, mistreated or stolen from another.*

As you can see from the Diagnostic Criteria, there is a propensity toward breaking rules. However, this does not necessarily mean that the individual with APD will necessarily engage in criminal activity. Oldham and Morris (1995) point out that, while APD is one of the two most common diagnoses among prison inmates (alcohol dependence/abuse being the other), not all convicted felons are necessarily diagnosable with Antisocial Personality Disorder.

So, even if the person with ADP isn't necessarily criminal, why are we talking about this diagnosis with regards to the workplace? What separates the con man from the top salesperson of the company? This is where Babiak's concept of the "successful industrial psychopath" comes in. Babiak contends that, often times, antisocial behavior and traits are not apparent to the casual observer, and that human resources professionals are not trained to detect psychopathy. If anything, the psychopath's charm, quick verbal wit, and intelligence may make them appear to be an excellent candidate for positions they apply for. Also, because these individuals are so adept at making a good impression, it's not uncommon for interviewers to be taken in (Hare, Forth, & Hart 1989). In a research study illustrating this point, Eisenman (1980) had high school teachers rate psychopathic, drug-using students and nonpsychopathic students. The psychopathic students were actually rated as more "likable." Hare (1993) mentions a story about a colleague who was interviewing a prospective candidate for a job and found him to be quite brilliant. What the psychopathic applicant had done was to read some of the work written by this colleague and was actually using this information deceptively in order to create a favorable impression in the interview. This is different from an applicant who prepares for an

---

* Reprinted with permission from the *Diagnostic and Statistical Manual of Mental Disorders*, Fourth Edition. Copyright 1994 American Psychiatric Association.

interview and is forthright in presenting what they know or have heard about a prospective employer or company.

Babiak (1995) also contends that some corporations may actually *attract* subcriminal psychopaths. Consider a corporation that may advertise for an "aggressive, outgoing, dynamic salesperson, someone willing to take risks, who is adventurous and good at handling people." This is exactly what Widom (1977) did in a research study in which she placed an ad for just such an individual. Lo and behold, she found that a number of the people responding to the ad had psychopathic traits. Therefore, corporations that seek these "aggressive, risk-taking, dynamic" individuals may actually be attracting subcriminal psychopaths into their midst.

Okay, let's say this type of individual does make it past the gate and is offered employment within a corporate setting. Wouldn't the bureaucratic structure and the rigid corporate culture prove too frustrating for someone with Antisocial Personality Disorder? On the surface, this would certainly seem to be the case, as we consider the list of APD diagnostic criteria described above. However, given the psychopath's ability to remain cool, calm, and to lie or deceive their way out of anything, they sometimes thrive in a corporate environment. Remember, their goal is often to circumvent the rules, to manipulate the rules to their own ends, or "get over" on the system. Babiak (1995) describes a case of a "problem employee" named Dave, who was good looking, well spoken, and married with children. Dave's supervisor, Frank, soon noted several objectionable behaviors. Dave would storm into Frank's office, demanding the department secretary be fired. He would leave in the middle of meetings, and bully other team members who did not support his ideas. He often berated coworkers only to then compliment them or beg forgiveness. He shirked assignments and, when confronted on work that was not done, he denied these allegations. He would flirt with younger female employees and take expensive equipment home on the weekends that he was unauthorized to take. What was noteworthy about Dave is that, as frustrating as he was to fellow employees and his supervisor, he had endeared himself to upper management, who considered him to be bright, ambitious, and as having management potential. Dave would apparently identify Frank to upper management as the source of his problems, a ploy that is very common among these industrial psychopaths. In addition to the behaviors described above, Babiak points out that Dave also had lied on his résumé, blatantly stolen from the company, and used both company time and materials for his own benefit. And what was the outcome of this case? Those of you who have ever dealt with such an individual already know the answer—Dave was promoted. Why? Because of his charm, manipulative skills, and his ability to appear ambitious to upper management. The bosses perceived Dave as a dynamic, high-potential employee, and Frank was told "to leave Dave alone" (181).

Another interesting conceptualization of an APD subtype is put forth by Gustafson and Ritzer (1995) in what they refer to as "aberrant self-promotion." Aberrant self-promoters are hypothesized to be individuals who are similar to psychopaths in that they exhibit characteristics of exploitativeness, entitlement, grandiosity, superficial charm, manipulativeness, the need for dominance, and a lack of empathy and remorse. Aberrant self-promoters, about midway on the sociopath continuum, don't often stray over the line into criminality. Gustafson and Ritzer explain that they have chosen this term because the prime motivation of these individuals is to "further their own self-interest" (148). Aberrant self-promoters seek to be admired, envied, and perceived by others as being highly competent. However, Gustafson and Ritzer make the distinction that the aberrant self-promoter is not only someone who is driven to achieve but a person who will do so no matter what rules are broken or who they have to step on in order to achieve their goals. In the mind of the aberrant self-promoter, therefore, the ends *always* justifies the means. In explaining why they had undertaken research to prove this construct, Gustafson and Ritzer explain, "Perhaps not surprisingly, we believe that aberrant self-promotion, conceptualized here as a *pattern of characteristics* that theoretically comprises a subclinical form of psychopathy, provides a unique and worthwhile perspective on the 'dark' side of organizational life" (179). It's this "dark side" that you may be dealing with right now in your workplace.

The Antisocial Administrator

In a news story appearing in *Time* on December 11, 1995 entitled, "Is Your 401(k) at Risk?", an engineer who was about to retire and cash out his retirement account, found that all the money had been drained out of the account. He later discovered that the former owner of the company had pilfered approximatly $3 million from the 401(k) funds of his employees. The article goes on to explain that the U.S. Department of Labor has launched investigations into 310 companies on similar cases and has recovered over $3.5 million in stolen assets. In some instances, the funds had been pilfered from health care programs by corporate executives, leaving their employees with virtually no health care coverage.

Although it seems antithetical to think of someone who manifests subcriminal psychopathic tendencies rising to the top of an organization, there are many situations where this can and does happen. There are two factors that lends to this scenario. First, there are many instances where skills involving ruthlessness, conning, manipulation, and deceit combined with unbridled ambition are viewed as necessary prerequisites to advance within particular organizations. Like the old saying goes, "Nice guys (or girls) finish last." Subcriminal psychopaths are known for their extroversion, their charm, and their polished social skills, and it's not unusual for these traits to be rewarded within many organizations.

The second factor that can assist the subcriminal psychopath in gaining administrative authority is the intoxicating effect of power. It is possible to see individuals who may have "played by the rules" (at least to the outside world) in the past become psychopathic power mongers once they reach the top and are no longer restricted by having to answer to many higher authorities. This was aptly illustrated by Jack Nicholson's character in the film, *A Few Good Men*. Here, Nicholson plays the role of a Marine colonel who encourages, aids, and abets the murder of a Marine private under his command, a soldier who was "causing trouble" by requesting a transfer. In the dramatic, final courtroom scene, Nicholson justifies his actions and is in disbelief that anyone would consider his actions negligent, let alone criminal. So, too, the antisocial administrator will see nothing wrong with firing employees on Christmas Eve, sexually harassing a young female employee, pilfering money from the union pension fund, or squandering company funds on personal expenses. One great example of this attitude was the director of a well-known drug-treatment facility in the Midwest who had the patients of the facility dig his swimming pool, all the while rationalizing that their labors were "therapeutic." What is common to all of these situations is that the administrator with APD apparently thinks nothing of crossing boundaries or invading the space (or even the pension funds) of his or her employees. Again, given their utter lack of compassion and inability to experience remorse or guilt, it is not uncommon for these types to fire an employee three days before Christmas, to cancel an employee's hard-earned vacation plans on a whim, or degrade an employee in front of others—and not give it a second thought.

Antisocial behavior may take several forms, but the common denominator is that those working for this type of individual end up feeling abused, often humiliated, and powerless. To the family members and friends of these abused workers, the answer seems quite obvious. "Get as far away from this person as possible, and the sooner the better!" However, for the employee caught up in the web of one of these characters it's often surprisingly difficult to break free. This difficulty is where the common denominator between the criminal psychopath and the subcriminal psychopath becomes of paramount importance. That commonality is *charisma*. Consider some of the famous psychopaths mentioned at the beginning of this chapter. Although there were many factors contributing to Hitler's rise to power, would he have made it so far without his ability to convince the German people that he, alone, could bring Germany out of economic depression? Would Ted Bundy have been able to lure all those pretty young women into helping him without his charisma and ability to play the victim so well? (There were instances where Bundy would feign a broken leg in order to get young women to give him rides.) Would Charlie Manson have been able to convince his followers to murder Sharon Tate had it not been for the charismatic charm and power he held over them? So, too, the subcriminal psychopath often possesses a remarkable charismatic charm.

Brainwashing techniques, as taught for military purposes, involve extreme-opposite treatment of the captive, i.e., threatening them within an inch of their lives one minute, while treating them kindly the next. It is not unusual to see employees caught in the same pattern by their subcriminal psychopath adminstrators, becoming effectively "brainwashed" into thinking that their bosses are fine and that they, the employees, *must* be doing something wrong. Therefore, it's not unusual for an employee to feel that they can't go anywhere else or work for anyone else. "After all," they think, "who will want me?" This is very similar to the abused spouse who has been manipulated by the abuser to believe the same thing. Research tells us that abused spouses can and do leave, and there are also many instances where people do break free of the spellbinding hold of these individuals with APD.

Working with the Antisocial Personality Disordered Administrator

In *Without Conscience: The Disturbing World of Psychopaths Among Us*, Hare (1993) makes several cogent recommendations. He suggests that people *know what they are dealing with* and *don't wear blinders*. Hare warns us not to get sucked in by "props," as psychopaths are often quite skilled at making a good impression with the warm handshake, good eye contact, and a convincing smile. Skills like these are why they make such good impostors. Hare also suggests that one *set firm ground rules* and *be careful about power struggles*. This is excellent advice for the employee who finds themselves being taken advantage of by a subcriminal psychopathic boss who thinks nothing of having them work many hours of overtime without pay or has them give up their weekends in order to do "a little extra work." Setting limits can take the form of saying "No" to extra work hours and assignments or agreeing to a specified number of overtime hours per week. As Hare suggests, it's important to pick your battles, as most subcriminal psychopaths will often derive intense pleasure by winning these battles and, in doing so, humiliating you.

A colleague of mine once worked for a woman who manifested many of these subcriminal psychopathic traits. Although this male colleague worked very hard, it was never enough in her eyes, and he was constantly being accused of incompetence and of being unmotivated. When they finally had a showdown, my friend ended up leaving the agency under duress. I ran into him at a conference several months later, and he said that leaving the agency was the best thing that had ever happened to him. He went on to take a higher-paying administrative position and became the director of his own agency. Had he stayed in the situation, he would have continued to be miserable and depressed and would have continued to suspect that he really was incompetent and lazy. So, even though there may be instances when you may have few choices, or may be chained to a job by the proverbial "golden handcuffs," there may be other options out there that you've simply not considered. Just as it is often said that, when we look back on our lives, no one ever says, "I wish I spent more time at the office," I doubt that anyone ever looks back and says, "I wish I spent more time working for that nut case."

The Antisocial Coworker

Probably the best advice we could give to someone who finds themselves working side by side with an antisocial coworker is "Watch your back!" Very similar to working with someone with Narcissistic Personality Disorder, you may often find yourself expecting to work with this person in a spirit of cooperation and mutual support, only to find yourself feeling that you are shouldering the brunt of all the work and that you're feeling abused or manipulated by this person. Coworkers of subcriminal psychopaths often complain that they find them going through their belongings, that they will borrow money and not repay it, that they will shirk work assignments or will simply fail to show up for work. A friend recently related a story in which such a coworker had stolen the phone numbers of his contacts and clients from a data file in his computer and was proceeding to call these contacts and clients looking for new business. Another friend related a story of a coworker who went through her desk and found a prescription bottle for antidepressants. This antisocial coworker then brought the bottle to their boss with claims that my friend was "unstable." These are excellent examples of how antisocial coworkers will cross boundaries.

Working with the Antisocial Personality Disordered Coworker

Employees with APD are often quite adept at getting other coworkers to feel responsible for them. The absolute worst combination is an antisocial coworker and a codependent person who likes to take less fortunate people under their wing. Although it is admirable to want to help others out, when stuck with an antisocial coworker, you will often find yourself being taken advantage of. Again, because of their incapacity for feeling compassion, guilt, or remorse, they will take advantage of your good nature, your willingness to help, and will manipulate you time and time again. The codependent worker will often feel like they are working two jobs—their own and their coworker's. People with ADP can be quite variable in their behavior toward coworkers. They can present as "just one of the guys or gals" or they can be demeaning to coworkers, making insensitive comments and often being abusive. Subcriminal psychopaths are often quite skilled at reading people and reading situations, and in doing so, can often present a good facade to their coworkers while backstabbing them at every opportunity. They can be ruthless in their need to manipulate others for their own aggrandizement. Therefore, they will often present one face to coworkers, while presenting an entirely different facade to managers and supervisors. What is unique is how extreme this behavior can be—nice one minute and mean or vitriolic the next.

If you find yourself working with someone with APD traits or characteristics, here are some suggestions:

1. *Set boundaries.* You may need to do this verbally as well as physically. For example, make sure your desk is locked, your computer password is secure, and don't leave personal belongings or valuables around. Don't give this person personal information about yourself. Remember, anything you say can and will be used against you.

2. *Keep note of any indiscretions.* You may not want to take action on these right away, but it's always helpful to have ammunition in the event that you do need to justify your taking action at a later date. In situations like this, most managers will ask you to document what you have heard or experienced, so it's good to be prepared in advance.

3. *Keep someone you trust apprised of your situation or concerns.* If you find that you've fallen prey to one of these characters, at least let another coworker know what's going on, in case you need validation or support later on.

4. *Ask for help.* If your company offers an employee assistance program, don't be afraid to utilize these services. Some companies offer in-house EAP counselors who can help you decide what steps to take or can offer you support in dealing with this person effectively.

5. *Don't blame yourself and don't feel alone.* Many of us get caught in the web of these subcriminal psychopaths, but it is important not to feel guilty or responsible for their behavior (e.g., "If I were a better friend to this person, maybe they would change"). Also, it's important not to isolate yourself or feel that you are the only one who is being victimized by this person. If you are truly dealing with an APD coworker, chances are great that they have already burned other bridges and crossed other coworkers and bosses.

The Antisocial Subordinate

Probably no other situation strikes fear in the heart of managers, middle managers, and CEOs more than to have an APD subordinate What is often confusing for administrators who have antisocial subordinates is that they are often charming, and they appear quite devoted and loyal. They are good at making an impression and in convincing you that they can do the job and come through for you when "the chips are down." It is only after time has passed that you may begin to pick up on inconsistencies in their work. Or, you may have personal items missing from your desk or discover that the employee has been falsifying his time card. This is when you begin to see the dark side of these individuals. At first, there may even be a tendency to deny that these things are happening or that this employee is capable of such deceit. The social-psychology literature on Cognitive Dissonance Theory, originated with Leon Festinger's research (1957) in which he points out that, when one is presented with two competing ideas or attitudes, the individual will tend to resolve the resulting "dissonance" by steering toward that idea which will most expediently reduce the discomfort or dissonant state. Therefore, if you are in a state of dissonance because you have been told that your "loyal" employee, Fred, has presented your idea for expansion of the European market as his own idea, your first inclination might be to deny the claim or refute it, thereby reducing your state of dissonance. You may even hold on to this idea until presented with strong evidence otherwise. Naturally, if you were to confront Fred, he would talk you out of the accusation. "How could you ever think that I would do such a thing?" You would then walk away feeling guilty for unjustly accusing him. If Fred is truly antisocial, he will feel no remorse for either stealing your idea or for making you feel lousy for accusing him.

Working with the Antisocial Subordinate

If you find yourself in a situation like those described, all is not lost. The important thing is to *document everything*, whether it be a conversation with this person, materials that they have "borrowed," or ideas that you have discussed with them. It is often common that you will have a "gut feeling" or "gut reaction" to this problem employee long before anything surfaces regarding their inappropriate behavior. Therefore, it's important to listen to these gut feelings. Don't invalidate yourself—there are probably more instances where you will be right in your perceptions. If it does turn out that you have someone with APD working for you, it is important to talk with someone in your organization about your concerns. Someone who can serve as a reality check and whose perceptions you trust. It's also important not to get caught up in blaming yourself for their behavior. This is one of the "survival strategies" suggested by Robert Hare in *Without Conscience*, as it is common that others will take responsibility for the subcriminal psychopath's behavior. It is also common for psychopaths to have convinced others of the validity of their positions, so don't be surprised if you see yourself caught up in a bitter division of staff over who is right or who should be in power. Psychopaths have a way of convincing others of the merit of their arguments, and they often prey upon meek or weak-willed coworkers to promote their cause. Individuals with APD think nothing of taking others down with them, because they know that they can always go along their merry way, leaving for a new job while leaving a path of devastation in their wake. I once worked with a subcriminal psychopath in an alcohol and drug prevention program.

73

In his job interview, he presented as a "team player," someone who worked well with others and who relished challenges. He was about six months into the job, when rumors began to surface about his going over his administrator's head to talk with the Board of Trustees and the corporate CEO of the parent organization. He did this under the guise of telling them his ideas of what was wrong within the organization. In fact, he was trying to put himself in place for a better, higher-paying position. Once the program director caught wind of what was happening, this individual was summarily dismissed from his duties. What was amazing was how this person proceeded to be hired by about a dozen different programs within the same state. In each job, he would last about six to nine months before being fired. But with all the charm, deceit, and charisma of the antisocial personality, he had no trouble jumping right into another position. Having an antisocial subordinate is not the most comforting of situations to be in, as these individuals can often be quite cunning and ruthless. Hopefully, by following some of suggestions mentioned above, you can avoid becoming prey to their schemes and manipulations.

In Conclusion

Of all the personality disorders we will be discussing in this book, the antisocial personality or subcriminal psychopath is probably the most dangerous and most insidious type to work for, to work with, or to supervise. Not surprisingly, it's also the one disorder for which traditional treatment approaches seem to do the least. In fact, one of the unfortunate aspects about treatment is that some psychopaths actually become even more adept at manipulation after therapy because they've learned more about what others expect of them. Subcriminal psychopaths often are forced into treatment, in which case they merely "go through the motions" of treatment, as they are incapable of the emotional intimacy necessary for effective treatment (Hare 1993). In addition, they rarely feel that there is anything wrong with them—so why change? Another disturbing fact is that white-collar crime is quite lucrative, and the penalties for such behavior are few or meaningless. "The federal prisons for the wealthy and privileged . . . have tasty food, jogging tracks, first-run movies, and libraries . . . the federal prisons for the rich and privileged are a national disgrace"(Hare 1993). This quote is from Brian Rosner, the New York State assistant district attorney, who was speaking at the sentencing hearing of John Grambling, a man who had been convicted of a multimillion-dollar bank fraud. Hare makes the case that Grambling is the epitome of the white-collar psychopath in that he used charm, good social graces, and forged documents to swindle four banks and a savings-and-loan association of $36.5 million without ever pointing a gun at anyone.

All too often, administrators, and coworkers will look away when they discover an antisocial worker in their midst. Yet, there is a social responsibility, as well as an ethical duty, to take action. Perhaps Martin Luther-King Jr. summed this up best when he said, "He who accepts evil without protesting against it is really cooperating with it."

CHAPTER 6

The Borderline Personality Disorder: A Storm in Every Port

By way of introducing the borderline, consider this first-person story, told to one of the authors by a client:

> I just don't understand it. When Samantha first applied for the job, I thought she had everything we were looking for: she had charisma and smarts, she was charming and dynamic. The first few months were wonderful. She accomplished things no one else could do, and she had boundless amounts of energy. Better yet, everyone seemed to like her, which is not an easy thing to accomplish here, if you know what I mean. After a while, though, things started to change. People started complaining that she was getting involved with things that she shouldn't be. The VP from accounting told me that she was always telling his people what to do. She even tried to make them use a new accounting software package she had used at her old job. Then she got angry when they wouldn't! Little brush fires like that began to spring up all over the place. One of our human resources people called to tell me that she had had a couple of run-ins with the designers. I guess she just lost it with them and started screaming, "You are to shut up when I am talking to you. You never listen to me!" That's when things started to get weird for me. It's kind of hard to explain, but she got under my skin, if you know what I mean. I'd go to work and it was "Samantha this" or "Samantha that." It seemed that all I dealt with at work were "Samantha problems." She was on my mind constantly. What was weird was that I liked her. In a strange way, I was attracted to her. She was charismatic and sharp—she had energy. But things

got worse when other people began taking sides, and then it was the "pro Samantha" people against the "con Samantha" people. I could've wallpapered my office with angry memos that were fired about by both sides. Just when I thought things couldn't get any worse, I found myself thinking about her when I was at home and when I was on vacation. I even dreamed about her. But that's not even half of it. She started calling me at home and would even follow me to lunch just to complain about the people she worked with. Out of pure desperation, I called a big meeting with Samantha and the others, and I asked her to do some things a little differently. That's when the explosion took place. Pow! She lost it, big time. She screamed as loud as she could. Her whole body shook. She told me that I'd never liked her, and if I wanted to fire her, why didn't I just say so? She said she was going to sue me and the company and the "whole stinking lot of you." I couldn't believe it—it didn't make sense. After that, she started calling in sick and taking all of her vacation days. She left nasty messages on my answering machine. I started getting hang-up calls at home, which I knew were from her. I don't know if I can pin this on her, but we even got some orders that were bogus. Now she's got lawyers, and I've got high blood pressure, a headful of gray hairs, and I'm here talking to a shrink!

Does this scenario sound familiar? If you have ever worked with a person with Borderline Personality Disorder or with borderline traits, you're probably smiling and nodding right now. Maybe trembling. If you haven't worked with a borderline, consider yourself lucky. Being involved in a relationship with a borderline is like going on a wild roller-coaster ride with all of its highs and lows. At first they love you, and then they hate you; there is no in between. You find yourself more and more involved with them and enmeshed in their problems; much more than should be reasonably expected. The relationship is intense and stormy. They get under your skin and can upset your entire sense of well-being.

What Is Borderline Personality Disorder?

First of all, the name "borderline" is a misnomer; it really doesn't tell us much about the disorder. The term "borderline" originally meant a person who was "on the borderline" between having a neurosis (a group of disorders usually characterized by depression or anxiety) and psychosis (which is a much more serious type of disorder involving a break with reality). Today, the term is usually used differently, but not very consistently. What makes the problem worse is the fact that many experts in the field of borderline personality do not agree as to what borderline personality actually is. A lot more research is needed to fully understand the person with BPD (Borderline Personality Disorder). For the purposes of this book, however, we will stick to DSM-IV descriptions.

Out of all the personality disorders discussed in this book, the borderline is probably the most difficult to deal with and the greatest challenge to the organizational structure. This is due to the fact that the smooth functioning of any corporate structure is dependent on the ability of its people to work cooperatively with one other. The core problem of the borderline is the *inability* to have stable and sane relationships. They have an almost magical way of disrupting the lives of others around them. Borderline women are sometimes considered the female version of the male antisocial. The problems people have with the borderline seem to matasticize, like a cancer. Moreover, borderlines are usually quite impaired in other psychological areas as well, bringing with them a spectrum of problems ranging from depression and alcoholism to suicide attempts. They are notorious for their explosive tempers which can lead them to become abusive in the workplace. When cornered, they can become like vipers, lashing out wildly at others around them and not caring about the collateral damage. They are also known to be highly litigious.

An adaptation of the DSM-IV description of the borderline is as follows:

A pervasive pattern of instability in interpersonal relationships, self-image, and affects, and marked impulsivity beginning by early adulthood and present in a variety of contexts, as indicated by 5 (or more) of the following:

1. frantic efforts to avoid real or imagined abandonment.

2. a pattern of unstable and intense interpersonal relationships characterized by alternating between extremes of idealization and devaluation.

3. identity disturbance: marked and persistently unstable self-image or sense of self.

4. impulsive in at least two areas that are potentially self-damaging (e.g., spending, sex, substance abuse, reckless driving, binge eating).

5. recurrent suicidal behavior, gestures, or threats, or self-mutilating behavior.

6. affective instability due to a marked reactivity of mood (e.g., intense episodic dysphoria, irritability or anxiety usually lasting a few hours and rarely more than a few days).

7. chronic feelings of emptiness.

8. inappropriate, intense anger or difficulty controlling anger (e.g., frequent displays of temper, constant anger, recurrent physical fights).

9. transient, stress-related paranoid ideation or severe dis-associative symptoms.*

Let's take these one at a time. First of all, the borderline perceives rejection and abandonment in situations where there is none. It has been said that borderlines are "exquisitely sensitive" to rejection. Simply being late for an appointment is enough to make the borderline imagine that you don't like them and are trying to end your relationship with them. A slightly negative performance evaluation means that you want to get rid of them. They perceive rejection in any negative thing you might say to them. For example, one bank manager had a bank teller working for her who happened to have Borderline Personality Disorder. One day, as the bank was closing for the day, the teller asked her manager for a ride home.

The manager was talking on the telephone when the borderline teller had approached her, and indicated that they would leave as soon as she was off the phone. When the manager came out to the parking lot, she found the teller had already left, and the manager assumed that she had gotten a ride home from one of the other bank employees. On the way home, however, she saw the teller sitting outside on the curbside in the dark. She stopped her car, rolled down the window, and asked why she was sitting on the side of the road. The teller replied sarcastically that she didn't want a ride from her because the manager "didn't have time for her, she was too busy talking on the phone!" The teller had read an outright rejection into the managers business conversation.

Another hallmark of Borderline Personality Disorder is their involvement in intense and dramatic relationships. In a typical scenario, the borderline absolutely loves their mate, idealizing them and putting them on a pedestal. Shortly thereafter, however, an intense type of hatred begins to develop, often over the slightest hint of rejection. The borderline begins to make numerous accusations

---

* Reprinted with permission from the *Diagnostic and Statistical Manual of Mental Disorders*, Fourth Edition. Copyright 1994 American Psychiatric Association.

about their partners which simply aren't true. They find absolutely nothing good about you. This is because the borderline either loves you or hates you; there is no middle ground. This type of over-idealization and devaluation is also seen in the narcissist and is referred to as "splitting," a term we will discuss later. And, like the narcissist, borderlines can be highly attractive and captivating at first glance. (By attractive, we do not necessarily mean physically attractive. But there is usually some feature the borderline has that draws people to them.) Therefore, they usually have no problem luring people into their traps. Think, for example, of the Glenn Close character in the movie, *Fatal Attraction*. In many ways, that character epitomizes the borderline personality. One minute, she is seductive and alluring, but as soon as there are hints of the affair ending, she slits her wrists in a wild frenzy of hatred.

When you are involved with the borderline, the experience is similar to one of being in some artsy, European movie about a crazy and intense love affair: your lover shows up at four A.M. yelling and gesturing frantically outside your window. "Antonio, Antonio," she yells, "I love you so much! Why do you hate me? I will kill myself right here, right now, in front of you. Look, see, I am cutting my wrists!" She continues this dramatic display, screaming and gesturing wildly. The police show up and you're arrested on the spot and thrown into prison. She is in the cell next to you, and all night long she harangues you saying, "Why do you hate me? Why do you abuse me so?" All this, and all you did was to tell her that you didn't like her earrings! It's just like a bad B movie. Or maybe like a bad dream. If you want a great visual example of the borderline person-ality, go rent the video, *Fatal Attraction*. Or, if you're in a lighter mood, rent *What About Bob?*, both excellent movies with fantastic illustrations of what we're describing.

In addition to abandonment worries and stormy relationships, the borderline has core problems with identity issues. As we men-tioned in chapter 2, one way to conceptualize personality disorders is by thinking of the disordered person as lacking an essential piece in their personality structure. In the case of the borderline, what's lacking is perhaps the most important feature of a personality, and that is a *core identity* or *sense of self*. Borderlines usually don't know who they are or what they want out of life. In most people, these identity issues are usually worked out, for the most part, by adoles-cence. But the borderline lacks any substantial in-depth knowledge of who they are or what their core values are. Core values are about the things that we love most in life, the things that we aim our ener-gies and efforts at achieving, the things we want most in life, all of our hearts desires; in short, the very essence of who we are. Core values protect us from being overwhelmed by the day-to-day ups and downs of life. They are like beacons which guide us through the crazy vicissitudes of life. Without these core values, the borderline gets tossed around by every intense passion, temptation, and fad that comes his or her way. They'll use drugs, drink too much, spend too much, or want sex too much. They'll follow any new guru, diet, con artist, or alternative life style in a wild effort to discover who they really are. They'll go from relationship to relationship, each time hoping that this one will be the "right one."

Identity issues, in fact, can be seen as a central problem for the borderline, and many of the other symptoms stem from it. For example, the borderline's fear of abandonment and struggle with being left alone can be seen as a direct result of their lack of identity. If you are alone, and you have no identity or sense of self, there is *no one* in the room with you. For the normal, nonafflicted person who has a strong sense of self, this is not a problem, because "no matter where you go, there *you* are!"

Without a core identity, the borderline can become impulsive in any number of areas (eating, sex, spending, driving, and drugs to name a few), in a frantic attempt to fill the emptiness inside. One borderline legal secretary lost job after job because she would leave the office and drive to the nearest market the moment she got hungry. One aerobics instructor would hitchhike hoping that a man she could have sex with would pick her up. One borderline decided to buy "a few things" for his home and promptly went out and spent thirty thousand dollars which put him into immediate bankruptcy. It's easy to see how the borderline can bring a host of "brush fires" into the workplace, problems they are constantly trying to solve: alcoholism, gambling debts, STDs, divorce, hostile outbursts, and so on. These problems and the borderline's ill-fated attempts at solving them spiral quickly into a vast chasm of entanglements and confusion in which the borderline finds himself helplessly trapped. And while short-term psychotherapy or substance- abuse counseling can be helpful for alleviating some of these impulse problems, they often will not address the deeper and more substantive problems inherent in Borderline Personality Disorder.

The borderline is also well known for suicide threats and attempts. Due to the lack of identity and the incredible feelings of emptiness inside, the borderline often struggles with depression and intense feelings of inadequacy. This makes them highly susceptible to suicidal behavior. Moreover, the borderline is not above threatening someone with suicide, especially if they fear abandonment by that person or if that person has already left them. Abandonment will make them so angry that they will "go down with the ship," killing themselves in retaliation for the real or imagined abandonment. As adolescents, borderlines will often self-mutilate, cutting or burning themselves with cigarettes, for example. Sometimes the borderline's forearms will look like a spiderweb of scars from all of the real or manipulative suicide attempts. Many borderlines who self-mutilate will report that they cut themselves when feeling overwhelmed by emotional pain. The physical pain caused by cutting becomes more definable and therefore easier to deal with. Naturally, all suicide attempts and self-mutilation gestures have to be taken seriously, but the borderline is more likely to be manipulative with suicide threats than they are to actually carry them through.

The borderline's moods seem to change daily. One day they might appear to be energetic, happy, and optimistic and other days, for no apparent reason, they will slide into depression or become irritable and testy. They feel these emotions intensely, sometimes to the point of being unable to contain them without acting out in some way, like cutting themselves because they are sad or spending money when they feel alone. Furthermore, their feelings will color the way they think. It has been said that, to the borderline, feelings *are* facts.

It doesn't take much to get the borderline angry: constant anger seems to be at the core of the borderline's personality. It will leak out in cynical or sarcastic remarks and can sometimes explode into rages. When the borderline becomes angry, they hate everyone and everything, often attacking blindly and wildly. These attacks can come in the form of direct verbal or physical assault; abandoning the other before they themselves can be abandoned; suicide; or simply attacking themselves by engaging in some self-destructive act. This hatred can be highly toxic to those around them, and, in the organizational environment, may often lead to litigation as the borderline misinterprets the actions of others as being deliberately malevolent.

Finally, the borderline can have what are known as "dissociative" symptoms. Dissociative symptoms express themselves in the borderline as feelings of unreality. For example, the borderline will often feel as if their life is not real. Sometimes they will feel like they're watching their lives go by on a television screen, feeling detached and uninvolved in the things going on around them. Another theory is that the borderline will engage in self-mutilative behavior just to feel *something*.

There are three additional key symptoms that appear to be operating in the borderline. The first of these is the ability to "split" others around them, as mentioned previously. Splitting refers to the borderline's inability to make fine gradations in judgment and categorization. In other words, they see things only in black-and-white terms. Therefore they either see others and themselves as good or bad, competent or incompetent, loving or rejecting, and so on. There is no in between. Moreover, in an almost magical way, the borderline is capable of making those around them participate in this splitting process as well, making coworkers and friends take sides. For example, when borderlines are hospitalized in the wake of a suicidal gesture, they have a notorious reputation for splitting the staff. What happens is that some of the staff seems to take sides with the borderline, while others take sides against the borderline. The two sides clash with each other, one side supporting the borderline and extolling his virtues, while the other side sees the shortcomings of the borderline and constantly denigrates him. We have observed the same type of thing occurring in highly acrimonious divorce settings where both husband and wife are borderline. The two lawyers actually begin to clash in a personal and unprofessional manner, getting entangled in their litigant's issues. If experts are drawn into the fray, they, too, will clash to the point of becoming unprofessional and losing their objectivity. If other authorities, such as probation, welfare, or child protective services, are drawn into the battle, they, too, will be split and will turn against each other. You can see how in an organizational setting, this splitting of the staff can wreak havoc upon the corporation and corrupt its efficiency.

A second key symptom is the inability of the borderline to contain certain emotions without acting them out. For example, it is quite difficult for the borderline to grieve the end of a relationship without having it affect those around them or without their engaging in impulsive actions to alleviate the feelings of loss. So, for example, if the borderline feels rejected, they might have to drink, go out and spend money, or overeat. And, if they are experiencing feelings of loneliness and abandonment, they might go to a bar to pick someone up for casual sex. Another more subtle example would be the borderline criticizing someone because they are feeling angry. A great many of the borderline's impulsive types of behavior can be traced to the inability to "contain" and not "act out" their emotions.

Finally, another key symptom is the borderline's inability to respect and maintain boundaries. As we mentioned before, boundaries allow us to let certain things in while keeping other things out. A boundary can be physical, such as a wall, a fence, or a drawer, or it can be psychological, such as personal space, one's private life and thoughts, or personal duties on the job. Boundaries are essential to the smooth working of an organization, everyone needs to "stay in their own lanes." The borderline has a tendency to disrespect boundaries and invade them. That's why they give you the feeling of always getting under your skin.

The Borderline Administrator

If you've already read the other parts of this chapter, you probably know by now whether or not you have a borderline boss. If you do, you probably also know why you hate going to work every day. Indeed, it's a joyous day when you're fortunate enough not to butt heads with them. You also probably think more about your borderline boss than any other person in your life. You are angry and feel that they have overstepped your boundaries, way beyond what your job requirements call for. You kick yourself for getting involved with them or even for taking the job in the first place. You are asking yourself almost daily, "How can I get out of this mess I'm in?"

Your boss is moody, angry, inconsistent, he contradicts himself, he personalizes everything, he counterattacks even when there is no attack. He's sarcastic, seductive, and his life seems jam-packed with personal problems. He's fighting wars on numerous fronts while constantly trying to recruit you to do battle with him. Crazy things go on around you, and the simplest task, the most ordinary of interactions, the most routine of meetings turns into a trip down into the rabbit hole.

You never really know which boss you're going to interact with on a given day. The brilliant and successful supervisor, the happy supportive friend, the depressed, dejected puppy dog, the wildly vindictive psychopath, or the rejecting (or rejected) lover. You feel unsupported, confused, exhausted, and abused. Your workplace seems like a boat tossed upon a windswept sea. Better hold on tight!

Working with the Borderline Administrator

Working for the borderline administrator can have serious, negative effects on your career. In fact, out of all the administrators addressed in this book (with the possible exception of the antisocial personality disorder), the borderline administrator is the most toxic. You might seriously need to consider a job change. Furthermore, the more closely you have to work with a borderline administrator, the worse it is. Things might not be so bad if your contact with the borderline administrator is relatively limited. But day-to-day interaction with a borderline administrator has a high likelihood of being highly destructive to your mental and physical health and well-being. The more power they have over you, the worse it is, and the more helpless you will feel.

At the beginning of your relationship, you will notice that they most likely have idealized you and think that you're truly wonderful. If it's not too late, don't buy into it. Although you might be quite competent, you are probably not quite as wonderful as they're making you out to be. And, perhaps more importantly, when they begin to hate you, remember that you're not nearly as bad as they think. *Do not* judge your adequacy by the way a borderline administrator feels about you. Somewhere along the road they will usually wind up hating you just as they will anyone else they are involved with. In the beginning you probably saw the borderline administrator as being quite charismatic, and you most likely felt yourself drawn to that person. You saw them as attractive, dynamic—perhaps you were even a bit sexually attracted to them. After a while, though, you began to hate them. Try not to be too hard on yourself for your changing emotions—they bring that out in most everyone they work with.

You will notice yourself becoming more and more involved with your administrator on a personal level. He might have you, for example, take calls from his girlfriend and lie to his wife about his affair. (In fact, he might ask you to do a lot of lying to customers, bill collectors, and coworkers.) You might become involved in his legal affairs, and he might expect you to buy him alcohol, or, worse yet, make a drug deal. He might ask you to cover up for his drunken absences or even to destroy documents. He will ask you to take sides and expect you to do so.

Dealing with a borderline administrator is hard, but there are some guidelines you can follow. Remember, however, that negotiating interactions with a borderline is not easy, and the following advice still might not work.

First of all, do your work well. Don't give them a reason to seek you out. If your work is solid, you can be sure that you're on firm ground when you defend yourself, which will most likely be inevitable at some point or another. It's probably best that you do your work quietly, becoming something of a wallflower. Let them get involved with someone else.

Let the moodiness slide—it's not about you. Don't personalize or react to it and, for heaven's sake, don't let them get you upset or depressed. It's certain that they will misjudge you and your intentions, so don't ever look for validation from them. Stick to your agenda, which should be the business at hand. Don't become overemotional—it will only get them overemotional. Stay calm and professional, avoiding any personality stuff.

Never ask her to do you personal favors or get involved with her on a personal level *in any way*. Don't ask them to cover up for you or bail you out of trouble. They will only ask you to do the same in return and their requests will be much greater and require a much deeper level of involvement than the favors that you have requested of them. Remember, boundary violations and intrusiveness are natural for them.

If they do ask you to become involved on a personal level, defer politely. Say something like, "I'm sorry, sir, I just can't lie to your wife. I am quite busy, and I want to get back to my work, so I can do a good job for you." Let them know from the beginning that you are not a person who will take sides; do not agree or disagree with them, just listen to what they say and reflect back that you have understood them. They will eventually go somewhere else to complain. Let them know that you just want to do your job and be good at it. If their inappropriate requests continue, tell them you will report it to their supervisor. Let them know right from the outset that you are a straight shooter who will not get involved with them on a personal level, *period*. Then stick to that decision. Don't form any alliances with them, even small ones, such as telling customers white lies. They will be angry at first, and you might have to weather the storm. But, if you give in intially, the storm will only get worse later on. Because the borderline is sensitive to criticism and rejection, you may need to do some soothing as you are setting limits and boundaries. Compliment them on ways in which they have been a good boss. For instance, by complimenting them on their energy level or their creativity.

Another suggestion is to look around within the organization to see what status your boss has. Are other people complaining about her? Does she seem to be on the verge of being fired? Maybe you can wait her out if you're not too miserable. It could be just a matter of time before she is fired. She might also turn herself into rehab or relocate somewhere. She could be actively looking for a new job, as borderlines can be quite restless and easily bored. Can you wait her out? Don't overlook this strategy.

However, since many borderlines are energetic and creative, the organization might not be so quick to get rid of them. If this seems to be the case, consider suggesting an executive or corporate coach. These are mental-health professionals hired by the corporation or administrator to observe and aid the administrator in their day-to-day responsibilities, kind of like a live-in psychotherapist. This idea may sound extraordinary, but as personality-disordered administrators rack up millions in damages, this strategy is becoming more and more popular.

Finally, you might find yourself forced into position where you might have to "up the ante." For example, if they become too toxic, you might have to start documenting, or even secretly recording, your conversations with the borderline. You might have to go over their head and file a complaint against them. Or, you might be required to answer a lawsuit or to testify for or against the borderline administrator. But be careful before you take extreme steps—weigh the costs first. You have to ask yourself if it's really worth it. Would it be easier just to leave? Or could you just let it go? Once you become entangled with a borderline, it's hard to get out. They do not back down easily when threatened, and they will take you to the wall. They will drain you of enormous amounts of energy, time, and perhaps money. Do you really want this? Better think twice. It may be better just to leave.

The Borderline Coworker

Like the borderline administrator, the borderline coworker presents an enormous challenge. The hardest part is that you will most likely have some type of day-to-day contact with this individual, and their dysfunctional personality will begin to wear pretty thin.

Expect to be misperceived. Expect the hidden agendas. Expect that the person will hear rejection and criticism when you intend none. Expect to feel strange, seduced, weird, even dirty around the borderline. If other people do not make you feel this way, you can be sure it is the borderline working their special brand of magic.

More than anyone else in this book, the borderline will get under your skin, so you're going to need to maintain your boundaries. Keep it professional. You will feel that the borderline, like a giant swirling whirlpool, is constantly trying to suck you in. They will try to get you involved in a personal relationship or will try to have a relationship with you after work. They will most likely ask you to do special favors for them, cover for them, lie for them, or bend the rules. They'll ask for special consideration that you would not normally give to others. It will feel hard to resist them—they can be captivating. Don't be surprised if you feel drawn to them while, at the same time, feeling repulsed.

Working with the Borderline Coworker

Many borderlines come from chaotic and abusive childhoods. Try to keep in mind that your toxic borderline is a person who has probably been deeply abused and wounded. Like any wounded or cornered animal, they will tend to lash out and they will lash out, choosing the person closest to them as a target. Try to look beneath the anger, to the hurt feelings of a child that often lie beneath their anger. If you respond to the anger as hurt (which, in fact, it is) and do not retaliate, you will go a long way toward improving your relationship with them. We all have compassion for children who were physically abused or sexually abused. Try to keep in mind that this is probably one of those children, grown up. If you can, try to keep your heart open while knowing your limitations.

While exercising compassion, remember always to maintain your boundaries. If the borderline is too dysfunctional, you will need to let them know that you are just there to do your job and have no desire for a personal relationship with them. They will be hurt at first, and the work environment might be a bit tense, but it will be much better than going on a wild roller-coaster ride with them later on. You should have very little to do with them after work. Be sure not to get ensnared in their personal problems. Never ask them to bend the rules for you or to give you special consideration because they will ask you for the same some day. Never ask them to become involved in your personal life. Avoid even telling them about your personal life, because sharing anything with them sends them a clear message that they can do the same. Their life will be much worse than yours and the depth of their problems could easily entangle you. Stick to your job and minimize your interactions with them. Finally, you should understand that the borderline might back you into a position where you have no choice but to do some things that are unpleasant to you. This might take the form of having to report them to your supervisor for things like sexual harassment, physical or verbal abuse, or some other boundary violation. You might be called upon to testify in a lawsuit for or against them, or defend yourself against accusations which they have made against you. (Remember, for the borderline, feelings are facts and if you make them feel bad they will believe it is your intention to hurt them.)

The Borderline Subordinate

As in the case of Samantha at the beginning of this chapter, the borderline subordinate seems, at first, almost too good to be true. You believe you have made a good choice in hiring them and you have high expectations. Pretty soon, however, you began to see many conflicts springing up around you, most of which are of a personal nature. Your wonderful new employee begins arguing with those around them and they don't seem to get along well with others. You soon find yourself trying to solve those conflicts. You find that a great deal of your day is spent in dealing with the problems that this subordinate creates. After a while, they begin to attack you also. You feel enmeshed in issues you can't seem to extricate yourself from. It seems that the more you try to fix things, the worse they get. Soon, you find that you're thinking of the employee all the time, even when you're away from work. Perhaps you think of firing them, but it would be too difficult to replace them. It begins to seems as though the borderline subordinate is not just looking for you to be a good boss, but they may also be looking for you to be the all-knowing, all-loving, benevolent parent they never had. God forbid you don't meet these expectations. God forbid you are human and, therefore, imperfect.

Working with the Borderline Subordinate

One of the best solutions to the borderline problem is to have a good screening system. But this can be tricky. See the last chapter for more details. Educating yourself as to what the borderline is all about will help you avoid hiring one. This book and this chapter will go a long way in helping you to identify a potential employee who has Borderline Personality Disorder. Although it is most likely illegal to administer personality tests to screen for a personality disorder, you can still be on your toes during the interview process by asking questions about the nature of their previous relationships on the job. What kinds of things did they like? What kinds of things didn't they like? What type of people don't they get along with? What were some of the best things about their previous job? Some of the worst? Don't accept general answers; ask for specifics. For example:

Interviewer: How did you get along with your last boss?

Potential employee: Good.

Interviewer: What were some things that were good about your relationship with your boss?

Potential employee: We got along all right.

Interviewer: Tell me some examples about how you and your boss worked well together. Give me specifics.

The astute interviewer will look for signs of splitting, i.e., the borderline either loving or hating others, with no gray areas. Be aware of whether they speak critically of their boss or anyone else within their prior company, as this could be a hint of interpersonal problems. You should also look for evidence of stormy relationships and impulsive actions, like quitting over some small slight. Look for other signs of impulsivity as well. Is there evidence of alcoholism or drug abuse? Is there an overeating problem? Do they have a lot of parking tickets and unpaid fines? How do they handle money? Under what circumstances did the individual leave? Are they presently involved in litigation? Of what nature? Listen carefully. The stories they tell could be a foreshadowing of what is going to happen when they work for you. If they tell you, for example, that they have a lawsuit against their former employers, you could be next in line. Consider the stories they tell as a group. Is there a theme that connects them? Look at the various situations the potential employee has been in and ask yourself, "What is similar about these stories?" This is a technique psychologists use called a "situational analysis," a way we have of making sense of the varied and diverse things our patients tell us. Making sure to do this extra evaluation could really pay off in the long run.

Don't be afraid to go with your gut feelings. Did this individual make you feel uneasy? Did they respond inappropriately to simple questions? Were you confused by some of their reactions? Did they appear to be a bit oversensitive or overreactive to your questions? Were they defending themselves a bit too much over (mis)perceived criticism? Did they seemed just a bit too captivating or just a bit too good to be true?

If you happen to have a borderline subordinate working for you, make sure to take charge, as soon as you know who you're dealing with. Let the borderline know that you will not tolerate abuses in the workplace. Tell them that you will not let *anyone* who is working under you be abused. Tell them that if they have any problem with a coworker to come and see you at once. Put out the brushfire in a firm and authoritative manner: you're the boss, you have the right to tell them how to do their job. But keep it strictly business. Keep their personality characteristics out of it. Here is an example of what *not* to do:

Subordinate: I'm having a hard time phoning my orders in to the head office.

Administrator: How come?

Subordinate: That little snot on the other line always gives me a hard time. She is so sarcastic! She's always telling me that I forget to fill in the little blue areas on the order sheets. I'm not talking to her anymore. I can't stand it anymore!

Administrator: This is the third time you've had problems with other people. Why don't you just get along with other people? Why must you be so difficult? You don't seem to be able to get along with anyone. No one else here has these types of problems.

Subordinate: Why do you always blame things on me! You just don't like me, that's all!

A better way of handling it would be as follows:

Subordinate: I'm having a hard time phoning my orders in to the head office.

Administrator: How come?

Subordinate: That little snot on the other line always gives me a hard time. She is so sarcastic! She's always telling me that I forget to fill in the details on the order sheets. I'm not talking to her anymore.

Administrator: Part of your job is phoning in those orders. I know that she can be a real pain but we have to work with all kinds of people—that's a part of our jobs. Don't let her push your buttons; just do your job.

Don't be afraid to repeat yourself if they continue to complain. This is called the "broken record" approach. Keep on telling them that you expect them to do the job and to get along with other people. Remember, you're the boss and you have the right to expect them to do their jobs in an efficient manner.

Refuse to let personality differences interfere with their work. Tell them you expect them to get along well with others regardless of the other person's personality. Tell them you expect them to do their jobs regardless of personality conflicts. Tell them part of the job is to get along with others, period.

If possible, limit their contact with others. They might work well in a more isolated environment where there is not too much interaction.

Expect moodiness. Don't overreact to the small stuff, such as minor irritabilities, criticisms, or cynicism. Just acknowledge them. A simple statement, such as, "I understand the way you feel," or simply, "I hear you," will go a long way in making them feel validated, something they don't often feel. Don't tell them they shouldn't feel a certain way, as this is the real trigger area for them because their families so often wouldn't validate their emotions. When they respond to something with an inappropriate emotion—usually hurt, rejection, or anger—don't respond in kind. Briefly acknowledge their feelings and continue to stick to the business task at hand. Repeat yourself if you have to, and don't let yourself be sidetracked.

If things really begin to get out of control, document everything. Keep a written record of every conversation. Managing the borderline requires a good deal of energy, and you're the one who has to decide whether or not it is worth it.

Firing the toxic borderline is always an option, if need be. Make sure you have a good procedure for laying off individuals and some documentation of the problems they have caused. Be present when they clean out their desks to leave. You might consider having another witness there as well. Get them off the premises as soon as possible. Consider a buyout so they are not in the workplace causing problems (a buyout is a financial "deal" one offers an employee in order to make their termination more acceptable). Once again, keep it professional and not personal. Avoid a lengthy termination letter that itemizes the borderline's inefficiencies, as there is a high likelihood that they will respond with retaliation to such a letter. Be factual. Avoid using terms that could possibly give the borderline grounds for a sex, race, or age discrimination case. The borderline will often scrape the bottom of the barrel to find ammunition for retaliation. Don't give them any. Stick to the objective circumstances from the organizational viewpoint. For example, don't say that the person was annoying; rather, they could not achieve this or that goal. Be squeaky clean. Take the high road.

Change access codes. Lock things up. You might even need to change some of the locks that the borderline has access to. If you have a legal department, check with them. Is it possible for this individual to have a case against you? Leave a paper trail and document *everything*.

In closing, you should consider input into your counseling or EAP program in your organization. Workshops on personality disorders can be highly useful. EAP programs should be skilled enough to treat Borderline Personality Disorder, as well as the other disorders that can spring out of Borderline Personality Disorder, such as alcoholism or drug abuse. With an informed staff, the risk of letting the borderline run roughshod over the corporation should be significantly reduced. Make sure HR knows what Borderline Personality Disorder is, and be sure to use therapists who can treat it. But remember, even psychotherapy cannot cure borderline. The best hope is to make them into a better functioning borderline.

CHAPTER 7

The Perfectionist: The World of the Obsessive Compulsive Personality

The battle to keep up appearance unnecessarily, the mask—whatever name you give creeping perfectionism—robs us of our energies.

—Robin Worthington

Did you ever hear the joke about the priest, the doctor, and electrical engineer who were playing golf together at a country club? Their game was slowed down by a foursome in front of them. When they saw the groundskeeper, they asked, "Why are these guys taking so long?" The groundskeeper replied, "Those are the four firemen who were blinded in the terrible fire at the clubhouse last month. We let them play here for free." To which the priest replied, "Oh those poor souls. I will pray for them." The doctor replied, "I know a famous ophthalmologist in Boston, and I'll call him to see what he can do." The electrical engineer, who was quite impatient, replied, "For God's sake, why can't you have them play at night!?"

What's noteworthy about this joke is that it so aptly depicts Obsessive Compulsive Personality Disorder (OCPD). It describes the practical, logical thinking of these individuals, while at the same time pointing to their seemingly inherent lack of compassion and basic sense of humanity. For the person with OCPD, it is much more important to be right or to do things perfectly than to do things that are in keeping with emotional propriety. Their decision-making processes are based purely on what's rational or logical, not usually on what's popular or what will make people around them feel good. You will recall that one of the characteristics of all personality disorders is a certain rigidity. For the obsessive compulsive personality it's one of the most distinctive features. Most obsessive compulsives (OCs) will see things from one point of view and have difficulty considering other factors. Their goal is to make the "perfect" choice or come up with the "perfect" solution. This tendency can make the OC's life miserable when constantly confronted with the imperfection of people around them or with life in general.

OCP disordered individuals can also seem very emotionally aloof or distant, but not quite in the same way as the schizoid or schizotypal personalities discussed below. Obsessives often do not intend to distance themselves from others, as a schizoid might do. Instead, they may feel set apart from others or may feel different because of difficulties thay have in connecting with others emotionally Also, since many interpersonal relationships are not predictable or perfect, obsessives may shy away from the unpredictability inherent in such relationships.

You may be saying to yourself, "What's so wrong with trying to get things right, in striving for perfection?" Actually, it's not that it's "wrong." It simply causes numerous problems when OCs are in situations which demand flexibility or the ability to look at issues from various points of view. Most relationships, whether they be work relationships, friendships, or love relationships, usually require flexibility. People in successful relations must have the ability to compromise, to be able to see things from others' points of view, and to be able to perceive the emotional nuances or shades of gray in a situation. This is where the OC falls short. For them, things are usually seen as black or white. They firmly believe that there are "right" answers and "wrong" answers and OCs often feel that they have the market cornered on what is right, which is defined as what is logical, not necessarily on what's kind or compassionate. This ability to make make an emotionally nuanced evaluation is what Goleman (1998) refers to as "emotional intelligence." It's not uncommon for OCs to have difficulty or deficits in emotional intelligence while rating high in rational intelligence. These two areas of intelligence are so often divergent in the OC that it gives them the appearance of having a learning disability. People often expect that if a person is intelligent in one area, that they will be intelligent in all areas. Yet, we know this to be far from the truth.

A good illustration of this split in intelligence is offered by the relationship between the rational, logical Mr. Spock and the sensitive, intuitive Captain Kirk on *Star Trek*. Spock would usually have a solution to any problem based upon what was practical and logical. Kirk, however, would always be stuck weighing out the ethical dilemmas, the nuances of the various problems they would encounter. Dr. McCoy often mocked Spock for his being more "computer-like" than human. While most decisions involve taking both emotional response and logic into account, those with OCPD are somehow unable to see things in this way. In a work setting, this can result in ruffled feathers and hurt feelings. In one company, it was logical to hold the monthly staff meeting one year on September 11. However, the OC person planning the meeting did not take into account that Yom Kippur fell on that day, and the Jewish members of the department were all quite offended by this oversight.

Oldham and Morris (1995) refer to Obsessive Compulsive Personality Disorder in their chapter on "Conscientious Style." At one end of the continuum, they see individuals who are conscientious, i.e., productive, hardworking, orderly, organized, and preferring things to be done correctly. On the other end of this continuum are those individuals who take these positive traits to the extreme, the people who suffer with OCPD.

OCs are naturally attracted to the types of occupations where issues can be defined in black-and-white terms, or where logic and reasoning are desirable skills to possess. Any of the science occupations are probably at the top of this list and computer sciences, law, accounting, and mathematics would also fall within this spectrum. In the medical profession, it's interesting to see more OCs falling into highly technical specialties, such as cardiology or surgery. Medical training generally requires a great deal of discipline, so it naturally attracts more OCs. This is certainly not necessarily a negative fact. If, for example, you were scheduled to have major surgery, you would probably want a surgeon who would make sure every potential problem is covered and every sponge is counted before they close you up. However, is it a coincidence that most medical schools now offer courses on "bedside manner"? In these courses, medical students are "taught" how to best deal with families in crisis. These skills would include how to tell them compassionately that a loved one has died or how to let them know that their father, mother, sister, son, or daughter has only six months to live. This would be a daunting task for anyone. For someone with OCPD it is nearly impossible, existing outside the realm of his or her logical world.

Individuals with OCPD are naturally very attracted to any field dealing with computers. They can spend hours in front of the computer, with little rest or nourishment, and find that they are quite satisfied with this life. Most techies, however, seem to have difficulty with both written and verbal communication. Their spouses often complain that they have to drag things out of them, or that they never talk about how they feel. With regards to written communication, anyone who has used a computer or purchased a new program can testify to the fact that the instructions and manuals are often poorly written. This may have something to do with the relatively arrogant attitude of many OC "techies." One programmer who was in counseling for work-related problems with coworkers admitted that he had absolute disdain for anyone who could not understand the basics of his program. Therefore, he'd decided that they didn't deserve to have rudimentary explanations as to the sequential procedures of the program in the technical manual.

In these technical fields, efficiency and creativity are often rewarded with promotions to supervisory positions. This promotion takes the contented computer techie from the computer monitor to the conference room or other situations where they must interact with others. This environment is where problems can begin. In the insightful article, "When Techies Manage," Lewey and Davis (1987) expand on this theme. They conclude that the skills that allow one to advance in the various technical fields are quite different from those skills that allow one to advance in supervisory positions. Often, techies find themselves being promoted to administrative positions, only to find that they lack the necessary managerial skills needed to work effectively with their employees or subordinates. In supervising others, there often are no clear-cut answers to problems. For example, if one of the programmers is coming in late because he or she is going through a difficult divorce, but they are still getting their work done, is this just cause to fire the person? Lewey and Davis note several different techie personality types: "the thinker," "the technical guru," "the track star," and "the Vulcan." Each of these personality types could fall within the framework of an obsessive compulsive personality; however, the thinker and the Vulcan appear to be prime candidates for having OCPD. The thinker, for example, is described as being adept at analytical skills and critical thinking. The thinker is driven to find the perfect solution, which often results in ambiguous management decisions, as they become overwhelmed by all the options or possibilities of a particular situation or problem. They often become paralyzed by overanalyzing the problem and, in doing so, will often frustrate those whom they manage. The Vulcan is, of course, patterned after Mr. Spock. For this type of manager, logic is the key to their existence. Vulcans have difficulty taking their employees' or subordinates' feelings into account. Instead, they make decisions that affect the lives of those who work for them without any consideration of how the decisions will impact their organization. Vulcans will often fail to motivate their workers, because they don't see the necessity for words of praise or encouragement. The employees under the Vulcan often end up feeling undervalued and a "why bother" attitude can then permeate the workplace. Obviously, although OCs are probably overrepresented in technical or scientific fields, these fields have not cornered the market on OCs. There are many other occupations that are likely to attract those with OCPD, and it is also likely that many people in managerial or supervisory positions may suffer from this disorder. One supermarket manager, for example, would spend hours admonishing subordinates to straighten shelves and keep things in impeccable order while other, more important tasks, such as making certain the milk was refrigerated as soon as it was delivered, did not get done. For those with OCPD, control is of utmost importance.

What Is Obsessive Compulsive Personality Disorder?

According to the DSM-IV, the following are listed as the diagnostic criteria for Obsessive Compulsive Personality Disorder. In order to meet the criteria for the diagnosis, a person must have at least five of the following:

> A pervasive pattern of perfectionism and inflexibility, beginning by early adulthood and present in a variety of contexts, as indicated by at least *five* of the following:
>
> 1. perfectionism that interferes with task completion, e.g., inability to complete a project because one's own overly strict standards are not met.
>
> 2. preoccupation with details, rules, lists, order, organization, or schedules to the extent that the major point of the activity is lost.
>
> 3. unreasonable insistence that others submit to exactly his or her way of doing things, or unreasonable reluctance to allow others to do things because of the conviction that they will not do them correctly.
>
> 4. excessive devotion to work and productivity to the exclusion of leisure activities and friendships (not accounted for by economic necessity).
>
> 5. indecisiveness; decision making is either avoided, postponed, or protracted, e.g., the person cannot get assignments done on time because of ruminating about priorities (do not include if indecisiveness is due to excessive need for advice or reassurance from others).

6. overconscientiousness, scrupulousness, and inflexibility about matters of morality, ethics, or values (not accounted for by cultural or religious identification).

7. restricted expression of affection.

8. lack of generosity in giving time, money or gifts when no personal gain is likely to result.

9. inability to discard worn-out or worthless objects even when they have no sentimental value.*

In reviewing many of the DSM-IV symptoms listed above, it should be noted that many of these symptoms relate directly to workplace behaviors. For example, criteria 1 and 5 deal with the perfectionism and the resulting indecisiveness that often interferes with task or project completion. These are very difficult traits to cope with, particularly if you are a middle manager who's getting pressure from administration to meet deadlines while your OC employee is stalled in completing their assigned tasks. Criteria 2, "preoccupation with details, rules, lists, order, organization . . ." and criteria 4, "excessive devotion to work," can both lend to increased productivity in some settings or situations, but the tendency to lose "the major point of the activity" seriously undermines any gains from the behavior. Such was the case with an OC senior partner, who would make a point of going around changing light bulbs in the office while important case assignments went untended. As for criteria 3, many workers know the pain of working for someone who is so controlling and demanding that their creative talents are stifled, their motivation to achieve is quashed, and their sense of identity and autonomy is taken from them. These symptoms will be discussed in greater detail later in the chapter.

The Obsessive Compulsive Administrator

As alluded to earlier, many of the traits or characteristics of OCPD lend to one advancing to managerial positions. The OC's seemingly strong penchant for organization, rules, and structure often make them appear to be excellent candidates for administrative types of positions. Yet, with the true OC, these "strengths" are often their

---

* Reprinted with permission from the *Diagnostic and Statistical Manual of Mental Disorders*, Fourth Edition. Copyright 1994 American Psychiatric Association.

downfall. Again, we refer back to the DSM-IV criteria regarding the lack of generosity in giving of one's time, money, and so on, and the general lack of emotional expression. So, in working for someone with OCPD, you can expect to be working for a rather tough task-master, someone who places efficiency and productivity above all else. Just as OCs are tough on themselves, so, too, are they tough on everyone else.

In working for someone with OCPD, don't expect to get much in the way of praise, compliments on a job well done, or monetary rewards, such as raises or bonuses. After all, as far as the OC admin-istrator is concerned, outstanding performance is a given. Unfortu-nately, those of you who work for an OC manager or boss will often feel taken for granted or unappreciated. Remember, too, that OCs are rather joyless people, so the workplace that the OC administrator creates is rather somber, serious, and totally work oriented. Subordi-nates often report feeling that their life is not their own, that they are "owned" by the company, as extra hours and weekend work become part of the corporate norm, rather than the exception. You probably don't feel valued by your boss, nor do you feel that your hard work is valued. So, while your colleagues working for other managers are out after work for social get-togethers or golf outings, or while they're attending conferences in tropical resorts, you can expect to be slaving away at your desk or work station. In coming up with a familiar example of an OC administrator, we could think of no better example than Ebenezer Scrooge from Dickens' famous work, *A Christmas Carol*. Scrooge meets at least seven or eight of the nine diagnostic criteria of the DSM-IV. He expects Bob Cratchett to dem-onstrate the same devotion and work ethic that Scrooge does. He also expects that Cratchett will work long hours and forego evenings and holidays in order to be at work, abandoning any pleasure in these holidays ("Bah, humbug!"). He has difficulty in expressing affectionate feelings for others. He is totally inflexible when it comes to values and work ethics. And when it comes to being miserly, Scrooge wins the prize. Yet, Bob Cratchett remains faithful to Scrooge, no matter how badly he's treated. In today's nomenclature, we would probably refer to Bob as being somewhat of a "codepend-ent" (i.e., someone whose life is made miserable by the miseries of others). However, we are not suggesting that people have to remain under stranglehold of OC individuals and become their obedient slaves, as Bob Cratchett did. Bob saw no alternatives and no way out, but there do exist some useful suggestions we have for dealing with managers and bosses like Ebenezer Scrooge—so you won't have to wait for that miracle on Christmas Eve.

Working with the Obsessive Compulsive Administrator

It's important to understand the inner workings of the OC administrator in order to better cope with them. By remembering their insecurity, their low self-esteem, their need for control in order to diminish anxiety, you may be able to avoid overpersonalizing or taking too seriously their criticisms or admonishments as a means of coping with this type of boss or manager. Remember, they are just as hard on themselves as they are on you. The advantage you have, however, is that you eventually get a break (even if you do have to work overtime), while the expectations never let up for the OC. They are the quintessential workaholics, and we can guess how hard they are on themselves and how work becomes the "be-all and end-all" of their entire existence. Doesn't seem like much fun, does it? Another approach to take is to is to try to learn from your OC boss. For example, you can learn from the positive aspects of their work habits, e.g., instances where they are being efficient or when they are able to accomplish tasks in a timely way. In looking at their behavior this way, you can use their good example as a model and ignore their bad habits.

The following is a list of other recommendations:

1. *Be clear about exactly what your OC boss expects from you and what they want you to do.* One of the common problems that staff have with these managers is that they often find themselves loaded them down with work assignments, one on top of the other, with little or no consideration for the amount of time that it takes to accomplish these multiple tasks. Therefore, what you will need to do is to ask your manager what they see as the most important task or assignment. This will help you avoid guessing what you should work on first, and the resulting frustration when you discover that you guessed incorrectly. The OCPD manager has no idea that you are overloaded, mostly because they expect that you will take on as much as they do, and asking them this question will help clue them in. It is also important to ask for specific guidance by asking direct questions, e.g., "Would it be okay for me to approach this problem by asking for a meeting with payroll?", or "Would it be okay for me to write out some ideas for you to review? Then you can let me know which ones to pursue further."

2. *Be clear with yourself and with the OC boss that there are only so many hours in a day.* One of the problems that people working

for the OC boss will often report is that they are expected to do superhuman amounts of work every day. Let's face it, there are only twenty-four hours in each day. Therefore, there is a limit to the amount of work you will be able to do. This is where you need to be realistic with yourself and also with the OC manager or boss. Don't fall into the trap of thinking that you can do all the work expected of you. After all, the OC boss, being merely human, is incapable of all that they expect of themselves. Don't let your boss think you are capable of superhuman feats. As Oldham and Morris (1995) point out, "They [OC managers] equate overtime with devotion to your job; often they think that if you go home on time, you're going home early. Never let this type of boss know that you think the workday ought to end at 5:00 P.M. Put in a little overtime every once in a while and always make sure the boss knows about it. But don't come in late the next day or take an extra-long lunch to compensate for that extra time; these bosses are very mindful of rules and regulations, especially those concerning timeliness" (79).

3. *Be complimentary to your boss or manager.* It is important that you compliment your boss, but you cannot do so in a patronizing way. You may thank them for specific ideas or help they may have given you, or thank them for mentoring you. Even though this may seem like you're kissing up, it's really not. You are simply trying to speak to the aspect that drives the OC boss, their need for perfectionism and their need to outperform everyone around them. What you're doing is to help allay their anxieties or insecurities. But, we cannot stress too highly, that it's important to be sincere in your praise and avoid patronizing.

4. *Be a team player.* Even though you're being overloaded with work and are probably really angry, it's better that you not voice your complaints in a negative, complaining way. You'll do better to portray yourself as a willing part of the team who is really trying to achieve the goals set before you, but can only do so much. Yet, this does not mean that you are quitting the team or taking your ball and going home. Instead, you'll do best to convey, "I'll try my best, even if I'm unable to achieve the goals or deadlines you've set before me."

5. *Don't get into debates or arguments with this type of boss or manager.* What OCs share in common is both their attention to detail and their inability to admit when they're wrong. So,

don't get into debates, because even if you win, you'll lose. It's better to defer to their way of doing things rather than to debate the merits of your cause. Better yet, try to present your idea while mentioning how they might have inspired the concept.

6. *Don't expect praise or emotional support.* One of the major symptoms that most OCs manifest is their inability to express feelings to others. Therefore, if you're working for an OC boss, don't expect them to praise your good work. However, if you mess up in some way, you will be certain to hear from them. For example, let's say you announce to your boss and coworkers that you're getting married. Most of your fellow workers will respond with congratulations or kidding remarks and will generally share in your enthusiasm. Not so, the OC manager. Instead, they will probably be more apt to ask you how much time you plan to take off for your honeymoon or some other detail, such as who will be covering your job while you're away. This type of reaction is evidence of their emotional constriction and possible lack of emotional intelligence, or possibly their focus on a strict adherence to rules. The same would hold true if you experienced the death of a loved one, the announcement that you or your mate is pregnant, or that your daughter or son was just given a full scholarship to an Ivy League college. Their reaction would be quite similar: "Does this mean you'll be taking time off from work?"

7. *Be specific and to the point when reporting any information.* Remember, the OC type of administrator often thrives on data and facts. Like Detective Friday from *Dragnet*, they want "just the facts." Don't bother them with emotional appeals, lengthy excuses, or trying to talk to them about your weekend. You can also add office gossip to this list. They're usually not the least bit interested in these things. Also, if you've made a mistake or screwed up in some way, it's usually better to admit the mistake, take it on the chin, and be prepared with a list of ways to remedy the problem or ways to avoid the same pitfall in the future. Toropov (1997) suggests that it's usually a good idea to take notes at any meeting you have with this type of administrator in order to create a paper trail of tasks you've been asked to work on.

As Oldham and Morris point out, OC or "very conscientious" bosses or managers "can be overly critical, demanding, and even tyrannical when you make just a small mistake" (79). Yet, in spite of being very rigid and lacking interpersonal skills, these individuals can be extremely competent. The goal, therefore, is to learn from them, before they drive you crazy.

The Obsessive Compulsive Coworker

Finding yourself with an OC coworker can also be a blessing or a curse, depending on how invested this person is in getting along with others and being a good team player. If you're working with an OC coworker who sees herself as part of the team and is concerned with fitting in, you probably won't find yourself too stressed out by their behavior. They are likely to be okay to work with, although at times their nit-picking and attention to detail can be a pain in the neck. In these instances, it's best to tell your coworker when to back off or to simply state that you "will take their comments under advisement." Be tactful and try not to hurt this person's feelings. After all, you have to work with them every day, so it's usually better not to come on too strong or become too annoyed. They may very well perceive themselves as being helpful, not annoying.

If, on the other hand, you're working with an OC who is insecure or is in competition with you, then you need to watch your back. This person will not only take great pride in finding fault with your every mistake, but they will also take delight in sharing this with other coworkers, or worse yet, your boss. One biology professor who was up for tenure couldn't believe it when one of his colleagues, who was also up for promotion, pointed out each small error the first professor had made in the book they were writing together. What was worse was that his coauthor also announced these mistakes at the department meetings.

Working with an OC Coworker.

Here are some tips and strategies to safeguard yourself against the idiosyncrasies of your OC coworker:

1. *Try to keep a collegial, or "team-based," type of relationship.* Obviously, this is not always possible, but you may find it helpful to recognize the strengths of the OC coworker and see how their strengths can balance with yours. Perhaps by dividing the work, so that they can obsess over details while you work on other tasks, can produce a more congenial atmosphere. It is better to recognize that each of you have

strengths and if you figure out ways to work cooperatively, rather than competitively, you are both better off. This might not always be easy, as OC's can be very insistent on doing things their own way.

2. *Don't personalize their criticisms.* OC coworkers can often come across as quite critical or sometimes even demeaning in their criticisms of your work. This may give them an air of superiority, but again, you must consider the source. These negative comments often come from very insecure individuals, people who probably grew up with a barrage of negative feedback and criticisms from their parents. So, it's better not to let the comments get to you. Instead, respond with, "Gee, thank you. I wasn't aware of that," and let it go.

3. *Stress your positives.* If you're working with an OC who likes to run you down to other colleagues or coworkers, you may need to do some damage control by stressing your positive accomplishments rather than getting into a contest with him. You may need to "toot your own horn" a bit or keep your boss appraised of your progress or accomplishments. Don't get into playing the game or into a competitive battle, as this may be exactly what the OC wants. After all, if they win, so much the better for them. It will serve you better to rise above getting into a contest as to who can be more nit-picky.

4. *Be patient and tolerant.* Often, the OC coworker can make even the most sane person a bit crazy. Again, it is best not to get hooked into their behavior. The OC coworker may not feel that they have much of choice in what they do or say. Fortunately, you do. So try not to focus too much on what they're doing or saying. Instead, it is more productive to focus on your own work.

5. *Try to help them stay focused and keep deadlines.* If you're working with the more benign type of OC coworker, then you can be of great help to them in trying to keep them focused on tasks and deadlines. You can do this by encouraging the work they're doing and downplaying their need to do all tasks perfectly. It is better to encourage them to at least turn in a draft or do an approximation of the task at hand rather than to let them procrastinate because they feel the need to do it perfectly.

6. *Stay true to your own goals or tasks.* Remember that one of the symptoms of OCPD is that this individual feels that things must be done *their way*. They are very controlling individu-

als, and it's very likely that they will try to control you as well. You'll need to set boundaries and be clear that their way of doing things may not be necessarily what is comfortable for you. Try to stress to them that it's okay for each of you to have different styles of doing things. Don't try to change them—which would be an exercise in futility—but make it clear that they should also not try to change you.

The Obsessive Compulsive Subordinate or Employee

Depending on your work setting, having an OC under your management can be either a blessing or a curse. They can be great assets because of their attention to detail and the amount of energy they'll devote to doing their work perfectly. As you'll recall from the DSM-IV criteria, OCs will bring to their jobs an "excessive devotion to work and productivity." This, naturally, can be a plus, as it may help to set a higher standard for other, less productive, employees. The down side is that these employees often require a great deal of personal supervision in order to keep them in a productive mode. Individuals with OCPD will often get lost in details, to the point where they lose sight of their goal. One OC computer programmer set a goal of trying to paint his apartment while on vacation. When he returned to work the following week, a coworker asked how the painting had gone. He explained that he never actually got the job done because he started by straightening out his magazine and CD collections. This reorganization became such an all-consuming task that he never got to pick up a paintbrush. His behavior at work was similar, in that he would start on tasks with all good intentions, only to be distracted by some minor tasks. This type of distractibility is somewhat similar to that which would be seen in adults with Attention Deficit Hyperactivity Disorder. However, individuals with ADHD often exhibit a host of other symptoms and problems in the workplace. Some examples of symptoms include daydreaming, having trouble reading because of being easily distracted, and jumping from one thing to another without completing tasks (Weiss 1996). This is different from the OC employee, who may have difficulty staying on task or may have difficulty staying organized, but for different reasons. Those with OCPD are often driven by anxiety, a need to conform or to be perfect, resulting in a certain rigidity and inflexibility that the person with ADHD lacks. What OCPD and ADHD share in common is that people in both groups tend to be quite intelligent.

In supervising those with OCPD it's important for you provide noncritical, nonjudgmental, supportive guidance. This can be accomplished by talking with the employee about how you and they seem to have different work habits. You can explain that in order to keep things more on track you'd like to work with the employee to come up with a way to provide better structure for their job so as to maximize their performance. In order to do this, you may need to take large tasks and break them down into more manageable pieces for the employee. You might even set up regular times for you and the employee to work together in modifying some of their work patterns. Yes, this project would be time consuming at first, but you're actively helping to initiate some productive work habits that can be helpful in managing other tasks that come along, and you're doing it in a supportive, nonthreatening way.

Working with the OCPD Employee or Subordinate

The following are some specific suggestions or recommendations to help you manage your OCPD employee:

1. *Be specific about what tasks you want the employee to work on.* It's usually better to give specific tasks so they're less likely to veer off track. Don't assume that the employee will anticipate what problems may come up or how to handle roadblocks. One OC accountant became immobilized when she was unable to gain access to some documents she needed to complete an audit. When her manager simply instructed her to ask a particular person in the accounts receivable department for the information, the audit was easily completed.

2. *Ask for regular updates on progress.* Regular updates will allow you to see if the OC employee has gotten stuck and will help you avoid the crisis that could occur when you simply assume that they are working independently and that all is well. Be casual and sensitive when asking for updates—it is important that the employee not feel singled out or picked on by your questions. Hopefully, the employee will see this attention as an attempt on your part to keep them on task and help maximize their potential.

3. *Try to avoid getting frustrated or making critical remarks.* You'll find that it's more productive to keep your frustrations to

yourself and to avoid dumping on the employee if they are procrastinating over a project. You'll get better results by being supportive. Goleman (1998) speaks of Shirley DeLibero, the head of the New Jersey Transit Authority, as an example of an administrator who provides plenty of praise and positive feedback, but will also give constructive feedback with suggestions for improvement when an employee has goofed up in some way. DeLibero feels it is essential to let employees know what they can improve and feels that it is a disservice not to provide them with corrective feedback. This is the best tactic for correcting a wayward OC employee.

4. *Set clear expectations and boundaries.* If the OC's procrastination is getting in the way of their productivity, and all other approaches have failed, it's best to be clear that this behavior will not be tolerated. As indicated above, it is better to set deadlines that the employee can handle. If you've worked to set realistic deadlines do not give extensions, as this may inadvertently encourage more procrastination. On the other end of the continuum, you may have an extremely conscientious OC employee who is overly functional. These employees will not only do *their* job, but they want to do everyone else's, too—including yours. Therefore, it's important to set boundaries with these employees as well, but let them know when you want help, being very specific about what you want them to do. If you adopt too passive a management style, the OC will take this to mean that they are allowed to take control of others' job responsibilities.

5. *Establish your authority.* As we said earlier, managing an OC employee can either be a blessing or a curse. The curse of working with these individuals is that sometimes their attention to minute detail can give them the appearance of higher competence, a competence that they feel transcends your own. The OC employee may claim that they "have to catch all your mistakes." The worse-case scenario is when the OCPD employee will vie for your job, trying to achieve recognition for being "perfect" or "the best." Be firm and exercise your authority to make certain this doesn't happen.

In Conclusion

Working with or for a person with Obsessive Compulsive Personality Disorder can have its advantages, disadvantages and, certainly, its challenges. As annoying as their behaviors and attitudes can sometimes be, they are often more annoying to those people who buy into their criticisms or their attempts to prove their superiority. They say that in presidential elections, the incumbent always has the advantage, because often all they have to do is to "act presidential." Perhaps the same advice can be applied here, especially if you're working with someone with OC, or they're working for you: act presidential. Don't get into debates or petty arguments with these individuals. After all, even though Mr. Spock was the most intelligent crew member on the *Enterprise*, Captain Kirk was skilled enough at maintaining his command to ensure that he would be the one to make the final decision.

It's also important to keep in mind who these people are and what makes them tick. As the famous neo-Freudian analyst and author, Karen Horney, pointed out, individuals with OCPD, live by "the tyranny of the should" (1950). They find it hard to make decisions, to complete tasks, or to evaluate their own behavior or the behavior of others because of their obsession with perfection. These individuals must be right all the time, and they must win all the time, and to concede or negotiate feels to them like a fatal concession. Just as they can be quite miserable, they have a penchant for making those around them miserable—if you let them.

CHAPTER 8

The Dependent Personality Disorder: Till Death Do Us Part

For some time now, I have said that codependence is not just a relationship disease, and a good codependent does not need someone else on whom to practice his or her disease. A codependent can be codependent with a fence post.

—Anne Wilson Schaef

Hey! Did you hear the one about the codependent who fell off a cliff? Someone else's life passed in front of her eyes! (Rim shot, please.) Still another joke circulating is, "What does a co-dependent say after making love?" Answer—"Was it good for me, too?" (Bada-boom, bada-bing!) Although these jokes may be in bad taste, they make their point all too clearly: There are some people who value other people's feelings and wishes even more than their own. It is these people that this chapter is all about.

Recently, there have been many books, news specials, and talk shows about codependency, which is actually a popular name for Dependent Personality Disorder, a disorder originally identified by Freud almost one hundred years ago. Dependent Personality Disorder (DPD) is found more frequently in women than men, and is typified by a type of clingy, yet accommodating, personality style that's marked by overinvolvement in another person's life due to a fear of being rejected or alone. When people hear the word codependent, they usually understand it to refer to spouses of addicted or abusive people. But the term Dependent Personality Disorder can be applied to anyone who stays in a relationship primarily to avoid fears of being independent or alone. Often, these individuals will put up with varying levels of abuse so as not to be abandoned. This is not because they are masochistic, as was once believed, but because the alternative to taking this abuse is that they must leave the relationship—this option is just too scary for them. The principal idea behind DPD is, "If I make myself as lovable and accommodating as I can, you will not desert me." Unfortunately, this strategy rarely works.

As individuals go through life, they must strike a balance between being an independent, autonomous person and being responsive to the needs of others. In the case of DPD, the individual is clearly overly concerned with attending to and gratifying the needs of others. They desperately want to be approved of by others and, consequently, are willing to subjugate their own needs to accommodate the desires of important people around them. As a result, they must put up with the variable moods and whims of others. They appear to be, at least on the surface, eminently agreeable and ingratiating. But on the inside, they can be highly resentful of surpressing their own needs to accomodate the needs of those around them.

What Is Dependent Personality Disorder?

Individuals with Dependent Personality Disorders have a powerful need for approval, attention, and affection from others, and because they are so dependent upon this approval, they need constant reassurance that the important people will not desert them. Dependents *hate* to be alone. If they are left to rely upon their own judgment, they can often freeze into a passive mode of inactivity. Lacking in self-esteem, they are quick to downplay their strengths and personal opinions while clinging to the opinions and strengths of others. Ever agreeable and self-effacing, they are constantly searching for guidance in carrying out any type of workplace duty with which they are not already highly familiar.

The DSM-IV criteria for Dependent Personality Disorder follows:

> A pervasive and excessive need to be taken care of that leads to submissive and clinging behavior and fears of separation, beginning by early adulthood and present in a variety of contexts, as indicated by five (or more) of the following:

1. has difficulty making everyday decisions without an excessive amount of advice and reassurance from others.

2. needs others to assume responsibility for most major areas of his or her life.

3. has difficulty expressing disagreement with others because of fear of loss of support or approval.

4. has difficulty initiating projects or doing things on his or her own (because of a lack of self-confidence in judgment or abilities rather than a lack of motivation or energy).

5. goes to excessive lengths to obtain nurturance and support from others, to the point of volunteering to do things that are unpleasant.

6. feels uncomfortable or helpless when alone because of exaggerated fears of being unable to care for himself or herself.

7. urgently seeks another relationship as a source of care and support when a close relationship ends.

8. is unrealistically preoccupied with fears of being left to take care of himself or herself.*

The fact that the individual with Dependent Personality Disorder has difficulty making everyday decisions without an excessive amount of advice and reassurance from others is perhaps the quality that makes this person a potential problem in an organizational setting. Also, the dependent will not be one who will rely upon their own instincts and self-motivation to get tasks done correctly, due, in part, to the fact that they can be deficient in self-confidence. The astute observer will notice that their nonverbal communication lacks a repertoire of assertive behaviors: they will tend to mumble and speak softly, with deference and lack of assurance. They will often walk stoop-shouldered and not make eye contact. Rather than confront, they will placate. They will go to great lengths to underplay their accomplishments or any strength. Indeed, they might even consider themselves highly incompetent and inept; new tasks and promotions frighten them because they don't feel qualified or competent enough to do them. This is highly ironic, because many dependents spend hours of their lives ministering and attending to others and are, in fact, hypercompetent.

---

* Reprinted with permission from the *Diagnostic and Statistical Manual of Mental Disorders*, Fourth Edition. Copyright 1994 American Psychiatric Association.

Because of this lack of self-confidence, the individual with Dependent Personality Disorder usually tends to gravitate toward stronger and more assertive people who will give them direction. Usually, they will cling to powerful individuals for guidance and sustenance, feeling weak and helpless when not intimately connected to this other human being. They will idealize this person, seeing them in the most favorable light possible, considering them almost omnipotent while ignoring their shortcomings. Indeed, the dependent person will often latch on to another individual with the almost magical belief that there is some inherent, inseparable bond between them. Unless the individual they've chosen is the type of person who has a personal need to constantly direct another and have another in their service (for example, see the chapters on Narcissistic Personality Disorder, Antisocial Personality Disorder, and Obsessive Compulsive Personality Disorder), this clinging type of behavior may actually drive the needed person away, producing the exact result the dependent fears most: *abandonment.*

If this disorder is not too severe, these individuals can be great "cheerleaders," standing on the sidelines and cheering for their champion. They will be highly supportive, doing exactly what they're told to do and worrying (often for nights on end) that they will not do it correctly. In fact, these people who have "healthy" subtypes of the disorder appear to have a great capacity to compassionately care for their fellow human beings and to love them unconditionally. They are highly trusting, and it doesn't take much to keep them happy—just a little appreciation, if you please. Gracious, thoughtful, and considerate of other people's feelings, these individuals can make wonderful coworkers. Problems arise, however, when the disorder becomes more severe, as in the story of Sharon below.

Sharon, a thirty-two-year-old teacher's aide, first sought therapy at the suggestion of the school principal, someone she was particularly close to, who was taking Sharon under her wing. Although Sharon had worked as an aide for nine years, Sharon still required the advice of the teachers before starting any new project for the students, often asking for help daily.

Sharon was the younger of two sisters. She said that her childhood was "traditional" and "perfect," with her father being the strong figure on whom the rest of the family relied. Her mom was old-fashioned and took good care of everyone. From almost the day she was born, everyone treated Sharon like a "precious little doll." All of her needs were met. In school, her sister, Brandy, became her guardian. If ever anything was wrong, Sharon ran to Brandy to make it right, whether it was to protect her from bullies or to help her in her classes. Sometimes Brandy even did Sharon's homework for Sharon. Although Sharon was only an average student, the teachers like her because she was "sweet and well behaved." As a teenager, Sharon never learned to drive. Instead, Brandy always took her wherever she wanted to go.

The day after graduating from high school, Sharon married Tom, an appliance mechanic who reminded her of her father. Tom was Sharon's first and only boyfriend, and like her father, Tom loved the idea of having a wife at home who didn't work and didn't mind catering to him. For the most part, Sharon adored Tom and loved playing the role of the traditional wife, and she sometimes found it difficult to assert herself in the relationship, fearing that Tom might become angry with her.

Soon, however, Tom began to see Sharon as needy and suffocating. Without her own circle of friends, she insisted they spend every free moment together. Her days were usually spent with her mother and Brandy, with Tom dropping her off in the morning and picking her up again in the evening. Responding to her neediness, Tom eventually decided that Sharon should have more of an identity of her own, and he insisted that she enroll in junior college. "I want someone who I can be more to than just another Brandy," he stated. Sharon, however, doubted that she would have the confidence to follow through.

Six months into couples therapy, Sharon was beginning to learn how to drive. About the same time, however, Brandy was killed in a car accident. The effect on Sharon was devastating. With Brandy gone, Sharon begin to slip into depression, clinging to Tom even more tightly. In response, Tom began a process of extended emotional withdrawal and is now threatening divorce. Sharon cannot imagine how she would possibly make it alone (Millon and Davis 2000).

As is the case with many other personality disorders described in this book, the Dependent Personality Disorder also has variations or subtypes. Below we present brief sketches of each subtype, the names for which were created by Millon and Davis in their book *Disorders of Personality: DSM-IV and Beyond.*

The *disquieted dependent* is really a mixture of both Dependent Personality Disorder and Avoidant Personality Disorder. Many of these individuals seek out bureaucratic institutions to submit themselves to, which they look to for fulfillment of their security needs. The disquieted dependent is overly concerned about their security and safety and will often become enraged if the individuals or institutions around them cannot supply this. They will often isolate themselves from others, choosing to live their lives almost solely for the institution.

The *accommodating dependent,* when contrasted to the disquieted dependent, is much easier to get along with and is far more obliging. On the surface, they may appear to be quite cheerful They are usually friendly and outgoing and will have a warm and engaging quality about them. Similar to the individual with Histrionic Personality Disorder, they will often seek to become the center of attention through self-dramatizing behaviors. The strategy behind these behaviors is that they encourage others to take control of the dependent's lives. As the individual with Dependent Personality Disorder feels incompetent, this allows someone else to come in and support them.

The dependent who is of the *immature dependent* variety appears childlike throughout most of their life and even prefers childlike activities. Most of them find the demands of adulthood to be quite frightening, and they will tend to shy away. This lack of contact with the adult world results in their being naive and unsophisticated. Sharon, in the case history above, is a good example of an individual of this subtype.

The *ineffectual dependent* is a subtype that combines behaviors of both Dependent and Schizoid Personality Disorder. These individuals shy away from social relationships and will often choose solitary activities. Like the schizoid, they possess low energy levels and cannot seem to experience the highs and lows of a normal emotional life. Unlike the schizoid, however, they *do* appear to understand the emotional lives of others.

The *selfless dependent* is the subtype that exhibits the most extreme attachment behavior. In many ways, they are truly self-effacing and symbiotic, subjugating their own needs to build up the other. Fusing themselves with the other, they will actually adapt the behaviors, values, and persona of the other person. All seems to be fine with this individual and they can often appear to be quite happy as long as the relationship is intact. Major problems arise, however, when the relationship's threatened. Naturally, these individuals take loss badly, as their identity is defined by the other person.

Distance and Pursuit

There is a particular symptom of Dependent Personality Disorder that merits special attention here. Dependents often engage in a pattern of interaction known as a "distance-pursuit pattern." What happens is that the dependent, looking for security, begins to cling to a strong security figure, much like Sharon clung to Brandy and Tom. This other individual, in an effort to get some breathing room, "pushes" the other person away, rejecting the clinging efforts. Feeling this rejection, the dependent will cling even more, which, in turn, sparks further distancing behavior by the mate. This ongoing interaction becomes a vicious cycle, with the dependent pursuing and the other distancing. The escalations continue, with the distancing leading to more clinging behaviors, and the clinging behaviors, in turn, producing other distancing behaviors.

The story of Paul provides a good example of how this might operate in the workplace. Paul was a top advertising salesman who had Dependent Personality Disorder. Because he desperately sought the approval of his boss (who reminded him of his father) he often went to great efforts to make sales. Because Paul was highly motivated, he often met his quotas and made a good income. Paul's boss withheld compliments and praise, so Paul often felt inadequate and would "fish" for positive feedback from his boss. This fishing behavior only annoyed Paul's boss, who then made deliberate efforts to avoid praising Paul. This vicious cycle escalated until the animosity between them reached a peak, and Paul went to work for one of his boss's competitors. It is interesting to note that Paul's boss might also have had a personality disorder, Obsessive Compulsive Personality Disorder, which is typified by a withholding of praise and compliments.

Yet another factor about this distance-pursuit relationship is that, even if you are not habitually a distancer and you customarily do not withhold complements or praise, day-to-day interaction with these individuals, with their constant neediness and clinginess, will often *cause* you to begin to distance from them—thereby increasing their need to cling. It seems that the harder you struggle to distance yourself from them, the more enmeshed you become. Being aware that you are in such an interaction can go a long way in helping you rectify the situation more effectively.

The Dependent Administrator

As a general rule, dependents make better followers than leaders. If the person with Dependent Personality Disorder does make it into a leadership position, it's because they have gone to extreme lengths to please their own superiors, not because they are ambitious or entrepreneurial. You'll find that the dependent administrator shies away from conflict and confrontation. It would be unusual, therefore, for a dependent to make it into the higher echelons of management.

Nevertheless, many dependents do make it into management positions. One of the things that they will try to foster among the employees is a positive emotional tone in the working environment. They will want a harmonious and cooperative atmosphere. And because the dependent administrator values that kind of environment, they will shy away from confrontations and will not "take the bull by the horns." Problems needing a proactive approach will most likely be left unattended.

Another problem is that the dependent administrator will have problems functioning independently. Indeed, one of the most striking traits of an administrator with Dependent Personality Disorder is that they have problems making decisions and taking charge without consulting others. You'll find that they have a constant need to discuss, sometimes endlessly, the decisions they have to make. Therefore, if you're the type of person who likes to have their own ideas acknowledged and implemented, and you do not mind the lack of leadership, a dependent administrator will give you the opportunity to have a great deal of input into the organization. Furthermore, the dependent administrator will appreciate your being a "team player," especially if you can present solutions to problems that won't hurt other people's feelings. But we must warn you that you may find yourself discussing the problem continually without ever coming to a conclusion or seeing one instituted.

Working with the Dependent Administrator

One of the good parts about working for an administrator with Dependent Personality Disorder is that though they seek attention and approval excessively, they will probably give attention and approval in return. You will most likely find little thank-you notes or other tokens of appreciation. Beware, however, if you ever need them to take a position on your side against their superiors. It will be difficult for them to stand firm in this kind of confrontation as they will fear abandonment and the destruction of the positive emotional tone of the workplace.

Also keep in mind that the dependent administrator will not mind so much if you do some things on your own. Working for a dependent can be a chance for you to grow and stretch without being overly controlled and scrutinized, as you might be with an administrator who is narcissistic or obsessive compulsive, for example. But keep in touch with them—they will want to know what you are doing and will feel abandoned if you don't share your experiences with them.

Taking things personally is another problem with the dependent administrator. While personalizing issues is a problem with almost all individuals with personality disorders, it is particularly pronounced in the dependent. If you do not like one of their ideas, for example, they will see it as a rejection of their own self-worth rather than as a simple, rational decision not to accept their ideas. If you wish to transfer to another department, they will see that as a personal rejection and, perhaps, as a betrayal. If you function at work independently and do not include them, they will become angered at the apparent rejection. Reassurances to the contrary will go a long way, though. In fact, by spending time nurturing your relationship with your dependent administrator, you will find they will repay you by providing you with a nice place to work. Not always efficient, but nice.

The Dependent Subordinate

It's important to recognize that, if you have a dependent subordinate, they will never be the type of worker who will function independently or assertively in their interactions with others. In short, they will never be a super go-getter. The best you can hope for will be to make them into more functional versions of themselves.

Also, do not expect a dependent to give you an honest, straightforward opinion. Remember, the dependent is anxious to please and is likely to tell you something that they believe you want to hear. If you say to a dependent, for example, that you're planning to order such and such piece of office furniture, and then you ask how they like it, they are likely to commend you for your fine choice, even if they hate it. Furthermore, in the more severe cases of Dependent Personality Disorder, your subordinate might not even *know* what they want or like. This indecision is because they have never really formed personal opinions, relying too heavily on shaping their opinions to fit the expectations of others.

Always bear in mind that the dependent's chief motivations are security, safety, and acceptance. They will want to make your workplace the last one they will ever work in; they are in it for the duration! Moreover, the dependent wants to be loyal and pleasing to you, as they are looking for you to accept and appreciate them. Most likely, they will do a fine job. Reward them for their loyal service, if you can. They will most likely not ask you for raises, promotions, or

other forms of compensation, but they will expect signs of appreciation and will resent it if you don't offer them. Additional sick days,
inefficiencies, and, under more severe circumstances, disability
claims, resignations, and requests for extended leave are what to
expect from the disgruntled and unappreciated dependent. It would
be sad to reach this point, because of all the disorders in this book,
the dependent is the easiest to keep happy and productive.

Working with the Dependent Subordinate

You'll find that the major problem with dependent subordinates is that, because dependents are unsure of themselves, they are
hesitant to try new things or test their potential. They are frightened
of unfamiliar things and prefer the old, familiar, and customary. As
your organization is probably constantly changing, it's important to
find a way to teach the dependent new things and have them stretch
their wings.

One way of dealing with this problem is through the use of
"graded assignments," a technique used by psychotherapists to help
their patients overcome fears. The first step in this process is to give
the dependent a task that is only slightly more challenging than ones
they have already accomplished. When they have achieved success
in that, another slightly more difficult challenge is added, and so on.
Add only one task at a time and make sure that the task is only
slightly more difficult than the previous one. Overwhelming the
dependent with responsibilities that require high levels of assertive-
ness and independence all at once will only cause them to shut
down.

The Dependent Coworker

If your dependent coworker is of the normal variety, you should
probably consider yourself blessed. They will be thoughtful, depend-
able, accommodating, concerned about your welfare, and will probably be a good very friend. If anything goes wrong with this
relationship it will most likely be that some resentment has developed because you are not as considerate of them as they are of you.
If you are the appreciative type, all will go well. If appreciation does
not come naturally, you should work on it—a little will go a long
way with the dependent coworker. If anything, you will find that
they tend to become a little too involved in the more ·personal

aspects of your life. If you are the type of person who likes that kind of intimacy, fine; but it can be a problem for a person who prefers to guard his privacy.

If your coworker's disorder is more severe, you will most likely find that this person has attached themselves to you, and the relationship is a little too close for comfort. Furthermore, you will probably be tired of reassuring them and walking on eggshells, trying not to hurt their feelings. You may find yourself endlessly giving advice and taking on more of their responsibilities than you care to as they perpetually claim not to be able to do certain tasks. It is really not very helpful to you or to the dependent for you to take over, as it keeps them in a helpless position. Firm but polite refusal with reassurances will be most effective in these types of situations. For example, one solution would be to say something like the following:

Dependent coworker: I wonder if you could call customer Jones for me. He's really angry, and I know I'll become intimidated and tongue-tied. Would you mind?

You: I really don't want to do that. But, hey, I know you can. Just be firm but polite—don't let him browbeat you!

Dependent coworker: I just don't think I can do it! I can never do these types of things. Please do it for me. You're better at it than I am.

You: Hey, I don't like it either, and it's your job. It's really not so hard. Call him, and I'll listen over your shoulder and help you out. You can do it, it just takes some getting used to.

To sum things up, here is some good overall philosophy: Maintain a positive emotional tone in your relationship with the dependent—it's important to them. And, when the relationship hits a bump, reassure them that everything between the two of you is okay, but that some adjustments need to be made. It is important to encourage them when they face a challenge, but make it a point not to do things for them that they can do for themselves.

Working with the Dependent Coworker

You may very well find that you make seemingly innocuous comments that the dependent hears as rejection. Sometimes it's important to make the dependent understand that you are two individuals and need to be separate. The above conversation is a good example. In such cases, the dependent may begin to feel rejected, and you might need to make some efforts to restore your relationship. You can point out that you are not rejecting them, but rather their behavior. A good rule of thumb under these circumstances would be this: Every time you make a statement rejecting their efforts to lean on you and that the dependent may take as rejecting, add something that *reaffirms* their self-esteem. In the above example, the coworker says, "I don't want to do this," which is a statement the dependent may take as a rejection. But by adding "you can do it," the coworker reaffirms the dependent's self-esteem. This formula, of rejecting with praise, will take some of the sting out of your encouraging them to be more independent.

In Conclusion

Individuals with Dependent Personality Disorder are also prone to depression and anxiety disorders, such as panic attacks and phobias. A perhaps oversimplified way to understand this is that they are anxious about becoming separated from a safe and protective relationship, and that they become depressed about perhaps losing such a relationship. Indeed, the strong relationship between depression and dependency is one that has been historically confirmed by numerous researchers. Also, many people with Dependent Personality Disorder develop physical symptoms, such as fatigue and exhaustion. It is easy to see that by developing a patient role, the dependent is sure to get the type of nurturance they so desperately desire. Job stressors are likely to bring on or exacerbate these symptoms. It's interesting to note that many dependents who have physical symptoms often use them to make others pay attention to them, as well as to excuse themselves from having to function more independently.

Additionally, dependents might share some obsessive compulsive, avoidant, and passive aggressive qualities, as well, because these personality disorders are in the same "cluster" as Dependent Personality Disorder. The Histrionic Personality Disorder is another disorder that has similarities to DPD as both disorders rely heavily upon the approval and acceptance of others. One way to distinguish between the two is that the histrionic is active in trying to obtain nurturance, while the dependent is more passive. If you believe that you are working with a person with Dependent Personality Disorder, you should investigate the chapters on these other disorders as well.

CHAPTER 9

The Passive Aggressive Personality: The Ultimate Obstructionist

*Anger repressed can poison a relationship
as surely as the cruelest words.*

—Dr. Joyce Brothers

Have you ever been rushing to get somewhere and gotten stuck behind someone doing forty miles per hour in the fast lane? Have you ever loaned a jacket or sweater to a friend and every time they're supposed to return it, they claim, "Sorry, I forgot." Have you ever asked a friend or relative to do you a favor, like pick you up at the mall at a certain time, only to have them arrive forty-five minutes late, claiming to have gotten "tied up with something"? Have you ever asked your spouse, partner, son, or daughter to shut off the bathroom light when they're finished, only to find that they leave the light on over and over again, despite your pleas, yelling, or screaming? If so, you may have received the brunt of passive aggressive behaviors. By passive aggressive, we are referring to instances where a person expresses their anger by passive means, like showing up late for an appointment or failing to return a jacket they borrowed from you, because they were angry. Although many people may engage in passive aggressive behaviors from time to time, not all of them manifest a Passive Aggressive Personality Disorder (PAPD). Carl's story below is a good example of the disorder.

Carl is a forty-five-year-old alcohol and drug counselor. He has worked in the field for about the past ten years. Carl has been sober for the past twenty years, and he has not experienced any problems in his sobriety. He avoids situations where he would have drunk in the past and does not allow himself to get flustered over everyday stresses and strains. Carl prides himself on his "laid-back" attitude and lifestyle. He just doesn't let things get to him. Unfortunately, Carl has been unable to hold onto a job for any period of time, and he has had jobs at several well-respected treatment centers. Carl makes an excellent first impression. His résumé shows years of experience, albeit at many different agencies, and he has attended many continuing education workshops. The problems with Carl's work history, when one scratches beneath the surface, is that he does not follow direction, does not adhere to simple rules, and does not follow through with requests of his boss and/or coworkers. In one of Carl's first jobs, he did a fine job in counseling the alcoholics and addicts who came in for treatment. However, Carl would slack off when it came to completing paperwork, and he would arrive late for treatment-plan meetings and show up late for individual and group sessions. At first, Carl would promise his supervisors that he would change, but it was all to no avail. Instead, Carl would continue to avoid paperwork while making empty promises of change. His supervisor became more and more frustrated while Carl continued to maintain his attitude of "It'll get done when it gets done." He would even use the popular AA slogan, "Easy does it," to support his case. Eventually, Carl was let go from the job. He very quickly landed another job at another reputable agency, only to have the same thing happen. Carl also blew other excellent opportunities. In one instance, he had a chance to work on a writing project with a friend but the same thing happened. Carl would promise to do the work but wouldn't deliver. When confronted, he would become defensive or would rationalize that he had a different understanding regarding deadlines. Carl seemed to have a knack for sabotaging great opportunities. It usually came down to the same thing: Carl would start off with good intentions, but his lack of sustained effort would usually come back to bite him. In each of these instances, Carl would brush off the termination by rationalizing that it was somehow "their fault," certainly not his. If anything, he would reason, they were making unreasonable demands on him, and he was right to refuse. And so the pattern continued.

Like Carl, other people with Passive Aggressive Personality Disorder are often known for their laid-back attitudes and for not letting things get to them. If anything, they seem to pride themselves on their ability not to let things fluster them. Unfortunately, passive aggressive types have an uncanny ability to totally tick off people who must interact with them. With passive aggressive types, the cardinal rule is that the more demands you place on them, the more they seem to be provoked into their passive aggressive mode.

What Is a Passive Aggressive Personality Disorder?

What is noteworthy in Carl's story is that he typifies so many of the passive aggressive or obstructionistic behaviors that seem to go along with this character type. For example, outwardly, Carl seems cooperative and willing to work within the rules of the agency. However, what is so often seen with passive aggressive personalities is their covert (and sometimes overt) sabotaging. It has been suggested that the passive aggressive personality is in a constant state of ambivalence that stems from their struggle with assertive independence versus acquiescent dependence. Therefore, when faced with even a minor request, the passive aggressive may perceive the request as an intrusive demand, and their reaction is usually one of resentment (Millon and Davis 1996). They often are apprehensive about dealing with their resentments directly, usually out of fear that they will be chastised, humiliated, or rejected. Therefore, rather than expressing these resentments directly, they will take the low road and express these feelings through negative behaviors. Some of these negative or obstructionistic behaviors may include some of what Carl did. Outwardly, he would agree to complete tasks and be cooperative, but then would ignore the request. He would show up late for meetings or not show up at all or he would passively obstruct the work of others by letting written projects sit on his desks for weeks. Then he'd become defensive or even more stubborn when confronted with these behaviors. Passive aggressive types are usually suspicious of authority and sometimes even paranoid of the motivations of those in authority over them. They will, therefore, adopt a posture of "don't expect me to do anything other than what's required in my job description." Obviously, passive aggressives are not the best team players. They may complain of how unfairly they are treated, while pointing out that other coworkers are given preferential treatment. Millon and Davis point out that passive aggressive types often exhibit at least three of the following behaviors beginning in adolescence or young adulthood: 1) irritable affectivity (e.g., is high strung, quick-tempered, and moody; reports being easily piqued and intolerant of frustration); 2) behavioral contrariness (e.g., frequently exhibits passively aggressive, obstinate, petulant, fault-finding, and sulking behaviors; reveals a measure of gratification in demoralizing, obstructing, and undermining the pleasures of others); 3) discontented self-image (e.g., reports feeling misunderstood, unappreciated, and demeaned by others; is characteristically pessimistic, disgruntled, and disillusioned about life); 4) deficient

125

regulatory controls (e.g., fleeting thoughts and emotions are impulsively expressed in unmodulated form; external stimuli evoke rapid, capricious, and fluctuating reactions); 5) interpersonal ambivalence (e.g., conflicting and changing roles are assumed in social relationships, particularly dependent acquiescence and assertive independence; unpredictable and vacillating behaviors provoke edgy discomfort and exasperation in others) (547-548).

In reviewing some of the behaviors and characteristics noted above, it becomes obvious that individuals with Passive Aggressive Personality Disorder (PAPD) are rather negative, miserable folks who are rather discontented with themselves, with others, and with life. The old saying "Misery loves company" certainly applies here, but should be amended to read, "Misery loves miserable company," because it seems that the goal of the passive aggressive personality (PAP) is not just to have company, but to make you as miserable as they are, especially if you intrude into their space by making some request.

In Carl's story, it's not coincidental that he is a recovering alcoholic. While many individuals who are in recovery from chemical dependency are quite psychologically healthy and do not manifest any major psychopathology, it's quite common for many recovering individuals to continue suffering from self-defeating personality patterns or disorders long into their recovery. Such is the case with Carl, who continued to experience problems with social and occupational functioning, even though he reported no problems whatsoever in maintaining sobriety.

If you've had the misfortune of working with or for someone with PAPD, or they worked for you, you know all too well the essence of this personality type. They are quite difficult to work with, given their negativity and resentful moods and attitudes. They often become the "wet blankets" of the workplace, being quick to point out all that is negative in whatever task is being proposed or accomplished. PAPDs are often a boss or manager's worst nightmare, because they can't be counted on to produce any more than what they perceive is strictly within their job responsibilities. Such was the case with Carl, who would promise to deliver but somehow would never quite produce all that was promised. Individuals like Carl are masters at procrastination. Thoreau summed it up best when he said, "Procrastination is the deliverance that doesn't deliver." Perhaps the PAPD derives some strange satisfaction out of watching their bosses and coworkers squirm, while they leisurely go about their merry way.

Oldham and Morris (1995) propose a less pathological variation of Passive Aggressive Personality Disorder, which they refer to as the "Leisurely Style." They characterize individuals with this style as men and women who feel they have the inalienable right to enjoy themselves, to not be burdened by extra work, to maintain their freedom. They propose that these individuals are not set on obstructing others or making others miserable, but instead are intent on maintaining their own limits and boundaries. "They are not obsessed with time urgency or demands of the clock. To these individuals, haste makes waste and unnecessary anxiety. Leisurely people feel that they are just as good as everyone else and as entitled to the best things in life" (204). Oldham and Morris feel that this leisurely type can operate quite well in the workplace, even though they don't "identify with any outer authority"(212). They feel that these individuals are simply not go-getters, not the ones to take work home with them or worry about work after hours. In fact, Oldham and Morris propose that the favorite refrain of the Leisurely Style individual is, "It's not my job." Because of these less-than-desirable work attitudes, they suggest that leisurely individuals will do well in nine-to-five jobs, civil service or governmental jobs, and the military. Just don't expect to find them at the top of their organizations, as these individuals often do not aspire to become managers, nor do they inspire leadership. If anything positive can be said for the Leisurely Style individual, Oldham and Morris feel it is their free-spirited attitude and their ability not to let things fluster them.

However, when talking about the more extreme Passive Aggressive Personality Disorder, it's much harder to find positive traits. Of all the personality disorders presented in this book, the passive aggressive personality is probably the least troubled from an individual perspective, yet they are probably the most difficult personality type in the workplace. According to the DSM-IV, the diagnostic criteria for Passive Aggressive Personality Disorder is described as follows:

> A pervasive pattern of negativistic attitudes and passive resistance to demands For adequate performance, beginning by early adulthood and present in a variety of contexts, as indicated by four (or more) of the following:
>
> 1. passively resists fulfilling routine social and occupational tasks.
>
> 2. complains of being misunderstood and unappreciated by others.
>
> 3. is sullen and argumentative.
>
> 4. unreasonably criticizes and scorns authority.

5. expresses envy and resentment toward those apparently more fortunate.

6. voices exaggerated and persistent complaints of personal misfortune.

7. alternates between hostile defiance and contrition.*

Probably the main clue that you're working with someone with PAPD is your own sense of anger or frustration in dealing with this person. You may be angry with them for a number of reasons but mostly because you may find yourself working harder than they are, staying later hours, and worrying more about work, while they have an attitude of, "I'll get to it when I get to it." Their sense of "playing by the rules" is probably quite different from yours. As a result, you will stay up nights and work hours on weekends to get a job done, while they will take their sweet old time to accomplish similar tasks. Your sense of anger or frustration will naturally be compounded if the work you do is somehow intertwined or dependent on their getting their tasks done. In an office setting, the PAP can be insidious, wiping out your hard drive "by mistake" or losing the twenty-page proposal that you've been spending months working on. Often their piece of a work assignment will slow down an entire team, as their coworkers sit around waiting for the PAP to get their part of the project done. Unfortunately, in situations like these, offering help may result in finding yourself actually doing the project yourself and feeling even more angry or frustrated. PAPD can often overlap or be confused with other disorders.

Given their negativity and sullen moods, these individuals are often mistaken for being depressed. People with clinical depression can often be low in energy, they won't enjoy things as much (what's called anhedonia). However, you will usually see more anger and irritability in the PAP, more obstinance and passive resistance to what they perceive as demands. A depressed individual may want to accomplish the work, but will feel that they just don't have the energy to do so. It is also possible that some of the obstinance or forgetfulness could reflect an Attention Deficit Hyperactivity Disorder. It was once thought that most children and adolescents outgrew this disorder once they reached adulthood, but it's now known that this is not necessarily the case. Adults will ADHD will often present with behaviors similar to the PAPD; the distinction is that the individual with ADHD may indeed have forgotten an assignment they were supposed to complete or they may have gotten distracted or

---

* Reprinted with permission from the *Diagnostic and Statistical Manual of Mental Disorders*, Fourth Edition. Copyright 1994 American Psychiatric Association.

sidetracked by something else that caught their attention. In ADHD, these behaviors are not intended to anger or hurt the other person, as would be the case for someone with PAPD.

The Passive Aggressive Administrator

The concept of the passive aggressive administrator is something of an oxymoron, because there are few real passive aggressive types who truly aspire to administrative positions or leadership roles. Often, their passivity and their laid-back attitude make it such that they are not really perceived by others as being strong managerial candidates.

In the event that they do rise to the top, one would expect to see various passive aggressive maneuvers that are sure to frustrate even the most patient and loyal employee. For example, passive aggressive administrators will often schedule meetings and then fail to show up. They may specify that you are to open the office or workplace at a particular time, and then they will show up an hour or so later. If you ask for a raise, they will usually respond with, "I'll have to get back to you on that," and then they don't. They seem to derive some pleasure in seeing you squirm, while you weigh out when to ask again without appearing an impatient pest. Similar delay tactics are used for any project or proposal that requires a deadline. If someone within the organization asks for a document by a certain date, you may bust your hump to get the document to your boss well before the deadline. Then your boss will sit on the document, turning it in late and leaving you to look like the slacker. If you recall the role of the Captain (played by James Cagney) in the movie version of *Mister Roberts* you'll also remember some prime examples of an administrator who used passive aggressive manipulations. Every time that Mr. Roberts (played by Henry Fonda) would submit a request for transfer, the Captain would stall as long as possible and then would reject the transfer request, giving no logical reason. When the officers of the ship requested shore leave for the crew, the Captain summarily dismissed the request, again with no real justification. The Captain was indeed a miserable person who lacked compassion for his officers and crew, and he used passive aggressive behaviors as part of his strategy for making others as miserable as he was. If this story sounds familiar to you, read on.

Working with the Passive Aggressive Administrator

So, how does one deal with a passive aggressive boss or manager? The first thing you have to do is give up any hopes or expectations you may have of changing this person. Your anger, hurt, complaints, or objections will get you nowhere. If anything, your expression of these feelings may only serve to make the manager with PAPD more uncomfortable and more passive. Remember, these are individuals who have difficulty in expressing their feelings, especially expressing their anger. Therefore, the more confrontational you try to become, the more resistant they will become. You will be better off by developing some strategies for helping yourself cope more effectively with this type of boss. For example, if you're asked to produce a document by a particular deadline, you can make certain the date you submitted the document to your boss is cited in the document itself, so you can't be perceived as a slacker if your boss decides to sit on it. You could also let other administrators know that you have completed your work on the document by asking for some confirmation of some information contained in the document. This way, you are not setting out to make your boss look bad but you are making yourself look good. If your requests for a raise or vacation are continuously put off, you do need to be persistent. This can be done with nonaggressive, gentle reminders like, "Mr. Smith, I was wondering if you could look over my performance review soon. I am trying to make some plans for continuing education workshops and need to know what areas I need to work on." Or, "Ms. Smith, could you please look over my request for an increase? I'm in the process of refinancing my car, and it would be easier if I knew what type of raise I might be eligible for." Or in a half-kidding tone, "Mr. Smith, you didn't forget about my raise, did you? I know how organized you are, so you'll get to it soon, right?" By using traditional assertive statements like, "I'm frustrated because you forgot my raise," or, "I'm angry because you keep ignoring my request for a raise," you will probably only incite more passive aggressive responses and your request will be put on the bottom of the pile. On the other hand, you don't want to be too passive, because this doesn't work, either. The PAP motto is, "Out of sight, out of mind." Therefore, you will need to stay on top of any request, but in a nonthreatening, nonaggressive manner. Oldham and Morris suggest that you offer to help this person with tasks that they may find difficult or distasteful, thereby helping the process along. For example, "

Mr. Smith, if I work on the month-end budget for you, could you review my request for a raise?"

In terms of your career aspirations, you probably already know not to hook your wagon to their star. These types of administrators are a dime a dozen in civil service, the military, in some tenured teaching positions, or in corporate settings where seniority equates to job security. These managers or bosses are merely putting in time before they retire or before moving on to something else that really interests them. Therefore, they are not invested in making a good impression for themselves or for those unfortunates who happen to be working under them. Therefore, get out as soon as you can in a tasteful, nonbegrudging manner. It doesn't help to gripe about this person or to complain about their ability to shirk their job responsibilities and to skillfully dump them onto you. From their perspective, they are merely "delegating" tasks, which is something that managers or bosses are supposed to do. Yet, most people readily know who the producers and who the slackers are within an organization. Like the saying goes, "When you want something done, give it to a busy person."

The Passive Aggressive Coworker

Depending on the amount of interdependence of your work, the passive aggressive coworker can either be a major pain in the neck or an amusing diversion. If you become the sole confidante of this individual, you will probably be barraged by a list of complaints about how this individual is misunderstood by others in the workplace or how they are mistreated by the administrators within the organization. They may support these claims with various stories of how other coworkers are given preferential treatment over them or how others within the organization have far better "luck" than they do. Meanwhile, as you observe this person's work behavior, you begin to understand why they are passed over for raises or are treated differently from other coworkers. What becomes obvious is that this coworker expresses their frustration or anger by passive means, i.e., not coming to work on time, not completing assignments on time, not showing up for meetings on time, by being unaccountable for their actions. They have established a work pattern that is characterized by irresponsibility and procrastination. However, instead of accepting any responsibility for their supposed misfortune, the PAP will masterfully shift blame onto anyone and everyone they can.

What is even more frustrating than becoming the PAPs confidant is when you become the target of their passive aggressive behavior. Again, PAP coworkers have an uncanny ability to make your life miserable. For example, Mark and Tom were working on a written proposal that had to be in to the vice president of marketing by December 1. There were several attempts made by Mark to set up meetings with Tom, but Tom would always come up with some excuse or other for why he couldn't meet that particular day. Mark resorted to writing notes, leaving e-mail or voicemail messages for Tom, only to find that very few of these messages were ever returned. Out of frustration, Mark began to work on the proposal himself. He put in several long, hard nights, trying to get the proposal done by the December 1 deadline, which he finally did. But when it came time, to present the proposal, Tom was right there, talking about his ideas and contributions. Tom perceived himself to be the "idea person" behind the project, but Mark bitterly saw him as a selfish slacker. Eventually, Tom's procrastination and lack of real productivity caught up with him, and he was let go. But, before he was gone, he had successfully ticked off a number of other people on the job, including Mark.

Working with a Passive Aggressive Coworker

If you are working with an individual like this, the trick is not to get hooked into their problems with authority or their passive aggressive maneuvers. In other words, don't become responsible for their work and don't take on tasks that are really theirs to complete. Once you begin to shoulder their responsibilities, it will become difficult to get out of, as they will begin to expect that you will continue to do both your share of the work and theirs. It's also important that you not get hooked into making excuses to administrators or bosses for their lack of productivity. If you do become their mouthpiece, you may be perceived as being in collusion with the PAP. It is better that you stay focused on your own work and keep your distance from them. You don't want to be perceived by your boss as someone who also slacks off from doing work or someone who can't be counted on in a pinch. Therefore, it is better not to get overly involved with the complaints, procrastination, and delays of the PAP coworker. If you do find yourself cornered by this person, it is better to politely excuse yourself and let them know that you're trying to get some work done by a certain deadline. This may convey to them that you are the type of person who respects deadlines, or at very least, that you try to adhere to the rules. Also, if the PAP coworker does foist their list of complaints about bosses and managers on you, it is usually better not to agree with their attacks. If you do, you may later hear this individual use your name to help support their position. Something like, "I'm not the only one who feels this way. My office mate, Bob, feels exactly the same way I do." So, don't even nod your head in agreement, or you may find yourself being given a cardboard box to collect your personal belongings along with your PAPD coworker.

The Passive Aggressive Subordinate or Employee

If you have a passive aggressive subordinate, you probably have been pulling your hair out trying to figure out how to get rid of this person. After all, when most of your other employees are trying to do their work, the PAP is trying to figure out ways to avoid theirs. You may recall that, when you were in the process of hiring this person, the only reference you got was one that was vague, nondescript, and basically told you nothing. Usually, former employers are so glad to get rid of the PAP that they are probably doing cartwheels on the other end of the phone. Labor laws prevent the former employer from telling you the truth about these individuals.

The PAP employee is a master at avoiding tasks, rules,and obligations. They will complain that you don't understand or appreciate them. They will criticize your management skills and run you down every chance they get. After all, from their perspective, *you* are the problem, not them. This is where the lack of insight of those with personality disorders really becomes a major concern. You, as a manager, may begin to question your own sense of reality. You may have worked as a manager or boss for many years, perhaps even many years for the same company, and here comes this PAP individual who is certain that they are right and you are wrong. As a result, they are sullen and miserable and tend to make those around them sullen and miserable. As we've stated before, misery loves miserable company. When confronted about their attitudes or behaviors, the PAP employee will either become highly defensive, or they will spin tales of woe about problems and misfortunes. Or they could become quite contrite and apologetic—only to repeat the same behaviors at a later date.

Working with the Passive Aggressive Subordinate

The trick to managing someone like this is not to let them know how angry you are. Once you do, you've lost. As Elizabeth Kenny once said, "He who angers you, conquers you." Most PAPs derive pleasure from making others miserable. Therefore, the more angry or miserable you become, the better the PAP employee feels, as if they have gained some kind of power over you. In a sense, they have: they can make you feel angry—or so it seems. No one can *make* us feel anything. That may sound outlandish, but when you think of it, we are the cause of our own upset. Therefore, if the PAP is procrastinating over turning in a project, and you are upset, it is really because you're *choosing* to be upset. One of the unfortunate parts of having an employee like this is that they derive pleasure from watching you get angrier and angrier. But we are not suggesting that you become passive, too. We are merely suggesting that your angry reactions are probably not helping the situation. Remember, this employee, like many with PAPD, may be functioning at the level of a fifteen-year-old, so you'll get as much response from yelling at this person as parents do when they tell their teenagers to clean their rooms. It becomes an exercise in futility. PAPs and adolescents love to think that they can wield power by making others angry, so it's usually better to manage them by using different strategies.

One such strategy would be meeting them halfway. What we mean is working out a deal with this person in which you'll try to find out what they need to get the job done. You promise to fulfill this need (within reason, of course) in return for their meeting the deadline. It's as if the parent is saying to their teen, "I'll help you get started with organizing your room, but then you've got to see the job through." Another variation on this theme would be to offer an incentive once the job is completed on time. These incentives can be small, but still represent some token of recognition, like a day off. This strategy is similar to the parent saying to their teenager, "Once you finish cleaning your room, you can go out with your friends."

Naturally, all of the best-planned strategies may not work. It really depends on how invested the employee is in sabotaging their jobs, or how invested they are in getting you to overreact in anger. So, when all else fails, you need to document all the attempts you make to try to work with them. If you do decide to fire this person, it's crucial to have a good paper trail. In each of your interactions with this employee, it's best to document precisely what job or task you are expecting them to do, when it is due, and how you want it done. Don't leave anything to chance or assume that you and they are on the same page, because if there is a loophole for avoiding work, the employee with PAPD will probably find it.

Also, in confronting the employee with your dissatisfaction about their work don't expect them to take the feedback in a receptive way. If anything, they will look for some way to put the blame on you or to make you look responsible for their work deficiencies. Such was the case with Carla, a postal employee, who, when confronted by the postmaster with her poor work performance, blamed the postmaster for not giving her enough direction and supervision. Carla went on to defend herself by claiming that she was being discriminated against because she was a woman, which was clearly not the case in this particular situation. In fact, Donna, the postmaster, was also a woman and had met with Carla on several occasions to review her work performance and to make various recommendations to her. Donna was careful in these meetings to point out Carla's strengths along with her weaknesses. However, when it came down to it, Carla was not responding to the suggestions that Donna had offered. In essence, Carla was going to do things her way and at her own pace, which was not was in keeping with the demands outlined in her job description. Carla was eventually let go, but only after months of disciplinary actions.

Passive aggressive subordinates present special challenges to even the most competent, adept, and patient supervisor. It is very difficult to find unique ways to motivate these individuals and to bring them around to being part of the work team. Sometimes it becomes all you can do not to have their negativity spread to other members of the work group. Therefore, you will really have your work cut out for you.

In Conclusion

Whether you're a manager, a coworker, or an employee working for someone with Passive Aggressive Personality Disorder you probably already sense that this is one of the more frustrating types of individuals to be dealing with in the workplace. Their lack of insight into their behavior, their unwillingness to change, and their tendency to spread negativity make the passive aggressive personality one of the most difficult individuals to work with. They are poor supervisors, they do not like to be supervised, and generally don't like to be held accountable for their behavior. Unfortunately, these do not make for very good workplace behaviors or attitudes.

Another unfortunate thing is that passive aggressive personality types do not benefit much from psychotherapy. Usually, when they do end up in therapy, it's often because a spouse or partner has reached the end of their rope with this person and has forced them into treatment. But one of the prerequisites for therapeutic change is discomfort. For example, a person who is depressed seeks therapy because of the extreme emotional discomfort of feeling pervasive sadness. People with PAPD, are often not the ones who are uncomfortable, however. Their spouse, mother, father, partner, coworker, or boss may be uncomfortable with their behaviors, but they probably aren't. Therefore, they often have little motivation to change. This is very similar to the adolescent who comes in two hours past curfew, worrying his or her parents sick. The parents yell and scream while the obstinate teenager just rolls their eyes in boredom. They have suffered no consequence, no discomfort; so, why change? Often, when people with PAPD do end up in therapy, they will bring the same passive aggressive behaviors to the treatment milieu—showing up late for appointments, canceling appointments at the last minute, or "forgetting" to bring in their insurance forms. Even the most patient of therapists can reach a point of exasperation, knowing that they could be putting their time and effort to better use for those patients who really want to change. So, too, is the dilemma of the boss, the coworker, or the employee working with a Passive Aggressive Personality Disordered individual. You cannot change them—the trick is to learn some strategies to cope with their behaviors, or, in essence, not to have them change you.

CHAPTER 10

The Avoidant Personality: "On the Watering of Wallflowers"

Charlotte taught courses in computer programming at a small parochial college in New England. In spite of the fact that she has been teaching for ten years, Charlotte has achieved only the rank of Assistant Professor, and her salary is well below average for that institution. This disparity is because Charlotte will not participate in the required committee meetings or make scholarly presentations to the college community, both needed for advancement. When it comes time for her to be evaluated, she usually calls in sick and has canceled on several occasions. Weeks before a scheduled evaluation, Charlotte usually begins to suffer from panic attacks. She develops insomnia and has often lost as much as ten pounds. She becomes panic stricken during the evaluations and begins to mumble, even though she's a skilled lecturer in class. Consequently, her evaluations are poor, in spite of the fact that she is highly knowledgeable in the field of computers and she has even published several articles in computer journals. "I don't need a promotion," she was heard to say. "I'm happy just the way things are." A promotion would require her to chair committees, which would simply be too frightening to her.

Charlotte's parents were divorced when she was young and she didn't see her alcoholic mother much. As a child, Charlotte's concert violinist father, practiced continually. He was constantly worried about losing his job. Tragically, an accident damaged one of his hands and he was unable to continue in his chosen profession. He obtained some compensation from the accident, which they lived off of when Charlotte was small. Quite overwhelmed and perhaps burdened with having to raise a child on his own, Charlotte's father disciplined her by insisting on academic excellence while continually criticizing grades that were less than perfect. Consequently, she grew up never feeling quite good enough. In spite of the fact that Charlotte was almost a straight-A student and was accepted by an Ivy League school, Charlotte attended the local state school so she could stay at home. She attended graduate school at that same college.

Charlotte's life is quite routine. Every morning she goes in and teaches her classes and then will run errands, do her shopping, have her hair done, and so on. On weekends, she either rents videos or grades papers. On rare occasions, she will attend a computer workshop. The only people with whom she socializes are her father and a girlfriend she grew up with, but who lives in another city. About once a year, around the holidays, they will get together. She will sometimes visit carefully selected chat rooms, where she will exchange surface pleasantries with others in the virtual community, careful never to reveal much about herself. Her life is dull and ordinary, and there is little joy. When asked why she doesn't date, she says that she is afraid of date rape. At age thirty-five, she is considering seeing a doctor for her panic. Twice now she has made appointments, only to cancel them. Charlotte has an Avoidant Personality Disorder.

What Is Avoidant Personality Disorder?

People with Avoidant Personality Disorder seem to melt into the woodwork. They reticently absent themselves from situations that would subject them to scrutiny. They avoid any situation or change in personal circumstances that might bring them into the public eye. Meetings, parties, presentations; in short, *any* situation where there is a possibility of being on display is strictly avoided. Rather, they withdraw into their own private world of inadequacies and self-doubts. And, although they might appear on the surface to merely be reserved, even confident at times, on the inside they are a bottomless cauldron of nagging doubts and insecurities. While other individuals in the organization engage in forms of self-promotion, the avoidant is happy to merely be a wallflower. Indeed, being invisible is their goal. Because they believe that if others in the organization really got to discover them, they would know exactly how inadequate these wallflowers actually are and would reject or even fire them.

The avoidant is a first cousin to another personality disorder called Schizoid Personality Disorder. At first glance, the schizoid and avoidant appear to be identical. Indeed, some researchers feel that they are simply variants of each other. But what makes the avoidant different from the schizoid is that the schizoid *doesn't wish* to have interactions with other individuals. The avoidant, on the other hand, wants very much to have interactions with others. They feel compelled to avoid interactions because they're afraid that they will do something stupid or embarrassing and will then be rejected. Another difference is that the avoidant can have a rich emotional life, whereas the schizoid is emotionally flat. In fact, the avoidant often experiences intense anxiety, whereas the schizoid can't.

Avoidants constantly scan the social environment for signs of possible scrutiny or criticism, rigidly regulating their outward appearance to appear calm and reserved. Consequently, they never allow themselves to simply be themselves with any regularity or spontaneity. In short, they are the embodiment of the expression "self-consciousness."

As with the other personality disorders, experts are somewhat divided as to what symptoms make up Avoidant Personality Disorder. However, as in previous chapters, we will rely upon a DSM-IV definition.

DSM-IV symptoms for avoidant personality disorder are:

1. avoids occupational activities that involve significant interpersonal contact, because of fears of criticism, disapproval, or rejection.

2. is unwilling to get involved with people unless certain of being liked.

3. shows restraint within intimate relationships because of the fear of being shamed or ridiculed.

4. is preoccupied with being criticized or rejected in social situations.

5. is inhibited in interpersonal situations because of feelings of inadequacy.

6. views self as socially inept, personally unappealing, or inferior to others.

7. is unusually reluctant to take personal risks or to engage in any new activities because they may prove embarrassing.*

---

* Reprinted with permission from the *Diagnostic and Statistical Manual of Mental Disorders*, Fourth Edition. Copyright 1994 American Psychiatric Association.

The symptom of key importance to this chapter is the fact that the avoidant will shy away from occupational activities that involve significant interpersonal contact. This is because they feel that people are watching them very closely and will misjudge them and evaluate them negatively. In most workplaces, an employee's performance is sooner or later, and in one way or another, evaluated. Someone is usually watching them and making sure they're doing their jobs correctly. Also, formal evaluations are usually required in larger organizations as a prerequisite to promotions and raises. Evaluations of this kind can be the avoidant's worst fear. Consequently, they will be drawn to work activities which, although far below their capabilities, might allow them to remain unobtrusive. They will find ways to avoid evaluations, either by not taking the position in the first place, becoming absent when an evaluation is scheduled (like Charlotte), or by making excuses as to why they shouldn't have to be evaluated ("I'm not looking to be promoted anyway"). When these strategies fail, the avoidant experiences intense anxiety throughout the entire evaluative process. By avoiding any kind of attention, avoidants become classic underachievers who never fully realize their potential—and its accompanying rewards—in the workplace.

Most of us realize that, when we become involved with another individual, there are really no guarantees whether or not we will be liked and accepted. New relationships are always somewhat risky. But, for the avoidant, the risk of becoming involved with someone without an almost ironclad guarantee of being liked and accepted is next to impossible to endure. The story of Marianne and William, below, provides a good example.

Everyone in the dormitory knew that Marianne liked William. She would call or stop in almost daily, making up excuses to see him: she needed help with her algebra, needed to borrow a computer disk, and so on. When William appeared uninterested, Marianne stepped up her efforts, massaging his back while she told him she did not have a date for Friday night. William suggested she go with another student whom Marianne knew. Marianne got close to William and whispered in his ear, "I think I would prefer someone like you." But William remained unresponsive in spite of the fact that he felt incredibly attracted to Marianne. Marianne's best friend, Tiffany, sat next to William in their English class. She would tell William that he needed to pay more attention to Marianne, because she liked him. William would reply that he did not think so. Tiffany could not believe her ears. She said, "Of course Marianne likes you! She asked you out last Friday. And besides, she told me herself that she likes you." William replied, "She didn't ask me out. She said she wanted to go out with someone *like* me. We're just friends."

Needless to say, the relationship never got off the ground, and William missed an opportunity to have a relationship with someone who cared, all because his acceptance would not be absolutely guaranteed.

When avoidants do finally get involved in a relationship they exercise a great deal of restraint. Rarely do they express affection freely or talk about their emotions or other things that are meaningful to them. Consequently, individuals who are involved in a relationship with the avoidant rarely know how strongly the avoidant feels about them. The simplest types of self-disclosures can be embarrassing or humiliating to the avoidant so they are reluctant to express them. One avoidant was afraid to have her boyfriend spend the night because he might find out that she liked to read when she was in the bathroom. Amazingly enough, the two were eventually married. He began to complain, however, because she was reluctant to have sex because she was ashamed of her body.

Another symptom of avoidant personality disorder is that the avoidant is constantly worried about being in social situations where they might be negatively evaluated. Office parties and other social gatherings, even lunch with a stranger, will be an opportunity to fret and worry. They will agonize as to what they should wear, what they should say, and what so-and-so might think about them or say to them. God forbid if the social gathering includes game playing or an athletic event. The avoidant will be absolutely miserable throughout.

This anxiety makes avoidants inhibited in social situations. They are afraid of expressing personal opinions or even taking a point of view. One avoidant student would always let her boyfriend order for her, because she did not want to feel that her choice was "stupid." Avoidants prefer to remain quiet or simply to give short answers—to elaborate is frightening. Because of their fears, they will often mumble or, worse yet, become paralyzed to the point of being speechless. When this happens, it only increases their tendencies to avoid these types of situations. It is important to state here that part of the avoidant's fear stems from the fact that they do not see criticism for what it is. Rather than seeing it as relating to the specific issue to which it's addressed, they take it as an assessment of their total value and worth as a person. If they fail a test, they are a failure. If a supervisor suggests that they need to improve their writing skill, they are a horrible employee. If they misplace a report, they are idiots. Rather than experiencing the total dejection of being so inferior, they would rather just stay far away from other people.

Not only does the individual with Avoidant Personality Disorder fear being negatively evaluated by others, but they constantly evaluate themselves negatively as well. The avoidant sees themselves as fundamentally incompetent, foolish, and inept. They feel that they can never measure up to what others expect of them. Even when presented with evidence to the contrary, the avoidant maintains the belief that they are inferior. A laboratory technician, for example, believes that he was not masculine enough for a woman to be interested in him, in spite of his good looks, athleticism (he ran marathons), and the fact that he built his own house from the foundation up.

As a result, the avoidant prefers to stay in his old familiar surroundings and not venture out into unknown territory which can present surprises, which they feel unprepared for. Being unprepared, they risk shame and humiliation due to the inferior performance they anticipate.

Psychotherapists who have worked with Avoidant Personality Disorder often talk about another symptom of the avoidant. They remark that the avoidant will talk about and greatly exaggerate obstacles and dangers associated with meeting new people or engaging in new activities. For example, an avoidant bank teller who was in psychotherapy was told by his physician that he needed to exercise and lose some weight. He considered joining a gym but quickly decided against it. At first, he ruled out the idea because even the closest gym was much too far away. When asked exactly how far it was, the avoidant allowed that it was only five miles away, but he complained that he would have to drive to the heart of town, which sometimes could be congested. However, at the most, it was a half hour there and a half hour back, if he went right after work. When the therapist suggested an alternate route, the bank teller replied that it would be too expensive. At that point, the therapist told the patient that the gym had a ninety-day special for $100, with no other commitments required. Again, the patient resisted, stating that he would need to buy sneakers as well. Eventually, the therapist was able to get to the heart of the matter: the avoidant was just embarrassed that he would not know how to use the equipment there and would look foolish to the other, more experienced members.

Like the other personality disorders, Avoidant Personality Disorder can be conceptualized as a continuum or spectrum of personality. People with avoidant personality disorder differ in the severity of their symptoms from mild to severe. Normal variants are simply individuals who possess less intense symptoms of Avoidant Personality Disorder. The normal type of Avoidant Personality Disorder has been described as sensitive, vigilant, or hesitant. They feel most comfortable in very familiar settings and have relatively few friends. They are polite and reserved and care very much about what others think about them. They are not risk takers. It's important to understand that the more normal variant of the disorder is not simply a shy person. An avoidant often harbors a good deal of resentment, whereas a shy individual will not. Also, a shy individual will not exhibit the anxieties of being evaluated nor have the same type of family history and its accompanying high set of standards.

Personality researcher Theodore Millon and his coauthors (2000) have described four other variations of the avoidant personality disorder. The *conflicted avoidant* possesses features of the passive aggressive personality (also referred to as a negativistic personality style). This personality style is a combination of the pattern of avoidance, coupled with the obstructionistic and passive expressions of anger exhibited by the passive aggressive personality. They are more vocal in their complaints that others are not meeting their needs for nurturing and care, thus they become petulant and resistive. The *hypersensitive avoidant* exhibits features of Paranoid Personality Disorder. They might believe, for example, that others are laughing or making fun of them as they unrealistically believe that others are watching or judging them constantly. The *phobic avoidant* has features of a Dependent Personality Disorder combined with the avoidant personality. Like the individual with Dependent Personality Disorder, the avoidant also avoids a close personal relationship due to a basic mistrust of others to accept him. The conflict between the desire to cling and the desire to flee is displaced onto a "symbolic substitute onto which to project or displace their fear and anger" (146). Charlotte did not date, for example, because she claimed that she had a fear of date rape. In other words, the fear of date rape became a more acceptable substitute for her conflict between wanting closeness yet feeling terrified of rejection. The *self-deserting avoidant* combines avoidant with depressive features. These individuals retreat into themselves in order to seek a fantasy life. Drawing into themselves, however, only makes them even more keenly aware of their perceived deficiencies, thereby making them even more depressed.

There are many other symptoms an avoidant can have in addition to the avoidant ones. Like all of the personality disorders, a pure type is rarely found, and you will find that the avoidant has other symptoms from the "C" cluster disorders, and you may find those chapters helpful as well (dependent, obsessive compulsive, and passive aggressive).

Also, Avoidant Personality Disorder is often referred to as the "anxious" personality disorder, because avoidants will often have other anxiety problems as well. One of these is a "Generalized Anxiety Disorder," which is a disorder characterized by excessive worry, being on edge, being overly concerned with potential disasters ("My son will surely break his leg in this soccer game"), and a general inability to stop worrying and relax. They are hypervigilant and fear that something bad will happen at any given moment. Another anxiety problem is an Obsessive Compulsive Disorder, in which the person has intrusive and unpleasant thoughts, such as the inability to stop thinking about an automobile accident they had witnessed. These thoughts continue to hound the individual and they believe them to be inescapable. A compulsion is a behavior that a person feels compelled to perform, such as washing their hands. Obsessions and compulsions go hand in hand. "I can't stop thinking about germs (the obsession), so I have to go and wash my hands (the compulsion)." Some researchers believe that this disorder distracts the avoidant so they don't dwell on their inadequacies.

Avoidants will often complain about vague physical symptoms (which are most likely psychological in origin) and exagerrate actual sicknesses, usually to justify their avoidant behavior ("I just feel that this headache won't let up long enough for me to go to the luncheon today").

And finally, the avoidant can be depressed. In fact, depression is a common diagnosis among avoidants and if they do enter psychotherapy, this is usually the reason. It's easy to see how the avoidant can be depressed, with little social interaction, isolation, constant self-criticism, and the fear of criticism by others, in spite of the avoidant's efforts to avoid them. And the avoidant constantly berating themselves for not being good enough. These are not exactly the conditions for feeling confident, secure, and happy.

The Avoidant Administrator

As a general rule, you will rarely find an avoidant administrator, especially within the higher levels of management, unless they are promoted for their technical rather than their people-management skills. Most avoidant administrators will be mid to lower level. If you do have an avoidant administrator, chances are they will dislike meetings and almost all other types of interpersonal contact. In most cases, you will find the avoidant to be a distant administrator who prefers a hands-off approach.

One of the most common feelings that comes with working under such an administrator will be one of a lack of guidance. There will usually not be a clear sense of direction in the department. Also, you will find the avoidant to be noncommittal. If you ask for a raise, for example, they might reply, "Okay, I'll consider that." If they don't get back to you within a reasonable period of time, and you make the request a second time, they might say something like, "I have been working on it, you know," or perhaps some other stalling tactic. But the avoidant will just keep putting you off and putting you off. It would be far more productive to ask the administrator for a deadline as to when he *will* make the decision. Saying something like, "I know you've been really busy lately. There's no rush, just let me know when you'll be deciding. Do you think it will be in the next month?"

Also, keep in mind that the avoidant boss will not champion any of your causes or pet projects, or go to bat for you in anything that might put them out on a limb or make them more visible. Once again, you'll hear a flood of vague excuses for why. Don't beat yourself up about it. You might be on the money, but it doesn't matter how right you are—your avoidant boss just won't take the risk.

Working with the Avoidant Administrator

First of all, if you're the type of employee who likes to work independently, you will find that you are probably happy with an avoidant administrator. If, however, you are the type of person who needs reassurances, guidance, or a good deal of feedback, you will most likely be unhappy in the situation. Trying to get the avoidant administrator to change is like trying to push the proverbial river: it just doesn't work. It's going to move at its own speed and in its own time. Expect change to come at an almost glacial pace, perhaps only slightly faster than erosion. But don't despair, there are still some things you can do.

How about a role reversal? Even though they should be nurturing you and building you up, you might be better off being their supporter and coach. From a number of perspectives, it would be a good idea for you to encourage them and remind them of their strengths and their past successes. From an organizational viewpoint, this helps the avoidant supervisor do her job and make the organization run more smoothly. Plus, people encouraging one another is good for the corporate atmosphere and gives things a positive tone. From the point of view of the avoidant, support helps to build their self-esteem, bolstering their confidence and enabling them to have more interactions. Some coaching may even help them go out on a limb more. And from your own career perspective, being trusted by the boss isn't such a bad thing.

Don't expect the avoidant administrator to try out any of your suggestions if they require that the avoidant expand their horizons.

If you are an eager employee and are always wishing to try new things and take on new responsibilities, expect the avoidant to discourage you. (One avoidant administrator was nicknamed "The Brakeman.") They will likely give you reasons why something shouldn't be done and really not look at the reasons in its favor. This can be quite discouraging. If you have a new idea that involves some type of change, reassure your administrator that it will not involve them or that they will only be involved minimally. Try to explain to them that the new thing is similar in many ways to the old thing. If you want to institute a new reporting procedure, for example, tell them that it's no big deal, that new report formats have been introduced in the past and there have been no problems. Tell them that you will take responsibility, if that's realistic. If possible, try to make it clear to them that the more you do, the less they will have to do.

If you volunteer to take on some of their duties that involve personal interaction, they will most likely be grateful. One laboratory assistant made points with the boss by taking on her job of presenting a quarterly safety report, much to the relief of her supervisor. But her supervisor then gave this assistant more and more things to do, and, for a while, the assistant felt harrassed and overworked. What eventually happened was that the assistant became better prepared to do her supervisor's job and was eventually promoted into that position when the supervisor herself was promoted. Consider the long-term perspective of this strategy.

Unlike the schizoid administrator, it *is* possible to have a personal relationship with an avoidant administrator. Usually this comes after a long time spent working closely with the avoidant and the opportunity for them to discover that you can be trusted. But don't expect it to happen too soon. The avoidant will need a good deal of time to warm up to you. If you do develop a close, trusting relationship with them, they are likely to use you as a crutch in social situations. For example, at an office party, they will most likely spend the whole time talking to you and ignoring others. If you become a confidante, you will find that they ask you questions about other people and those people's feelings toward them. They will ask for reassurances from you, and you will become, in a sense, their social advisor.

But beware. At the slightest hint of rejection or disapproval, the avoidant will drop you like a hot potato. You will find that they don't return your phone calls, memos, and so on. They will become too busy to see you. In other words, they will *avoid* you. This serves dual purposes for the avoidant: the first is that it will protect them from being hurt again by you. This is a common defensive strategy used by the avoidant: If you can't find them, you can't hurt them.

The second purpose it serves is to hurt you back for hurting them in the first place. In other words, if you hurt them, they'll hurt you right back. You might have to think long and hard to figure out what you did to offend them because, most likely, you've done nothing wrong. They have only misperceived and misread your intentions. You might have to go a long way in explaining yourself to convince them that your behavior wasn't intended to be hurtful. You might say something like, "It was not my intention to criticize your comment at the meeting. In fact, I don't feel critical toward you at all. But I do feel that friends help one another, and I consider myself your friend. I just want to see you do well, because I like you."

And, finally, you will most likely be the one who has to go back to repair the relationship. Don't expect them to call you—you will be waiting forever. If the relationship is worth it to you, be the one who calls them. You should recognize that this will never be a fifty-fifty type of relationship. The avoidant will take for granted the fact that you will always be the one to reach out first. Live with it—it's really not so bad, is it? A little effort goes a long way here.

The Avoidant Coworker

If you are working with an avoidant coworker, you are most likely in one of two situations. In the first situation, you will find that you hardly know this person at all, in spite of the fact that you might have been working with them for long periods of time. You may have noticed that they are easily embarrassed, often showing physical signs such as blushing and the avoidance of eye contact. You might think they're stuck-up or conceited. Perhaps they blend into the woodwork, and you hardly notice them at all. They might have a nickname such as "Nowhere Man" or "The Invisible Woman" or perhaps "The Incredible Shrinking Violet." You have learned not to ask them to do things with you because they will always say no. In fact, you might all but ignore them. They might just have no effect on your life whatsoever.

In the second scenario, you might have befriended this coworker after putting in quite a bit of effort. For some reason, they have decided they can trust you. They can be good and loyal friends. But perhaps you might find them too clingy in social situations. They will expect you to spend most of your time with them and to give them the bulk of your attention. They will, most likely, ask for your assurances. They will need to know if they are doing the right thing.

You might have even discovered by now that they expect you to perform some of their more interpersonal job duties. For example, they may approach you and say, "Why don't you go tell the boss that we need more lighting in this room?" Or, "Why don't you take this phone call? I don't want to talk to her." You might find that you're always encouraging them to do certain things, such as go out to lunch with someone or attend a certain function. They will most likely not want to go anywhere unless you are with them, acting as a type of security blanket. They might even ask you to have special input into making key decisions in their lives, such as telling them what type of car to buy or where to rent an apartment or what gym to join: You have become one in their small circle of trusted friends.

Working with the Avoidant Coworker

In most cases, working with an avoidant coworker isn't much of a problem at all, as they usually don't make waves or cause problems; they simply wish to be left alone. What will happen, most likely, is that there will be certain jobs that they request you to do that they find unpleasant. Usually these jobs will be of an interpersonal nature, such as taking phone calls or confronting certain coworkers. If you wish to be kind, and this is your choice, be reassuring. Tell them that they are capable and have good skills. The conversation might go something like this:

Coworker: Could you call Mr. Franks for me? I'm kind of busy, and he's upset that he didn't get his modem.

You: Come on, you can do this. It will only take a minute of your time. You're pretty tactful anyway—remember how you handled your son's principal? I'll listen and help you out, if you like.

If they persist, just repeat yourself. Remember, you don't have to do this, it's their job and they are responsible for doing it.

If you don't feel like being someone else's coach or mentor, that's a legitimate choice as well. If this is the case, be firm. Let them know from the beginning that you're not one to do other people's work. Simply defer politely by saying something like, "No, thank you, I don't want to do that right now." You might have to watch them squirm and become quite anxious in the beginning, and maybe even listen to some whining. But they will eventually get the point and leave you alone.

Sometimes finding out what they are interested in can help you strike up a relationship with them. They will most likely be reluctant to talk about it. However, many avoidants can be quite artistic or creative. Many of them have interesting hobbies, and many like the arts or the theater. Be bold. Approach them, introduce yourself. Don't be put off by their seemingly cool behavior; remember, they want a relationship but are frightened. Instead of asking them what types of things they like to do, a remark that might require too much self-disclosure from their point of view, simply ask them what they *did* this past weekend, for example. Expect to do all the relationship work. Don't be deterred by their seeming lack of desire to be involved in a relationship. Keep plugging away, show them that you really like them. It takes a thick-skinned person to do this, one who's not easily rejected or put off. If you are sensitive to rejection yourself, this might not be the friend for you.

Finally, if you have not already done so, go back and read the section on working with an avoidant administrator. You'll find some good tips there as well.

The Avoidant Subordinate

You'll know that you have an avoidant working for you because they are quiet, unobtrusive, usually won't make waves unless they are asked to try something new, and they will appear to simply blend into the background. Rarely will they cause problems and will be scarce at any social function organized by the corporation. You'll see a great deal of resistance when the avoidant is requested to take on job duties where they might have to demonstrate a greater degree of competency or to be more in the public eye. Even working with strangers is difficult for them. Simply being moved to a new department within the organization can be terrifying to the avoidant, and they might make every excuse not to be moved. When one parole officer, for example, found out that he was being transferred to the next county, he became enraged and used up all of his vacation and sick days. In spite of the fact that he would be given a car to commute, he complained of the travel time, the inefficiency of management in making such a decision, and the fact that he would no longer have time to participate in his hobby, which was reading Civil War history. Because the man was Hispanic, he complained that he was being singled out because of his race and considered filing an unfair labor practice. Only after he discovered that the new supervisor was an old acquaintance of his did he acquiesce.

Individuals with Avoidant Personality Disorder usually are unable to profit from job evaluations. Evaluations are like stakes which pierce the heart of the avoidant. This is because they perceive the evaluation as a criticism of their ultimate worth and become so distraught that they can't see any positives in the evaluation. One avoidant chemist, named Sam, called his therapist in desperation. Although he was attending psychotherapy sessions weekly, he requested an additional session. Concerned, his therapist asked why he needed the additional session. He replied that he had just gotten a horrible job evaluation, and that he would most likely be fired soon. When he actually attended the session with the psychotherapist, he produced the job evaluation. The therapist was shocked. Sam had, in fact, received a wonderful job evaluation, excelling in all areas but one. The evaluation simply stated that he needed minor improvements in the area of communication. Sam's seeing this evaluative mole hill as a mountain of criticism is highly characteristic of the avoidant.

Working with the Avoidant Subordinate

Avoidants can be very talented and competent people. They try harder, because they need to cover up their perceived deficiencies. You can get the most out of an avoidant by being a benevolent coach who always accentuates the positive and minimizes the negative.

When you have to evaluate the avoidant subordinate, make it clear to them from the beginning that you value them and their work. Tell them that, because it's a requirement that you evaluate them, you would like to form an alliance with them. Tell them you would like to collaborate, much in the same way a coach collaborates with his star players, to help them become better employees. Tell them that the evaluation is not to tear them down, but rather to build them up. Be encouraging. Say something like, "You know, out of the ten billion things you do well for us, it's a shame that this evaluation form only contains twenty items. If I could, I would write ten pages on what you were doing right and perhaps only a sentence or two of things that could use improvement."

Also, when it comes to evaluations, you might want to consider this option. Explain to the subordinate something psychotherapists have known for a long time. We explain to our patients that every personality trait has positive and negative qualities. For example, an aggressive salesman can be seen as pushy, or an accommodating coworker could be seen as "wishy-washy." A frugal and careful accountant might be seen as stingy, and a seemingly stuck-up supervisor might be simply confident. Each strength is its own liability. Telling the avoidant in an evaluation that they need improvement in the area of communication might be put this way: "You are a hard worker, and we really like that in you. But every quality our people have also comes with its own drawbacks. Hard workers sometimes get so absorbed in their work that they overlook the fact that they have to communicate their findings to others. It seems weird, but it's true. Take a break once in a while and let us know what you're doing. Keep us apprised of your good work and efforts." Staying positive is the best tactic.

We know that, as a supervisor, you have to play many roles. One of those roles is that of coach, taking an employee under your wing, and motivating them. This is even more important with the avoidant subordinate. In fact, you will find that thinking of yourself as a coach or a mentor is a good frame of mind to be in when dealing with the avoidant. Never put them into a situation that is way over their heads. Build them up gradually, encouraging them as you go along.

Like the individual with Dependent Personality Disorder, you might want to use a technique called "graded assignments." Start them off with something small and gradually give them things that are harder and harder to do as they continue to build confidence. Tell them that you will never ask them to do things that they cannot do or that make them feel very uncomfortable. But let them know from the outset that there will be things they are required to do that might make them feel somewhat uneasy. But, nothing more than they can bear. And let them know that you will be there to help them. And remember, this desire not to take on new work can actually be a God send if the workplace will benefit from their staying in a routine job where they perform routine and repetitive tasks.

The avoidant coworker is actually someone who is not so difficult to work with. The key here is understanding what motivates them. You need to understand and respect their need to go slowly, to be reassured, and to not be embarassed. The avoidant can be helped through psychotherapy, once they overcome their initial fear. This is true of the avoidant in many instances—once they get over their immediate fears of rejection and embarassment, they can function well.

Also, you shouldn't assume that, just because someone is evasive, they are necessarily avoidant. There is another type of toxic coworker who avoids people and who, at first glance, bears a strong resemblance to the avoidant. This coworker is the schizoid, the type we will be discussing in the next chapter.

CHAPTER 11

The Lonely World of the Schizoid

It was like falling into a hole. It was like falling into a hole, and it keeps getting bigger and bigger, and you can't get out, and all of the sudden it's inside, and you're the hole, and you're trapped, and it's all over.

—*Ordinary People*

Over a seventeen-year period of time Ted Kaczynski, the so-called Unabomber, killed three people and wounded twenty-three others. Although he probably had other psychological disorders, the Unabomber represents a good example of an individual with Schizoid Personality Disorder. And although the vast majority of schizoids are *not* violent, his case history reveals many similarities with other schizoid types.

The childhood of Ted Kaczynski was spent with parents who were socially withdrawn. When Ted Kaczynski was less than a year of age, he suffered from an allergy that required him to be hospitalized for a week. During that time, he had very limited contact with his family. After he returned home, his family reported that he became highly withdrawn. As a young child, Ted Kaczynski remained quiet and reclusive. It was reported that his mother spent many hours reading from *Scientific American* to him. As he became older, Kaczynski would never respond to greetings when he was spoken to by other children. In high school, he became interested in explosives, and though he liked blowing things up, he never really hurt anyone. He was not seen as angry but rather shy and immature. A very intelligent student, he finished high school in three years and went on to Harvard University, where he graduated at age twenty. One of his roommates commented, "I don't recall ten words spoken by him in the three years." In 1967 he received his Ph.D. in mathematics from the University of Michigan. He is remembered by his professors as being intelligent, serious, and quiet. Later that year, he accepted an assistant professorship of mathematics from the University of California at Berkeley but was seen as a poor teacher, in large part for his inability to relate to the students. One of his teaching evaluations included the comment, "He absolutely refuses to answer questions by completely ignoring the students" (Meyer 1999, 208). He resigned from his position in 1969 and, in 1971, moved to a cabin in Lincoln, Montana. The following description is particularly revealing: "the ten-by-twelve foot cabin had a table, two chairs, a narrow bunk, and a wood burning stove, but no electricity, indoor plumbing, or phone. He grew some of his own food; hunted rabbits, squirrels, and porcupines for food; and about once a week spent approximately five dollars for provisions at the Blackfoot Market in Lincoln. He traveled on a dilapidated, one-speed bicycle, pieced together from mismatched parts, even occasionally riding fifty miles into Helena, Montana. He didn't drink or smoke, and his only leisure activity was reading, as he frequented discount bookstores and the Lincoln library. He rarely spoke more than a few polite words to anyone. He was in part supported by periodic checks from his mother and received some money from his brother" (Meyer, 210).

Ted Kaczynski's desire to be alone, his lack of social skills, his repressed anger, and a family history that emphasizes intellectual rather than emotional development are hallmarks of Schizoid Personality Disorder. The word that best describes the schizoid is "aloof." Why is it that schizoids prefer a life of solitude and social emptiness?

For the most part, people do not function in a vacuum: we are social creatures and we have needs for contact with other individuals. However, we vary in the frequency and the intensity with which we wish to interact with other individuals. Some individuals desire to be with other people frequently and feel most comfortable when they're in the company of others. They are highly responsive to social stimuli and are usually referred to as *extroverts*. Other individuals have more of a desire to be by themselves and are more responsive to internal cues, such as their own thoughts and feelings. These people are often referred to as *introverts*. In the workplace, introverts are best suited for certain types of tasks that do not usually demand a great deal of interpersonal contact, such as working alone adding up figures in front of a computer. On the other hand, extroverts are usually best suited for positions that involve a great deal of human contact, public relations or sales, for example. A great deal of research has been done in this area and many human-resource offices are set up to test individuals as to which personality type they might be. One way to conceptualize the individual with

Schizoid Personality Disorder is that they have an extreme case of introversion; they have no real desire for the company of others. But it goes beyond that.

What Is Schizoid Personality Disorder?

When the disorder is not too severe, the individual appears to be simply shy or normally introverted. They seem relatively free from problems and usually do their jobs adequately, often working in a slow but methodical manner, usually in the background. They may seem a bit distant or cold, like wallflowers who do not become involved in the more social aspects of work. They are relatively colorless individuals who simply do their jobs. They do not seem to respond to emotional cues nor require the social rewards such as guidance, admiration, appreciation provided by others. They might even be seen as untroubled and easygoing.

But the individual with a more pronounced Schizoid Personality Disorder will show themselves to be unemotional and lifeless, highly undemonstrative and lacking in vitality. Possessing low energy levels, they may appear to be almost robotic at times, exhibiting clumsy and awkward movements. Schizoids lack spontaneity. They appear to be indifferent to human interaction and almost always will choose solitary activities over social activities. They will often appear to be in a "world of their own."

One of the key features about the individual with Schizoid Personality Disorder is that they are highly deficient in knowledge about human beings. Because they lack meaningful contact with other people, they never learn the intricacies and the "ins and outs" of human interactions. They do not understand things like the need for social contact or the need to be accepted. They do not seem to need the "emotional supplies" such as recognition, flattery, chatting, and sharing our lives with our coworkers, which so many of us seek out in our work environment. Often, schizoids may be insulted by someone and not even understand that they have been put down. Sarcasm and innuendo are all but lost on them. More sophisticated social skills, such as understanding hidden agendas, understanding nonverbal communication, and the need for "schmoozing" are lost on them. In fact, individuals with Schizoid Personality Disorder appear to be totally indifferent to the simplest of human interactions.

Schizoids live an almost emotionless life. They do not respond emotionally to situations that might cause others to respond in a joyous or angry manner. They appear flat, lifeless, and colorless. They appear to be unmoved by all the human emotions: in short, they are the embodiment of the word "apathetic."

Perhaps it's because of this lack of social interaction that they are severely deficient in areas about other human beings and social matters. Because they don't understand others, they have difficulties communicating. They simply don't understand the communication needs of their listener. Their communication style also appears to be loose, unfocused, and lacking in direction. They will not describe human experience accurately or in any detail but may very well be able to speak of the intricacies of the Internet or a computer-programming language in great detail. They will often speak in a monotone voice that rarely demonstrates any emotional expressiveness. They will almost always express themselves in a perfunctory and formal, albeit polite, manner.

The individual with Schizoid Personality Disorder has few introspective abilities and little awareness of self. They are not psychologically minded and rarely do they wish to engage in activities that involve any type of soul searching, introspection, or personal growth. Interestingly, this often results in a rather self-satisfied and complacent self-image. They are not prone to using sophisticated defense mechanisms to protect themselves against stress (which is often caused by individuals encroaching upon their lives); rather, they will almost always simply withdraw.

If these individuals do have friends at all, the relationship is fairly superficial, and most of the energy is put into the relationship by the other person. Often times, a family member will take an interest in the schizoid's life and try to nurture them and include them in their social activities. If the personality disorder is not too severe, schizoids will sometimes marry. Although they may remain married and avoid divorce (especially if the person that they marry also has a need for distance in a relationship), their spouses will often complain that they are distant, cold, and uninvolved in family life. They will almost always prefer a peripheral role, whether it's at work, in relationships, or other social settings.

Another important feature of Schizoid Personality Disorder is that they almost always prefer dealing with inanimate objects that require small amounts of energy, such as watching television, working on the computer, or reading. Often, they can become quite skilled in these or related activities such as electronic repair, computer programming, and so on.

Many schizoid individuals lack even a rudimentary understanding of basic human behavior. They simply do not understand the "rules" of social interactions, which can make working with them difficult. The following vignette serves as a good illustration.

One schizoid hospital administrator on the first day of his job approached his African American secretary and tried to tell her a joke, feeling that this was something he had seen other administrators do in the past. Unfortunately, the joke included a crude racial slur which only made his secretary feel highly uncomfortable, coughing and turning away from him. The man's lack of understanding of the nonverbal emotional cues expressed by his coworker, his mechanical and clueless imitation of social interaction, and the odd nature of this behavior are the calling cards for the individual with Schizoid Personality Disorder.

It is important to understand that schizoids do realize that they have to function appropriately in the organizational environment in order to keep their jobs and to maintain some semblance of normality. Although they may have a personality disorder, they are not stupid. They are often aware that they need to behave like others around them and not appear to be too strange. They are cognizant of the fact that other individuals around them tell jokes, smile, get upset, and relate to others in a manner that is different from the schizoid's and that includes various types of social etiquette and emotions. They will, therefore, imitate these behaviors in a rather mechanical, thoughtless, and lifeless way; but there is no substance behind these behaviors; they are all facade. After repeated contacts with such an individual, one begins to get the feeling that these copied behaviors are lacking in depth. Often they are reminiscent of behaviors one would see in a movie or in a play. An individual with Schizoid Personality Disorder may indeed model behaviors they've seen in a play or on TV, because they don't know any other way to behave in a normal social manner.

The Schizoid Personality Disorder, according to DSM-IV, is:

A pervasive pattern of detachment from social relationships and a restricted range of expression of emotions in interpersonal settings, beginning by early adulthood and present in a variety of contexts, as indicated by four (or more) of the following:

1. neither desires nor enjoys close relationships, including being part of the family.

2. almost always chooses solitary activities.

3. has little, if any, interest in having sexual experiences with another person.

4. takes pleasure in few, if any, activities.

5. lacks close friends or confidants other than first-degree relatives.

6. appears indifferent to the praise and criticism of others.

7. shows emotional coldness, detachment, or flattened affectivity.*

Usually perceived as loners, they have few, if any, friends and usually relate to only one or two family members. Their communication patterns with others are characterized by a lack of focus and purpose and may seem disjointed and not to the point.

It's important to mention the fact that Schizoid Personality Disorder sometimes resembles the Avoidant Personality Disorder, which is covered in chapter 10. The reader who believes they might be working with a schizoid individual would do well to read that chapter as the interventions are quite different. While neither the schizoid nor the avoidant personality has close friends, the avoidant actually desires close friendships but is afraid of rejection. This is quite different from the schizoid, who has no real desire for close relationships at all. Another distinguishing factor is the "flatness" of emotionality exhibited by the schizoid, as well as the odd nature of their behavior. Individuals with Avoidant Personality Disorder are more fearful and anxious than the schizoid, who usually does not appear to be anxious. Sometimes even the best clinically trained psychologists have difficulties distinguishing between the two. This is further complicated by the fact that many individuals with Schizoid Personality Disorder are good at "faking it." Often, as previously mentioned, their superior intellect enables them to recognize the fact that they have to relate to others in a certain way.

Another important point is that sometimes individuals from other cultures who do not understand our culture or brand of "in your face" type humor will often appear to be schizoid. This is usually due to their discomfort and lack of knowledge about the culture rather than a personality disorder. Naturally, it would be astute of their coworker to treat them with sensitivity about this difference.

It's easy to see how an individual who doesn't understand the basic needs of others is insensitive to nonverbal cues, does not understand social etiquette, and has no need for contact with other people, can wreak havoc in a work environment, especially if their job requires social contact. If, however, the individual with Schizoid Personality Disorder is allowed to work in a nonsocial environment,

---

* Reprinted with permission from the *Diagnostic and Statistical Manual of Mental Disorders*, Fourth Edition. Copyright 1994 American Psychiatric Association.

emotional evenness often serves them well in the decision-making process.

Here is a pretty good way to recognize whether you're working with an individual with Schizoid Personality Disorder. One of the more striking things that we've noticed when talking with schizoid individuals is that when they are asked to describe a person they have frequent contact with, they seem unable to do so. If you asked an average individual, especially one who is relatively socially oriented, you can almost picture that person in your mind as they describe them. The schizoid individual will describe the people in their lives in only a few vague adjectives, making it very difficult for you to picture the person in your mind. For example, when a factory worker was asked to describe his wife of fifteen years, he could only say of her, "She's nice, but she can be annoying sometimes." This description doesn't give you much of a feel for what his wife is like, does it? This inability is often one of the first signs of Schizoid Personality Disorder that we encounter when we are conducting psychotherapy with a schizoid individual. We consider this to be one of the more reliable pieces of evidence that a person indeed has Schizoid Personality Disorder.

The Schizoid Administrator

In the workplace, these individuals often hold highly technical positions. The field of engineering, for example, appears to attract a great many people with Schizoid Personality Disorder. Most often, they are highly successful and, as a result of their success, may be promoted to managerial positions. It is here that the problems begin. Individuals who are adept at the technical aspects of their job often will be promoted to managerial levels as a result of their outstanding technical abilities. But the schizoid qualities that attracted the individual to the technical position in the first place will be the very qualities that will inhibit them in being an effective manager. Often, these people are highly frustrated by their promotions and find their managerial positions highly stressful and unrewarding. They tend to manage others like they would like to be managed, that is, with very little management at all. Their subordinates will often complain about the lack of direction that they receive. Often these administrators will not build networks of peers, nor do they interface well with other departments. Scornful of "office politics," they often isolate themselves from others. If they are forced to interact with others, it will be on a strictly business type of basis. Quite often, the individual with Schizoid Personality Disorder values thinking and logic above human emotion. These individuals often appear as Mr. Spock on the old *Star Trek* episodes—devaluing all emotion and worshiping logic and thinking. As a result of this analytical thinking, they will often be unable to make effective decisions because of "paralysis by analysis." Moreover, they will often make arbitrary decisions regarding policy without taking into account how it affects the feelings of their subordinates. One college administrator, for example, could not understand why having a particular professor teach on weekends would be upsetting to him. After all, he would have a day off during the week. This administrator could not understand that most people use their weekends to interact with family and friends.

There are a few telltale signs that the administrator you're working under has Schizoid Personality Disorder. The first is their hands-off style of management. You will be given no discernible direction. When the schizoid administrator finally is forced to lead and issues some type of directive, they will often be vague or will delegate to another person. Individuals with Schizoid Personality Disorder will often isolate themselves in their offices, communicating to others infrequently or through some type of distancing mechanism, such as e-mail, memos, or telephone. They will almost never attend social functions and, if they do, will be one of the last to arrive and one of the first to leave. When there is contact, it's often forced and stiff, and there is a distinct lack of emotional responsiveness.

Another clue that you are working with a schizoid administrator is that they will be utterly insensitive to your emotional and interpersonal needs. They can often be cold, and you will feel a definite barrier between you and them. If you do find yourself having some type of contact with them, you'll feel a definitive apathy about your personal life. But individuals with Schizoid Personality Disorder are sometimes bright enough to learn how to fake it. They will say all the right cliches and homilies. "How are the wife and kids?" or "Nice weather today," for example. They will put on an appearance of being happy and social, but it's all on the surface and there will be no real depth to it. Please do not confuse this lack of concern with that shown by the narcissistic administrator who might be insensitive but is a lot more flamboyant and full of life. The schizoid is lifeless, perfunctory, and robotic.

Finally, you may want to be prepared for some unpleasant behavior. The administrator with Schizoid Personality Disorder can often erupt into unexpected anger and even cruelty. Many researchers believe that the schizoid individual harbors a great deal of anger inside. However, their eruptions are seldom direct. They prefer indirect means of aggression, such as extending working hours, not attending to things that their employees might need, or instituting measures that are insensitive to their employees' social and emotional needs.

Working with the Schizoid Adminstrator

If you have been struggling under an adminstrator with Schizoid Personality Disorder, you're probably all too aware of the problems inherent in your situation. Perhaps it feels a little bit like the example below.

Here's the situation: You've just had a two-hour meeting on instituting the new computer-billing program with the vice president in charge of computer operations. After 120 minutes of tedious, monotonal, and jargon-laden droning, everyone is still confused about what they are to do. Asking questions didn't produce any more clarification than the presentation did in the first place. People are muttering unhappily as they leave the meeting, "Now what do we do?" No one has even an inkling of what they should do next. Collectively, the staff begins to bemoan what appears to be their inevitable fate: to be kept in the dark forever. Someone suggests that two or three of you approach the president to tell her that this vice president, once again, has had difficulties communicating effectively. Off you go. After listening intently, she suggests what she believes to be a viable solution, which is for you to ask the vice president questions at the end of the meeting for clarification. You tell her you've been there, done that. She then suggests that each of you approach him individually during the regular work day to ask for clarification about areas that you don't understand. But you've been there and done that, too. Becoming somewhat frustrated, she then suggests that you write a memo asking in detail for clarification of exactly what you don't understand. You answer that you would not even know where to begin—you don't understand *anything*. She then goes on to say how the vice president is really trying, that she has spoken to him about this problem, and that you need to just give him time. After all, he's such a nice man and he's making an effort. Exchanging pleasantries, you depart. You look at your coworkers with the mutual understanding that you're all doomed.

Confronting the administrator with Schizoid Personality Disorder and telling them that they have some type of problem with withdrawal does not seem to have much of a chance to bear fruit. Bear in mind the fact that individuals with personality disorders are usually woefully unaware that they have a problem to begin with and will resent your saying anything that suggests they do. Therefore, going to a schizoid administrator and saying, "You know, boss, you have a tendency to withdraw from problems and not communicate effectively," will definitely be poorly received. And one certainly cannot overlook the fact that one of the major problems in confronting a schizoid administrator is the very fact that they *are* administrators and have power over your life in the organization: We don't believe that the schizoid is above retaliation. In fact, there is a great deal of evidence that many schizoids can have explosive tempers when pushed. And, even though they might have a personality disorder, individuals with Schizoid Personality Disorders who are in administrative positions usually know that they are *supposed* to be managing people and will try to give that impression. But because they lack the social skills to effectively mediate and remedy problems, they usually resort to punitive types of actions when they are forced to solve personnel problems. And, because they lack knowledge about the feelings of other individuals, they will most likely be surprised when these punitive remedies only anger their subordinates and cause deterioration in morale and organizational functioning.

But, as sticky as this problem seems, there are some solutions. As is true in dealing with all of the personality disorders, one must realize that the administrator above one is severely lacking in certain skills and, most likely, will never change. They are not ignoring you because of anything you are doing. It's not your fault. That realization alone usually will bring some comfort to the subordinates of such an administrator. Any effective measures in dealing with such a person require that you consider this individual's severe social limitations. Keeping this in mind, we suggest the following solutions.

If there is an outstanding problem that your boss refused to deal with, it may be useful to go to your boss directly and suggest a solution. A solution that requires a minimal amount of intervention by the administrator but which can achieve maximum future results should be well received. Something like, "You know, a lot of the workers are confused about how to use the new computer software. I think that I can get the software company to send one of their reps down here to work with us for a while, until were used to the new products." And, here is the key part; "It would avoid a lot of problems down the road. I don't think we want to get entangled with grievances and customer complaints, do you?"

This solution is good because it requires no future action on the part of the administrator and it is likely to protect them from future involvement with complaining and angry people. The schizoid's inherent lethargy, as well as their desire to remain unencumbered, makes this a useful and attractive solution.

It is also helpful, when approaching an administrator with Schizoid Personality Disorder, to speak their language. This language is highly logical, technical, and stripped of emotion. Don't cloud the issue by referring to people's feelings. For example, a group of faculty members were faced with a principal who wished to close down the faculty lounge and use it for storage. They changed his mind by keeping their anger to themselves and pointing out instead that it wasn't good for the students to see the faculty eating in their offices and making messes. Emphasizing the logical and the practical should be coupled with a communication style that keeps it "short and sweet." Long-winded explanations attempting to appeal to the administrator's sense of compassion will most likely only serve to freeze the administrator into inaction.

Finally, a novel idea that should be considered is the implementation of a support group (whether formal or informal, on premises or off, during or after working hours) in which subordinates of the schizoid administrator can meet to air their grievances and devise solutions to problems. Indeed, if the administrator is in too powerful a position and is running the organization into the ground, such a support group might be essential to keep the organization viable and protect your jobs. And while, in most cases, it would be wise to keep such a group discreet, the schizoid administrator might even welcome such meetings, as they serve their wishes to remain as un-involved as possible.

The Schizoid Coworker

It's really not that difficult to know when you're coworker has Schizoid Personality Disorder. The most striking feature of this relationship is that you simply do not feel a connection with the person. Schizoid individuals are notorious for being inconspicuous. Probably the most common reaction you'll have to them is wanting to ignore them. Moreover, you'll most likely be incredibly bored with any social interaction you may have with them. If you do interact with them, do not expected the schizoid to be emotionally responsive. It will feel like you are walking into a house full of empty rooms.

Sometimes the person with Schizoid Personality Disorder might appear to be stuck-up and cold. They usually will not speak unless they are spoken to. They might enjoy computers, model building, watching sports on TV, or rebuilding automobile engines, for example. Don't expect them to speak about anything regarding people or relationships at length. The key thing to remember is that this distance is not your fault—the individual with Schizoid

Personality Disorder is not rejecting you. They simply have little or no need for any type of human contact. It's not because of anything you did. In fact, your schizoid coworker might consider you the most important person in their lives. They are often satisfied, indeed almost overstimulated, to spend very short periods of time with another person. This is all they require. Don't be surprised if they talk about the same topic over and over again. This is safe territory for the schizoid and you are doing them a wonderful service just listening. Beware, however, of intrusions into the schizoid's space. A simple invitation to a party that you are having might be way too intrusive and cause the schizoid a great deal of discomfort. She might agonize for weeks and weeks, trying to figure out a way to say no. A touch on their hand or on their back can be a frightening experience for them. Indeed, even a handshake can be a stressful event for them.

Schizoid coworkers will not vibrate with your joys and sorrows. Although they might politely acknowledge them, most of the time this will be simple lip service. At times, they will be totally unaware as to what you might be feeling. For example, one schizoid administrator began to discuss a technical issue when their coworker broke in, "My wife just told me she was leaving. I think my marriage is about to end." The schizoid person nodded in acknowledgment, and then continued the technical conversation! It is amazing and shocking how pronounced their lack of emotional responsiveness can be.

Working with the Schizoid Coworker

Any effective solution for dealing with a schizoid coworker will require that you take into account this individual's special need to be alone. Keep in mind that they actually enjoy the silence between you—it does not make them feel uncomfortable. Do not be insulted if they prefer working by themselves or away from you. It will never be necessary to fill up the time with idle chatter. Do not feel sorry for them because they appear to you to be lonely; they prefer it that way. In fact, they might even feel sorry for you, because you need to interact with others! Respect their need for space and distance; never be intrusive or try to force conversation or social interaction upon them. Do not feel obligated to include them in office parties—they will most likely be relieved that you never asked them to go. Be comfortable with the silence between you.

Believe it or not, the schizoid might even consider you a friend, even if they never speak much to you or interact with you outside of work. Don't underestimate the importance of your seemingly limited role in their solitary lives; you might just be all the social contact that they require. Even the scant contact you have with them might be important enough to save them from a life of total emptiness, even if they do seem somewhat uncomfortable during conversations with you.

The key here is to adjust your expectations. Don't expect the schizoid to be overjoyed that you're speaking with them. Begin with topics that you know that they are interested in. For example, you might ask them about the computer program they are working with or what type of car they like to drive. Ask them questions about the work they're doing, questions to which you're sure they have an answer. Stick with "thing" conversations rather than talking about people and relationships.

Be sure to adjust the amount of time you spend with them according to how they are feeling. On some days a simple hello might be all that they can handle. On other days, when they are feeling bolder, they might wish to speak with you for five or ten minutes, perhaps even longer. Go with the flow here. The key is to watch them closely and break off the conversation when your coworker appears to be becoming too uncomfortable.

Finally, don't overlook today's technology. Things such as e-mail, electronic games, and the Internet are excellent ways of communicating with the schizoid as the technology gives them much needed distance. One employee found that she could communicate more effectively with her schizoid coworker by interoffice mail, in spite of the fact that they worked just six feet away from one another. They exchanged jokes and news articles in this manner. This employee was able to discover a greater depth in her coworker and began to see him as a whole person. And yet another example involved two coworkers who rarely spoke to each other during the workday, but who played computer games over the modem with each other. In the future, our ever-expanding technology will surely provide even more areas for the schizoid to interact at a distance.

The Schizoid Subordinate

Individuals with Schizoid Personality Disorders are well-known for their ability to work with things rather than people. They can be highly technical and well versed in mathematics, engineering, and computers. They are often highly intelligent. The technical languages are the languages that they are most comfortable with. In fact, if the schizoid is not too lethargic, they can be quite skilled in working with their hands in a number of ways. Model building, mechanics, arts and crafts, home repair; in short, anything that does not require interpersonal contact, yet requires the mastering of some skill, is attractive to the schizoid. Computers, in particular, offer the schizoid a unique opportunity to interact in a nonpersonal and nonthreatening way through either e-mail or chatrooms. Moreover, computers give the schizoid a chance to be productive while escaping human contact.

It is an interesting fact that the individual with Schizoid Personality Disorder, despite having a psychological disorder, can be quite self-sufficient. They are able to work with minimal amounts of supervision. This makes them excellent candidates for working alone or at home. You need not feel guilty about having them work by themselves—they prefer this. And they are usually conscientious and will get the job done with minimal amounts of supervision. They do not require a great deal of praise or recognition. The danger here is of the schizoid making errors because they are not getting feedback from the corporate body. Sometimes the schizoid employee can all but vanish; they are very good at making themselves inconspicuous. There is a tendency on the part of the organization to ignore them. This, of course, should be avoided.

Individuals with Schizoid Personality Disorder might not mind routine or even tedious jobs if these activities will keep them away from others. Keep in mind that they might not mind the safe and predictable rather than the new and adventurous. Schizoids are known for not being very ambitious. They might not be concerned with advancements in the company, especially if that means a more complicated lifestyle with greater interaction with others.

Probably the most prominent sign that an individual working for you has Schizoid Personality Disorder is the fact that you're almost totally unaware of his presence at work. As mentioned throughout this chapter, these people are unobtrusive, to say the least. Perhaps other individuals have complained about him, stating that he does not communicate key information effectively, or perhaps that she is a little "weird." Sometimes the schizoid may be the butt of jokes circulating around the office. The following is an example of how this might work.

Martin had been employed as a social worker in the food-stamp branch of the state welfare office for six years. At the age of twenty-eight, he was still single and almost never dated. When he did, it was almost always the woman who asked him out, as he was a fairly handsome man and dressed well. As a result of his dependability and tendency not to "make waves," he was promoted to a supervisory position after several years. The social workers around him, mostly women, knew about his awkwardness with the opposite sex. After each and every weekend, one or two of his subordinates would ask them how his weekend was. Most of the time it was uneventful. However, on several occasions, he replied that it went well, and that he had taken a young lady out to dinner or a movie. The women would tease him, asking if he'd kissed his date or if he "got any." Martin did not understand that the women were asking him these questions to make fun of him and always answered in his monotone voice, "No, not this time." On one date, a woman aggressively manipulated him into his bed by deliberately getting her clothing wet, taking it off, and getting into his bed, claiming she was cold. She told him she would have to stay the night until her clothing dried. She told him to come to bed with her, and he put on his pajamas. Obviously frustrated, the woman asked him for his pajamas, and he took off the top and gave it to her, keeping the pajamas bottoms on. After several more attempts, the woman turned over and went to sleep. When he told his coworkers, they were hysterical at his naivete, and at his willingness to broadcast it. They spread the story throughout the agency. When people confronted him about it to tease him even more, he would, once again, honestly explain what had happened, totally unaware that these individuals were poking fun at him. As a result, his subordinates lost respect for him and he was ineffectual at his job. Martin's story is a good example of a schizoid's cluelessness causing disruption in the workplace.

Problems can also arise when the schizoid subordinate, due to their lack of ambition and energy, doesn't do what they are supposed to do. One parts manager, for example, would not spend enough time looking up in his catalogs whether a particular part was available. He enjoyed cataloging and just "being around" the parts. He just didn't like helping folks. This would obviously frustrate the mechanics who needed those parts.

Yet another problem that can arise is when the schizoid subordinate individual does not communicate effectively. Naturally, efficient and timely communication is essential to the smooth workings of any organization. The situation can worsen when management confronts this individual, demanding (often aggressively) that they sharpen their communication skills. This can aggravate the situation, because it makes the schizoid individual withdraw even further into their shell. It's important to understand that withdrawal is the first and foremost defense mechanism the schizoid individual utilizes. And, withdrawal can take many forms, such as an increase in absenteeism, increased daydreaming and, worse yet, increased silence.

Working with the Schizoid Subordinate

The key to making a successful intervention with communication problems is to somehow let the schizoid know, without scaring her, that she needs to communicate more effectively. The first thing to do would be to allow yourself plenty of time to talk with the individual. If you feel time pressures or feel agitated with the schizoid's seemingly withholding posture, you will only tend to make matters worse. In fact, you may wish to schedule several such sessions, just in case the first one doesn't work.

Avoid asking this subordinate questions that require only a yes or no answer, for they will be only too happy to oblige. You will then find yourself doing most of the thinking and most of the communicating, a result counter to your goal. Asking an open-ended question such as, "Could you please describe what you plan to do about this?" rather than, "Are you going to fix this?" holds a much greater chance of being successful. Be sure to allow plenty of time for the individual to answer. There might have to be a prolonged and uncomfortable period of silence, but make it clear to them that you expect a detailed answer by not interrupting and not asking a different question until what you have asked has been thoroughly answered. If you still do not get the information you require, ask for specifics by using who, what, where, when, and how types of questions.

Be sure that your nonverbal communication conveys the idea that you *expect* a detailed answer. You can borrow here from the training in nonverbal communication that psychologists receive. We are taught a skill called "active listening," whereby we communicate through verbal and nonverbal behaviors that we are listening and expect more information. To do this, look squarely at the individual with whom you are speaking and nod your head frequently, saying things like, "Umm-hmm" and, "Yes, go on," or simply, "Tell me more." Saying the word "Yes" with a slight upward inflection in your voice as if you were asking a question, can be highly effective. Remind the person of the topic you're discussing if they get too far off the beaten path.

"I don't know" or shoulder shrugs should not be allowed to end the conversation. One clever response to this type of answer is to say, "I understand that you don't know, but if you *did* know, what do you think your answer would be?" You may not think that this seemingly obvious deception would work, but it is surprisingly effective. If all else fails, suggest an answer. Say something like, "Well, I've seen other problems like this. One way that we dealt with this problem in the past was to ... Why don't you do that?"

You'll want to treat your attempts like experiments. Try something and then observe the results. If the individual with Schizoid Personality Disorder changes their behavior, you were on the right track.

Finally, take advantage of the fact that the schizoid individual prefers to work alone. Assign them tasks where they have the opportunity to work alone, if at all possible. This person will work very well alone in his or her own cubicle on a computer all day. If it's not absolutely necessary, don't force them to go to meetings or social gatherings. Give them jobs where contact with customers is limited. (The exception to this might be if the person has highly technical skills that she is able to communicate effectively, and if this person can be trusted in a position such as technical support.) Don't be afraid to give them routine or repetitive tasks, such as posting ledger entries.

You might find that the schizoid subordinate works well with their hands and might do very well repairing equipment or working in a machine shop. Bear in mind that the schizoid individual prefers to work with things rather than with people. One schizoid individual, even though he had an advanced degree, ended up working in a business machine repair shop. He lived in a one-room apartment above the repair shop, and he often brought the machines up to his room to work on in the evenings. He enjoyed doing this and was proud of his skill. His technical expertise, coupled with his willingness to put in extra (and unpaid) hours, made him a valuable employee.

In Conclusion

In today's society, more and more organizations are relying upon the aid of psychotherapists to help with personnel problems. Individuals with drug addictions, alcohol problems, stress or anxiety problems, and even interpersonal issues can be helped and learn to function more effectively in an organizational setting. Unfortunately, the individual with Schizoid Personality Disorder does not usually respond well to psychotherapy. It does not take an astute individual to recognize the fact that, at the heart and soul of psychotherapy, lies a close, interpersonal relationship between the client and the therapist. This is the very thing that the schizoid individual cannot maintain. Consequently, most individuals with Schizoid Personality Disorder do not seek or stay in psychotherapy. If they do, it is because of another overlying psychological disorder, such as anxiety or depression, or referral by a family member. Usually, when they realize that there is no quick answer to their problem and that they have to engage in an interpersonal relationship in order to be helped, they will quit. There are, however, some instances in which individuals with Schizoid Personality Disorder do benefit from psychotherapy. The safe, non judgmental, warm, and supportive environment of therapy might just be enough for the schizoid to begin to open themselves up to another individual, especially if their disorder is not too severe. Despite its limitations with this population, psychotherapy, as an option, should not be overlooked.

Like its distant cousin schizophrenia, Schizoid Personality Disorder remains a mystery to researchers. In spite of advances in psychopharmacology and psychotherapeutic techniques, Schizoid Personality Disorder remains stubbornly resistant to treatment. Nevertheless, by taking into consideration and addressing the schizoid's desire to be alone and unfettered, one can affect necessary strategies when dealing with such an individual.

CHAPTER 12

The Paranoid Personality: The Loneliness of Suspicion

What loneliness is more lonely than distrust.

—George Eliot

In 1951, Herman Wouk published *The Caine Mutiny*, which is about a Navy ship captain, Commander Queeg, who was found to be psychologically unfit to effectively command his ship, the U.S.S. *Caine*. The executive officer who took command from Queeg was subsequently put on trial for mutiny. This book was later made into a movie starring Humphrey Bogart, who played Commander Queeg. In the famous, unforgettable court scene, Commander Queeg literally wins the case for the attorney defending the executive officer when he begins to decompensate on the witness stand, ranting and raving about all the injustices that the officers and crew had cooked up against him. In the court scene, Dr. Forrest Lundeen, a Navy psychiatrist, is testifying on behalf of Commander Queeg regarding his mental status. He is being cross-examined by Lieutenant Greenwald, the Navy attorney who is defending the executive officer. Dr. Lundeen testifies that Commander Queeg, like all adults, had problems to which "he adjusted . . . inferiority problems brought on by an unfavorable childhood." Lt. Greenwald asks if Commander Queeg would be likely to admit mistakes. Is he a perfectionist? Was he likely to hound subordinates about small details? Does he tend to blame others for his own mistakes? He then asks, "Doctor, isn't distorting reality a symptom of mental illness?" To which Dr. Lundeen replies, "Certainly not, in itself. It's all a question of degree." Lt. Greenwald then asks, "Would such a personality be inclined to feel that people were against him, hostile to him? Would he be suspicious of subordinates and inclined to question their loyalty and competence?" To which Dr. Lundeen replies, "It's all part of it. Such a man, by nature, is constantly on the alert to defend his self-esteem." Greenwald then asks, "If criticized from above, would he be inclined to think he was being unjustly persecuted?" Lundeen replies, "Well, as I say, it's all one pattern, all stemming from one basic premise, that he must try to be perfect." Finally, in the most poignant part of the cross-examination, Lt. Greenwald asks, "Doctor, you've testified that the following symptoms exist in the commander's behavior: rigidity of personality, feelings of persecution, withdrawal from reality, perfectionist anxiety, an unreal basic premise, and an obsessive sense of self-righteousness . . . Is there an inclusive psychiatric term, one label, for this syndrome?" To which, Dr. Lundeen reluctantly replies, "It's a paranoid personality, of course. But that is not a disabling affliction."

Doctor Lundeen quite aptly describes many of the symptoms of Paranoid Personality Disorder. The diagnosis is well-confirmed when Commander Queeg takes the stand and talks of the disloyalty of the officers and crew, blames them for blunders that were clearly his own doing, and rants about how they were out to sabotage his command. His restless manipulation of two silver ball bearings confirms the diagnosis for all in the court room. As discussed in chapter 2, individuals with personality disorders usually do manifest "rigidity of personality," a lack of insight into their own character and how their behavior affects others. With the paranoid personality, one would also see a hypervigilance to any possible slight or perceived disloyalty and a suspiciousness about the motives of others. Their striving toward perfection are thought to rise from feelings of insecurity and may be based upon past humiliations. Such was the case with Commander Queeg, who is describe as having insecurities regarding his "short stature," the "low standing" in his class at the Naval Academy, and the hazing he was subjected to there. In response to such insecurities and humiliations, those with Paranoid Personality Disorder (PPD) often construct a pervasive view that the world is a hostile place to live in, that it's a "dog-eat-dog world" and, therefore, one needs to be on guard or vigilant for any signs of threat, hostility, or humiliation. What is central to the PPD, however, is that these individuals often manifest angry or aggressive feelings themselves and will therefore "project" these feelings onto others, i.e., "I am hostile toward him," becomes "He is hostile towards me and will humiliate me, given the chance." Through hypervigilance, suspiciousness, and by maintaining strict interpersonal distance the individual with PPD never gives *anyone* the chance to humiliate or derogate them.

The Caine Mutiny also provides an excellent illustration of a situation in which an individual in an administrative position, who possesses tremendous authoritative powers, places those under them in jeopardy because of their stubbornness, their need to be in control, and their constant need to be right (perfectionism). It's not surprising, therefore, that these individuals pose especially acute difficulties in the workplace. Whether it's on the bridge of a naval vessel, in the boardroom of a major corporation, or in a work crew of a utility company, individuals with PPD do not "work and play" well with others.

What Is Paranoid Personality Disorder?

Before proceeding further, we need to clear up any possible confusion about the term "Paranoid Personality Disorder." In the DSM-IV the term "paranoid" appears in two different diagnoses, "Schizophrenia, Paranoid type" and "Paranoid Personality Disorder." The symptoms of Schizophrenia, Paranoid type have some overlap with PPD, but these disorders are qualitatively very different. For example, in order to be diagnosed with Schizophrenia, Paranoid type, one would have to exhibit hallucinations and/or delusions (e.g., "a false personal belief based on incorrect inference about external reality and firmly sustained in spite of what almost everyone else believes and in spite of what constitutes incontrovertible and obvious proof or evidence to the contrary. The belief is not one ordinarily accepted by other members of the person's culture or subculture (394). The Paranoid Schizophrenic would also exhibit marked disturbance in functioning, e.g., in work, social relations, and self-care. The essential feature of Schizophrenia, Paranoid type is a preoccupation with one or more systematized delusions or with frequent auditory hallucinations related to a single theme. Usually, these individuals exhibit unfocused anxiety, anger, argumentativeness, and violence. So, with the Paranoid Schizophrenic, we see a person who is out of touch with reality and who has difficulty operating in reality.

Those with PPD, on the other hand, usually operate within the boundaries of reality, except for those areas where they misinterpret the actions or intentions of others. While this "misinterpretation" does have a delusional quality, it's not to the extent of the Paranoid Schizophrenic, whose delusions of persecution or grandiosity will take on bizarre qualities. For instance, it would probably be the Paranoid Schizophrenic who is convinced that he is Jesus Christ and that, because of this special stature, others are out to cause him harm or crucify him. The DSM-IV symptoms of PPD include:

A pervasive distrust and suspiciousness of others, such that their motives are interpreted as malevolent, beginning by early adulthood and present in a variety of contexts, as indicated by at least four of the following:

1. suspects, without sufficient basis that others are exploiting harming or deceiving him or her.

2. is preoccupied with unjustified doubts about the loyalty or trustworthiness of friends or associates.

3. is reluctant to confide in others because of unwarranted fear that the information will be used maliciously against him or her.

4. reads hidden meaning or threatening meanings into benign remarks or events e.g., suspects that a neighbor put out trash early to annoy him.

5. persistently bears grudges, i.e., is unforgiving of insults, injuries or slights.

6. perceives attacks on his or her character or reputation that are not apparent to others and is quick to react angrily or to counterattack.

7. has recurrent suspicions, without justification, regarding fidelity of spouse or sexual partner.[*]

Although the symptoms noted above suggest that PPD is a rather unitary, well-defined disorder, experts in the area of personality disorders recently have noted some subtypes of PPD that warrant mentioning. In 1996, Millon and Davis revised an earlier conceptualization of PPD subtypes: 1) the *fanatic paranoid* acts in a "haughty and pretentious manner, are naively self-confident, ungenerous, exploitive, expansive, and presumptuous ..."(706). Fanatic paranoids expect to be viewed as the center of attention and expect to be admired and valued, however, when faced with humiliation or the reality of being insignificant, they will dismiss these events and often go to great lengths to reestablish their image; 2) the *malignant paranoid* is considered to be a variation of the *sadistic personality*. These individuals are characterized by their "power orientation," the

---

[*]   Reprinted with permission from the *Diagnostic and Statistical Manual of Mental Disorders*, Fourth Edition. Copyright 1994 American Psychiatric Association.

need to dominate or control others. Most often, these individuals were subjected to constant parental antagonisms and harassment. There is a sense of justification in their antisocial behaviors, as their approach to the world is one of "do unto others before they have a chance to do unto you"; 3) the *obdurate paranoid* is the anxious type, usually growing up in an environment of strict parental overcontrol and punishment. They grow up believing that strict adherence to rules and keeping within approved boundaries will free them from the guilt they felt growing up. However, the harder they try, the more anxious they feel. These individuals essentially sacrifice their own identity in the belief that others will recognize their efforts, and when this result fails to happen, they feel angry and mistreated; 4) the *querulous paranoid* is characterized by a negativistic personality, irritability, and affective instability. The family milieu that querulous paranoids grow up in is often marked by this same erratic emotionality, with parents being affectionate one minute and irrationally hostile the next. The person growing up in this environment learns to give up any hopes of being nurtured or approved and adopts a worldview that others are given preferential or undeserved treatment, which they will never receive. This paranoid subtype is, therefore, often found to be obstructionistic, fault-finding, aggressively negativistic, sullen, and resentful; 5) the *insular paranoid* is the most likely to decompensate into a psychotic episode, especially if subject to public humiliation. They often harbor deep resentments from past hurts that seethe near the surface. This anger then creates anxiety, because it jeopardizes the insular paranoid's sense of security. As long as their anger remains suppressed, they are sometimes able to function on a satisfactory basis; but once this anger breaks through to the surface, they decompensate rather quickly. One client comes to mind, a man who was working as an electronic technician for a local cable TV station. At first, he was able to make a good impression based upon his past experience in the field. However, once the director began to criticize him, he began to fly into rages, becoming suspicious of the director's motives, and feeling the director was out to get him fired. These delusional thoughts gave rise to even more oppositional, obstructionistic behavior, which then did result in his being let go from the job.

The Paranoid Administrator

The position of the paranoid administrator (CEO, middle manager, or office manager) will have a large bearing on how their personality style will affect their work and relationships with subordinates. The

CEO will be constantly vigilant for any signs of disloyalty within the company and will also be very wary of competitors.They'll watch for any possible leaks of information to the outside and will also keep a sharp eye on the political climate within the board of directors. They will think nothing of monitoring the activities of their staff. This was well portrayed in the movie, *The Firm*, where the attorneys were expected not only to do quality work but also expected to act in certain ways, attend certain functions, and belong to certain clubs. The "corporate culture" often dictates what is appropriate and what is not with regards to both workplace and leisure-time decorum. A paranoid administrator will see to it that their subordinates are towing the line in this regard and will interpret any transgressions as signs of disloyalty and betrayal.

Those in middle management may demonstrate similar behaviors, but sometimes to a lesser degree. They may mistake ambition for disloyalty or interpret the highly motivated worker as someone who is out to take their job. For that reason, a paranoid manager may make it difficult for an ambitious worker to move ahead within the organization (Oldham & Morris 1995). If this adminstrator is convinced and reassured that the employee is loyal and can be trusted, the paranoid manager may be quite generous with praise and rewards. The key is that the paranoid manager must feel that they are in complete command and will react quite harshly or strongly when they feel they are not in control of the situation.

All the paranoid administrators that we have known usually want to be kept abreast of what is going on in each of their departments. So, those working for someone like this are wise to prepare both verbal and written documentation of the goings-on within their department or work group. The expression "It is better to ask forgiveness than to ask permission" does not apply here. You are certainly always better to check things out with this type of administrator and to keep them posted on new developments and any rumors that may be circulating within the organization. It is better to err on the side of overcommunicating than undercommunicating, as anything not openly conveyed to this type of manager or CEO can and will be interpreted as a sign of disloyalty or a signal that something is awry. Even though you may request to be given difficult assignments as a means of proving your motivation and ambition, don't expect to be given these assignments. Paranoid administrators often operate by the old adage, "If you want something done right, do it yourself," which is based on the worldview, "I can't really trust anyone to do this task as well as I can."

Working with the Paranoid Administrator

When working for an individual like this, you should not expect much praise or much in the way of support. For example, if you were to do an outstanding job on a project, you would do best to give praise to this administrator for their support, encouragement, and creative input instead of waiting for positive feedback from them. Don't take too much credit, or you will find yourself being given a cardboard box and escorted by a security guard to clear out your office. Paranoid administrators are notorious for their lack of compassion in situations where they feel they have been overlooked or betrayed. Naturally, the security guard must be there to make certain you don't steal any important corporate secrets or paper clips!

As another example, say you call in to take a few days off, because your favorite aunt has passed away and you must fly to Toledo to attend her funeral. Most administrators will express their sympathies and offer condolences. The paranoid administrator will be short on sympathy and long on suspicion. They would probably like to see a copy of the death certificate and will not be reassured by a picture of you beside the casket. Although they may not ask for this kind of validation, you may want to provide some verification anyway. In the paranoid administrator's mind, you are probably going off to be interviewed by their competitor or are lying on a beach in Bermuda, so again, it's better to overcommunicate. Reassure them that their goals are your goals.

The Paranoid Coworker

What is it like to work with someone who manifests this type of character style? Since these individuals usually prefer autonomy, it's not likely that they will derive much pleasure from interacting on any work projects with you and may perceive such a work assignment as a "necessary evil." Naturally, they will be hyperalert to anything that smacks of criticism, so it's best to steer clear of this type of communication. These individuals will also be quite vigilant to whether you're advancing more quickly than they are, and whether you are considered to be more politically connected within the organization. Individuals with PPD often want to be part of the "in crowd" but seem to lack the skills and trust to pull this off. Instead, they will watch from the outside and often become more isolated from the work group as a result. They may feel that you're out to steal their ideas or take credit for their work. Therefore, it's best to be clear in your communication with these individuals as to what your intentions are and that you believe in giving credit where credit is due. Also beware of their filing lawsuits or grievances against you, if they feel they have been treated unjustly. We have seen that the majority of lawsuits are filed by this type of coworker.

Working with the Paranoid Coworker

Although the coworker with PPD may appear to be very autonomous, confident, and independent, they often will need your respect (Oldham & Morris 1990), so it's not a bad idea to express or demonstrate your respect where possible and where it does not seem patronizing or insincere. It is also better to develop, if possible, a sense of cooperation with this person, rather than getting competitive with them. Competition will only breed a sense of mistrust. Avoid teasing or humor at their expense (Oldham & Morris), as these individuals are naturally rather thin-skinned and usually don't like being made fun of or being the brunt of jokes. If you're accused of disloyalty or some other transgression, don't be flip and dismiss or invalidate the concern. Instead, it's better to reassure this person that you respect them and that you want to maintain a good working relationship with them. As indicated earlier, paranoids will often try to pass blame onto others. If this occurs and you find yourself being the brunt of the blame game, Oldham and Morris suggest that it's probably better to talk with this person and express your feelings about the situation without criticizing or finding fault. Naturally, the thing to avoid is getting into a debate with such an individual. They won't fight fairly and will see the situation as highly threatening

The Paranoid Subordinate

Having someone working for you who manifests PPD is no picnic. Although these individuals can often be excellent workers (especially the obdurate paranoid subtype), they are difficult to manage when it comes to giving feedback and helping to shape their work habits. Because of their tendency to misinterpret the intentions and motives of others, they will often become angry and easily offended by seemingly benign comments or constructive criticism. What may be helpful criticism to one worker becomes a major slight or humiliation to the paranoid employee. Performance-review time becomes a major pain in your neck, as you anticipate the defenses going up, the threats to call their attorney, their threats to report you to the Labor

Board, and similar such defensive posturing. Even a suggestion like, "Could you work on getting to work on time?" becomes a major federal case with the paranoid employee. It's so difficult to offer feedback that most administrators will tiptoe around these individuals, having found that it is better to avoid conflict, if possible. It won't be long, however, before someone upsets the apple cart. Such was the case with a janitorial worker who was referred for a psychological evaluation to determine fitness for duty. Upon entering my office, the employee asked if he could record the session for his attorney to listen to at later date. I agreed, and the interview proceeded. He then went on to explain to me, in precise detail, how long it should take to clean the sinks, empty the garbage, take the garbage out, sweep the floors, and so on. His complaint was that he felt that his fellow coworkers did not allow him the proper amount of time to perform each of these tasks in the "correct" manner. He had timed each task down to the split second, and what was irking him was that his coworker and foreman, whom he had threatened a lawsuit against, had been performing their jobs more quickly and probably less efficiently, presumably so that they could get their shift over with more quickly. The paranoid employee felt that their disruption of his routine was a direct attempt to humiliate him. At one point in the session, after listening to twenty minutes of time schedules, I felt like screaming, "You're talking about collecting garbage—this is not rocket science!" For the person with PPD, this often is the type of triviality on which their life is focused. This example speaks to the narcissistic edge that Millon talks about, i.e., that they feel they are so special or important that people actually go out of their way to harass them. This is not to say that some individuals with PPD are not harassed by their coworkers or superiors. Unfortunately some people get a charge out of harassing others, and the PPD individual is sometimes very easy to set off. Beck and Freeman (1990), in their treatment of PPD, indicate that the therapist must often sift out who the malevolent individuals are in this person's environment, and part of their treatment involves developing better instincts regarding who they can and cannot trust, rather than to assume that no one is trustworthy.

Although individuals with PPD often function better when left to work more independently or with little supervision, not all job situations are able to afford their workers that kind of autonomy. At one point, I thought one of my PPD patients had found the ideal job when he decided to become a park ranger. Although he liked the work itself and enjoyed being out in nature, he still had to interact with a supervisor and fellow park rangers. Even this somewhat minimal contact was enough to keep him on guard, hypervigilant, and mistrustful of their intentions.

Working with the Paranoid Subordinate

It's important to keep paranoid employees informed in a friendly, nonthreatening way. It is also good to give them feedback on how they are doing, but to play up the positives enough that any negative can be suggested with a minimal amount of disruption or perceived threat. Don't ask for much personal information, nor should you disclose much about your personal life, as it will only lead to possible misinterpretations of your intentions. Keep your conversations with this person to the point, cordial, but somewhat impersonal. It is also best to be very specific about things you would like done, not leaving much to the imagination. Explain why you would like things done in this manner, so that this individual does not feel that you're singling them out in some way. Again, if changes need to be made, explain why.

Many work teams will often poke fun at one another or play practical jokes in order to break up monotony. While this may be fine for most work groups, if you have someone with PPD working as part of the team, you need to let the others know that it's not a good idea to tease one another or play jokes. This needs to be done without naming the paranoid as the reason for your concerns. Otherwise, you will just make things worse for them. One administrator of a social-service office was suspended from his job when several of his subordinates had played a practical joke on a fellow employee who was being transferred to another department. Although the practical joke was meant in "good fun," it backfired terribly. The staff had concocted a costume for this person that reflected their ethnicity, which turned out to be a caricature that was very offensive to another coworker of the same ethnicity. The other coworker had paranoid personality tendencies, and she interpreted the practical joke as a direct assault on her ethnic background. The whole office was disrupted over the incident, and it took the new administrator months before he was able to get the staff functioning as a team again.

Conclusion

As you can see from the descriptions above, if you find yourself in work situation with a paranoid personality, it doesn't mean that you must pack your belongings and move to another state. What we do suggest, however, is that you be mindful of your interactions with these individuals, weigh out what you say before you say it, and tread lightly. One of the ways that beginning therapists are trained to spot Paranoid Personality Disorder is to ask themselves if they feel they are walking on eggshells with the patient. If the answer is "Yes," then, chances are, you're either dealing with someone who is very critical or who is very paranoid. This does not mean that a working relationship is not possible, or that it is out of the question. There are instances where the paranoid person will develop trust in you, which has its positives and negatives. Once you are accepted or considered trustworthy, you will often become privy to family secrets and stories of betrayal. It is difficult, sometimes, to remain their friend, as your loyalty will often come into question. This is why people who interact with paranoid individuals often stay at arm's length. You would be wise to do the same.

CHAPTER 13

Other Toxic Coworkers

Throughout this book, we have provided you with various instances where some toxic coworkers, administrators, and subordinates may not actually manifest an actual personality disorder, but may instead be suffering from some other type of problem or disorder. Some of these individuals may *seem* like they have a personality disorder, but they really suffer from one of the disorders we will discuss in this chapter.

There have been two major studies investigating how many Americans suffer from various psychiatric disorders. These two surveys, called the Epidemiological Catchment Area Survey (Robins et al. 1988) and the National Comorbidity Study (Kessler et al. 1994), both came to some similar conclusions. They concluded that the three most frequently occurring psychiatric disorders were anxiety disorders (such as phobias and generalized anxiety disorders), mood disorders (including both depression and manic depression), and substance-use disorders (which includes both alcohol and drug addictions). Naturally, administrators, coworkers, and employees who have with these types of disorders will present problems in just about any work setting.

Because it would be too time consuming to list the diagnostic criteria for each of these disorders and to discuss how these disorders impact on administrators, coworkers, and subordinates we will discuss an overview of the main symptoms of each disorder and how these symptoms may present in the workplace.

Anxiety Disorders

Anxiety disorders are a group of disorders composed of some rather different and complex disorders. For example, under the umbrella of anxiety disorders are included Panic Disorder, Social Phobia, Specific Phobia, Agoraphobia, Generalized Anxiety Disorder, Posttraumatic Stress Disorder (PTSD), Acute Stress Disorder, and Obsessive Compulsive Disorder (OCD). Obviously, the common denominator to all of these disorders is anxiety. This anxiety is often experienced as both an emotion and a physical state, as the person suffering from anxiety experiences intense dread and racing thoughts, along with heart pounding and increased breathing rate. It seems that, for each of these disorders, anxiety can arise in different intensities and in various settings or situations. For example, a person with Panic Disorder will experience intense anxiety and will often fear they're having a heart attack. The panic is often extremely intense, but it may only last for fifteen or twenty minutes. For the person suffering from Panic Disorder, those fifteen or twenty minutes may seem like an eternity. The person suffering from PTSD may experience acute anxiety when presented with a stimulus similar to those associated with the original traumatic situation. A friend of mine who is a Vietnam veteran will experience incredible anxiety when he hears helicopters or smells diesel fuel, stimuli that were constants back when he served in Vietnam. The person with Obsessive Compulsive Disorder may experience anxiety if they're prevented from washing their hands or vacuuming the carpet for an hour, rituals that they perceive as helping them to decrease their anxiety. The person with a Specific Phobia has an irrational fear about being exposed to a specific thing, such as riding in elevators, a fear of doctors, or feeling anxious in an enclosed space. The person with a Social Phobia may feel anxious speaking in front of group, eating in a restaurant, or using a public rest room. Finally, a person with Generalized Anxiety Disorder may feel anxious to some degree nearly every day, without any rhyme or reason. They experience anxiety all of the time, regardless of the situation. So, how do these anxiety disorders cause problems in the workplace? Here are a few examples.

Some may think that it would be nearly impossible for a person in a leadership role to experience an anxiety disorder; but the reality is quite the contrary. There are many instances where bosses, managers, and other administrators can and do suffer from an anxiety disorder, and Panic Disorder is among the most frequently occurring on the list. Panic Disorder can be crippling for workers at any level, as it can often result in missed time from work, visits to the local emergency room, and a general restriction of activities. What folks with Panic Disorder often conclude is that they can prevent panic by leading a restricted, insular life. So, they begin to decline invitations to work-related conferences, meetings, company picnics, or other such events. This is why it's not unusual to see Panic Disorder coupled with Agoraphobia. Agoraphobia, which literally means "fear of the market place," is another subtype of anxiety disorder, whereby the person feels more anxiety the further they venture away from home. In some instances, people with Panic Disorder and Agoraphobia end up leaving their jobs or going out on disability, because they can no longer travel to and from their jobs without experiencing panic-level anxiety. It's often difficult for coworkers, bosses, and subordinates to understand what is going on with the person who suffers from Panic Disorder and Agoraphobia, as these disorders defy rational logic. If you've never experienced a panic attack, you naturally will have trouble relating to someone who dreads the mere possibility that they may have one.

Phobias are also high on the list of those anxiety disorders that most often impact work performance. The following are some examples: A vice president for a medical supply company suffered from a Specific Phobia of airline travel. For years, she would work her schedule around her phobia by traveling to various business meetings either by train or car. This resulted in quite a loss of time and efficiency for her and lost opportunities for advancement. Another example is the computer analyst who was anxious about using the public rest room where he worked, as often occurs in a Social Phobia. This man would actually travel twenty minutes to his home if he had to urinate. Yet another example is that of an executive for a large utility company who suffered from a fear of public speaking. His job required that he speak at various board meetings, energy commission meetings, and the like. He would often load up on Valium or take a few stiff drinks of scotch in order to fortify himself to speak in front of a group. Although it's not uncommon for many individuals with phobias to work their lives around their anxiety, they may not always be successful if their job depends on their performing certain job functions. One manager was let go from her job because she refused to speak in front of groups. What often happens in situations where individuals are asked to face their anxieties and fears is that many strive to continue living their lives around the phobia rather than facing them. Phobias about airline travel, public speaking, or urinating in public rest rooms must usually be confronted at some point if the person is to survive in the workplace.

A coworker who is experiencing an anxiety disorder may not be all that prone to admitting to or discussing their anxiety with you, depending on how close a personal relationship you have. For example, a coworker who experienced some traumatic event may not be likely to discuss this with you: that would be the case with Posttraumatic Stress Disorder. A car accident may be more likely to be discussed or revealed than an attack or sexual assault if they had been so attacked in the past.

What you may see is that person fading in and out of work, as their attention waxes or wanes. They may seem preoccupied or unable to focus. This type of behavior may be common with a person who is going through any personal crisis, such as a coworker going through a divorce or who is having a personal problem with a teenage son or daughter. However, with an anxiety disorder, the behavior may be more pervasive and usually does not depend on a particular situational crisis going on in the person's life at the time.

Anxious coworkers with Obsessive Compulsive Disorder may present as being fastidious or anxious over dirt and details. There is naturally some overlap between Obsessive Compulsive Disorder and Obsessive Compulsive Personality Disorder, but the essential feature of OCD is that these folks engage in very specific rituals or obsessional thoughts in order to allay their anxieties. For example, an OCD nurse might check and recheck and recheck again to make certain that the medication cabinet is locked, even though, rationally, he knows he locked it the first time. People with OCD may worry over the slightest thing that is out of order, and may have a need to have extreme control in their work environment. Anxiety disorders become detrimental when the coworker's level of anxiety interferes with their work, they feel too distressed to function, or where their anxiety impairs or interferes with their ability to relate to other coworkers. An administrative assistant who suffered from Generalized Anxiety Disorder once commented that she was so consumed by anxious feelings all day that she had a difficult time staying focused on her daily work tasks. She also found it hard to keep focused on her boss's schedule or those things her boss needed in order to function effectively.

If you have someone working for you who suffers from one of the aforementioned anxiety disorders, you probably have had to exercise a lot of patience. Anxious employees may take days off when they're in the midst of severe anxiety. They may come in late if they've had a panic attack or if they're anxious about some task they must perform during the day. They may shrink from making public presentations or will come up with excuse after excuse in order to get out of particular tasks. Again, they are not engaging in these avoidant behaviors in order to anger you, as would be the case with a Passive Aggressive Personality Disorder. They are avoiding simply in order to reduce their levels of anxiety. There is naturally an overlap between the Avoidant Personality Disorder (discussed in chapter 10) and some of these anxiety disorders. The difference is that individuals with anxiety disorders will usually tend to avoid particular situations or particular places, whereas the avoidant individual will tend to avoid interpersonal conflict almost completely.

It's sometimes difficult to motivate individuals with anxiety disorders because their levels of anxiety will usually take precedence over all other concerns. If flying to San Diego for a business trip translates into a hefty bonus for someone with a phobia of airline travel, the true phobic will likely avoid flying no matter what the incentive. Most phobics will learn to avoid jobs where they have to confront their fears. For example, if you have a phobia of snakes, you avoid working in climates where snakes are plentiful or you avoid working in jobs where snakes might be present, such as zoos, pet stores, or biology departments. However, while it's easy to avoid snakes, it is not quite as easy especially in some work settings to avoid things like air travel, public speaking, elevators, or other things that people often become phobic about. One systems engineer had actually forfeited obtaining his master's degree because his final project would have involved a lengthy oral presentation. Not having his master's held him back from promotions and salary increases.

In coping with a coworker, boss, or administrator with one of the aforementioned anxiety disorders, it's important to keep in mind that they may be battling the anxiety on a daily basis. They may be excellent workers when they are not in the midst of more severe anxiety, but when the anxiety hits, it can really derail their performance and efforts. We recommend that you try to be supportive of this person. You can do this by allowing them time off, to take a walk around the building, or to use relaxation exercises if they're feeling stressed out. While your overall approach would be one of support, you should also encourage this person to utilize employee assistance services. Obviously, these suggestions are easier to implement if you are the boss or coworker dealing with an anxiety-ridden employee or coworker. When dealing with a boss who suffers from anxiety, it's probably best to be supportive, but not to encroach on their turf. Find out from them how you can help. If, for example, they need to take time off, find out what tasks they want you to accomplish in the interim just as if your boss was out with some physical illness. This will usually go a long way in terms of building a less stressful working relationship. There may be times when you find yourself picking up the slack but, hopefully, not for long. We also suggest that you avoid become an enabler, i.e., someone who ends up enabling the illness to continue by doing all the work for that individual. Usually, if the anxious person is making efforts to deal with the problem through counseling or therapy, then you probably won't have to worry about being an enabler. If they are trying to work on their problem, you should begin to see improvement in this person's ability to manage their anxiety.

Mood Disorders

There are two major subtypes of mood disorder, Unipolar Depression and Bipolar Depression. Unipolar Depression refers to individuals who experience depressive moods that permeate their lives. The subtypes of Unipolar Depression (Major Depression and Dysthymia) really only differ in terms of degree or intensity. Individuals with Major Depression usually have difficulty functioning in everyday life. They feels pervasive sadness, and they often cannot sleep or will want to sleep all the time. People with major depression often lose interest in life—they lack energy, and nothing really seems to give them much pleasure. They usually withdraw from all social interactions. These individuals also report having difficulty in concentrating, which can often lead to difficulty with remembering things. Naturally, all of these behaviors can have an impact on a person's ability to perform their job. With Dysthymia, the person feels much of the same symptoms of Major Depression, but to a lesser degree. The person with Dysthymia usually is able to function, although the fact that they're depressed much of the day, every day, naturally will have an impact on their work performance. With Major Depression and Dysthymia, the symptoms must last for at least six months before the person meets the criteria to be diagnosed with these disorders.

The impact that depression can have on work performance is pervasive. Especially in those occupations that require social interaction, cooperation, and high levels of concentration. Workers suffering from depression will usually withdraw socially, physically, or emotionally. One middle manager talked about closing her door for hours while she sat in her office, crying and staring out the window. A motor-vehicle agency clerk spoke of how he couldn't hide from coworkers or customers at the front desk, so he would withdraw emotionally by his facial expression and lack of responsiveness. An outside salesman for a paper manufacturer spoke of how she would drive to a local park and sit and stare out at the duck pond all day. People suffering from depression usually have a way to withdraw. Because they find being around people to be emotionally draining work is emotionally draining and sometimes just getting through the day is all that these folks can muster.

In working with someone who is going through a depression, whether it be a coworker or subordinate, is usually better to be supportive. Offer to talk if the person wants to, but don't assume they will take you up on your offer. Also, your job is not to become their therapist, and it is usually best to encourage the person to seek therapy or to take the first step by calling employee assistance.

Naturally, you must tread lightly here. In making a suggestion such as this, you don't want your coworker or employee to think you are labeling them as "crazy." Instead, you might be better off speaking of their past accomplishments or the energy they were able to put into past projects, and how you see how hard they are trying just to get through the day. You may speak of other people (without naming names, of course) you've known who benefited from receiving counseling or medication, and how they were able to get back on track. In many instances, your coworker or employee may agree but may feel it's "not worth it." Depressed people often suffer from tremendous guilt and low self-esteem, which makes it difficult for them to feel they are deserving of your help, let alone the help of a professional. Some will feel that they just need to tough it out on their own. Problems arise, however, when their work slips to such a point that you, as a boss, must begin to cite them on their poor performance. Here, it may be necessary to take a stronger approach and mandate a psychiatric or psychological evaluation. Naturally, under the Americans with Disabilities Act, a person cannot be fired for a mental illness. However, medical leave may be granted for someone who is not able to perform their job adequately because of a mental illness.

With Bipolar Disorders, there are usually two phases: The manic phase is characterized by extremely high levels of energy, talking a mile a minute, sometimes grandiose ideas of things they feel they can accomplish, inflated self-esteem, thoughts racing, easy distractions and excessive activity in pleasurable, often risky activities (including gambling sprees, spending sprees, or sexual promiscuity). When individuals are in the midst of a manic phase, they are usually unaware of their condition or may be so energized that they don't want the feeling to stop. Unfortunately, what goes up must come down, and when these folks crash into depression, they often crash very hard. This is one reason why Bipolars are considered at risk for suicide. It's also not unusual for bipolar individuals to abuse alcohol or drugs, which just adds to their problems and can even further increase their risk for suicidal action or other dangerous, risk-taking behavior.

In working with someone who manifests a Bipolar Disorder, one would usually expect to see depressive behavior much of the time, since the depressive phase usually lasts much longer (usually four to six months or longer) than the manic phase, which usually lasts a few days to a couple of weeks, at most. Therefore, coping with the person with a Bipolar Disorder who is in the depressed phase is very similar to coping with Major Depression or Dysthymia. However, be prepared for a real roller-coaster ride during the manic phase. Manics can often wear out the people around them. They will often expect you to keep up with them. In a work setting, they can be creative and humorous (Robin Williams' stand-up comedy has a definite manic style, i.e., fast-paced and sharp-witted), or they can be demanding, argumentative, and quite caustic, making inappropriate remarks. The reactions of most coworkers or employees will be to steer clear of someone who is in the midst of a manic phase, although there are times when their energy levels can be contagious. The difficult part often is trying to do "damage control" in the wake of one of your boss's or coworker's manic phases. Missed days from work, coming in late, making outlandish demands on employees, or spending foolishly or recklessly may all be part of the manic behavior—a lot for someone to have to sweep up afterward. It is also unlikely that one can make an appeal to someone in a manic phase to seek help (or to resume their medication). It's probably easier for a boss or manager to corral the manic employee into seeking help or speaking with the employee-assistance professional. However, the boss or manager may not see the manic behavior if the employee "disappears" during the height of their manic phase. When employees take off from work for periods of time for vague "personal" reasons or vague medical reasons, it may be difficult to tell if the person is experiencing an emotional problem of some sort. That is why managers and administrators are often taught to judge by the employee's work behavior (e.g., work performance, tardiness, absenteeism), which are observable and can be documented. Unfortunately, it may be more likely to get the bipolar to accept a recommendation for evaluation or treatment once they begin the downward spiral into the depressive phase. The problem is that this is the time when the person is most vulnerable. Fortunately, when bipolar individuals do seek treatment, stay on their medication, and stay clear of alcohol and drugs, they often do quite well and make excellent employees, managers, and coworkers.

Substance-Use Disorders

One of the myths about alcoholism and drug addiction is that, in order to be considered an alcoholic or addict, one must drink or use drugs every day, and the person must have lost everything. With all that has appeared in the media (e.g., movies such as *Clean and Sober* or *When a Man Loves a Woman*), it's more widely accepted that alcoholism and drug addiction can take many forms and can affect many people. We always tell our students that alcoholism and drug addictions are "equal opportunity" diseases—they can, and do, affect anyone and everyone. So, in the workplace, no one is immune. What is tricky is that, even though alcoholism and drug addiction have a finite number of symptoms, the way in which these symptoms can be expressed is nearly infinite. The other tricky part is being able to see addiction in its early phases. The other unfortunate part is that most alcoholics and addicts will manifest denial of their disease, and denial of the unmanageability caused by their drinking or drug use. They see alcohol and drugs as their solution to problems, not as something that is causing problems. And that, in a nutshell, is what alcoholism and chemical addictions are: when a person's drinking or drug use causes serious life problems. Given their denial, most alcoholics and addicts have an elaborate "alibi system" in place, which consists of rationalizations, excuses, and justifications for their drinking or drug use. Often, the alcoholic or addict will project blame onto others, "My spouse is driving me crazy," or "The job is too stressful." Sure, husbands and wives do experience conflict, and certainly some jobs are highly stressful, but not everyone drinks or uses drugs in response to the stress.

How do substance-use problems manifest in the workplace? Usually by erratic behavior. The person may be fine and functioning one day, the next they can't even hold a pencil. They are making a million-dollar sale one day, and the next they are calling in sick. The list goes on and on. Erratic behaviors and mood are also found toward other coworkers or employees. They may be kind, helpful, and friendly one day, while caustic and surly the next, guilt-ridden and contrite the next. Sure, everyone has a bad day every now and then, but with alcoholics and addicts, there is a pattern of this type of behavior. Some alcoholics and addicts can be adept at not letting their addiction interfere with their jobs, especially in the early stages of the disease. So it's not unusual to see more subtle signs in which their addiction is impacting on their work. For example, lowered efficiency, missed deadlines, withdrawal from cooperative interaction at work, or sporadic absenteeism.

For the employee who is trying to cope with an alcoholic boss or manager, it is usually best to steer clear of them when they are in the midst of any drinking or drug use. Basically, trying to talk with someone who is drunk or stoned is a waste of time. It is much better to talk with them when they're not under the influence. If the alcoholic or addict is caustic or critical, as is so often the case, don't take their remarks seriously. Often, the feelings that are expressed when the person is under the influence or in the midst of a hangover are merely the by-products of the substance, and not the person's true feelings. Employees often feel intimidated by an alcoholic boss or manager, much like a child is intimidated by a mean, vitriolic alcoholic parent. We have worked with employees who have been in these situations and their options are, unfortunately, limited. For example, if they were go above their alcoholic boss (say, to the board of directors, board of trustees, or anyone higher up the ladder), they fear they will be perceived as disloyal and targeted for retribution. So, why take the risk, right? There are many employees who decide it is safer to suffer in silence and live to fight another day than to try to intervene in some way. Employee-assistance counselors would be an excellent resource to tap to help you deal with this manager or boss effectively and with less chance of retaliation. When this option is not possible, it's best to begin looking for another job or request a transfer to another work unit. Unfortunately, given the progressive nature of alcoholism and addiction, these situations tend to get much worse before they will get better.

With an employee or coworker, it is somewhat easier to intervene, because you're not dealing with the risk of losing your job. Again, in companies where employee assistance is available, it's better to consult with a counselor, as they will probably know the procedures on how to set up an effective intervention (a gathering of people close to the individual who confront him or her about the problem in a loving, caring way). There are other ways to intervene on a one-to-one basis, but these usually are not as effective as an intervention done by a group of coworkers and family members. Given the denial system described earlier, alcoholics and addicts are quite adept at "explaining away the problem." A crew foreman for an auto manufacturer once remarked that, after trying to confront an alcoholic employee one-to-one, he walked away feeling that he had done something wrong—or that he had the problem, not the alcoholic. One intervention that was done with a bank vice president included her husband, some of her colleagues, the bank president, and a couple of her friends. The woman accepted what all these folks were saying and went into rehab as soon as the intervention was over. Today, she is happy, sober, and has received several commendations for outstanding work. The moral of the story is that interventions can and do work. However, we know that it's not always possible to do a formal intervention. In those instances, coworkers often need to learn to detach from the coworker's alcoholism or addiction. This means that you accept that you are not responsible for this person's addiction, and therefore, naturally, you are not responsible for their behavior or trying to change them. You can still like this coworker while not necessarily liking what they do when they drink or drug. After all, it is the addict or alcoholic whom you are trying to detach from physically and emotionally. One commercial airline crew got along great when they were flying and doing their jobs. On layovers, however, most refused to socialize with one flight attendant, because she would drink herself into oblivion when they would go out, and the others would have to "baby-sit" for her, making sure she got back to the hotel safely. These coworkers did not want to be responsible for her behavior when she was drinking, and were perfectly justified in this decision.

Attention Deficit Hyperactivity Disorder (ADHD): A Special Case

Do you remember those kids in school who just couldn't seem to stay in their seats, much to the teacher's chagrin? Do remember how they used to blurt out answers before they were called on? Did they tease you and butt into your games? Well, those kids are grown up now and out there in the workplace. Attention Deficit Hyperactivity Disorder, usually referred to as ADD or ADHD, has received a great deal of attention in the past several years. It has been recently recognized that this disorder does not necessarily go away when the child grows into adulthood. And, as the workplace becomes more and more complex and stressful, problems with ADD employees become more apparent and costly to the organization.

Although ADD is not a personality disorder per se, we believe it is a special case that deserves mention here because, in several ways, it is related to a personality disorder. First of all, many individuals with ADD also have accompanying personality disorders, as well. Secondly, ADD has the same type of stability and pervasiveness that personality disorders have. In other words, ADD sufferers usually quite resistant to change, even through psychotherapy, and the disorder affects the individual in a wide range of circumstances. However, while many personality disorders have psychological roots, ADD has been shown to be a problem with physiological underpinnings. It is believed by researchers that individuals with ADD have areas of the brain that don't function correctly. Areas of the brain regulate planning and organization, that are believed to be underactive.

The most common symptoms of this disorder are inattentiveness, distractibility, and impulsivity. Some individuals with ADD are hyperactive, but some can also be hypoactive (underactive).

Inattentiveness is the inability to pay attention and to sustain attention. People with ADD *can* pay attention to things that they like to do. For example, they can watch television for long periods of time, play video games, and watch a movie, if it's interesting. What the individual with ADD can't do, however, is make themselves pay attention when they don't want to. We've all been in boring meetings or dull presentations where we have to force ourselves to pay attention. For the person with ADD, this concentration becomes a nearly impossible task that requires tremendous effort.

The second major symptom, distractibility, means that people with ADD are easily pulled off tasks by other distractions. Mr. Walker, a computer programmer, came to work at 8:45 A.M.—fifteen minutes earlier than usual—and sat down in his cubicle. He was behind in his work and needed to finish up to project by 10 A.M. Recognizing that he forgot to put sugar in his coffee, he got up to look for some. "This will only take a moment," he thought. On the way, he stopped to chat with three individuals who passed him. When he returned to his cubicle, he realized that he'd forgotten to put sugar in his coffee—which had gotten cold. He took it to the microwave, and started reading what was posted on the bulletin board next to the microwave. He then returned to his workstation and booted up his computer. He realized that one of the labels on one of his floppy disks was beginning to come off so he got up to look for another one. He looked at the clock and saw that it was already 9:20 A.M. and he still hadn't gotten any work done. Working frantically, he got it done by 10:05 A.M. but arrived at his staff meeting without the disk. Constantly being pulled off the main job by minor distractions and the resulting inability to prioritize tasks are hallmarks of workers with ADD.

Impulsivity, the third factor, expresses itself in many different ways in the workplace. People with ADD often "leap before they look," and this behavior often gets them into quite a bit of hot water. For example, they are quite prone to putting their foot in their mouth, speaking before they think things through. One middle manager, for example, told his supervisor that it was a "stupid" idea to change the lighting in his office. Had he not been so impulsive, he would have used a milder word and perhaps realized that his boss was only trying to be helpful. Yet another way this impulsivity expresses itself in the workplace is when the employee with ADD interrupts. They are notorious for doing exactly this. You'll find it very difficult to express yourself with this person constantly interrupting you.

These three symptoms make it very difficult for the individual with ADD to organize themselves. Most can be quite scattered: their desks are a mess, they are constantly losing things (especially those things that are required for them to do the job), they always are showing up late, leave many things unfinished and are well known for their tendencies to procrastinate. They have an inability to prioritize and to put things in a proper sequence. One secretary with ADD was constantly sealing envelopes before she placed the letter in them, for example. It is often very difficult to understand them, because they have problems organizing their speech. "Over there, in that. I wrote some letters the other day. You know, for the maintenance account. I couldn't find the folders, could you do that?" might be the way an employee with ADD would tell his secretary to file the letters in the filing cabinet.

Individuals with ADD often develop secondary symptoms beyond the primary physiological ones. For example, as a result of usually being "problem children," they were often criticized. By the time they get to be adults, they have become hypersensitive to criticism and avoid it by blaming others. Point out a flaw, and they are bound to respond by pointing the finger at someone else. Yet another symptom is that ADD people do not like to take direction; they don't like being told how to do something. As a result of the disorder, they have spent a lifetime learning to do things their own way, to work around the disorder. Another secondary symptom is argumentativeness. Because they're tired of being blamed for things and criticized, as well as always being told to do things differently, they hate to be wrong and will often argue at great length with you. Naturally, in a workplace setting where the ability to take correction and direction is essential to the healthy functioning of the organization, this behavior is toxic. And, it can be infuriating to those working around them.

Individuals with ADD can seem very insensitive and self-centered, much like the narcissist. But there are some differences here. This insensitivity stems from the fact that these employees have spent a great deal of energy trying to organize themselves. Consequently, they haven't spent a lot of time learning how to read other people and consider their feelings. Because of this necessary self-absorption, the employee will often talk incessantly and never really seem to listen to what other people are saying. A machine-shop worker with ADD once quipped that having ADD was like walking on a tightrope while juggling ten balls—it takes everything you've got. And everyone else in the organization keeps throwing you more, expecting you to juggle them as well.

Many individuals with ADD can be quite talented and productive workers, very valuable to the organization. Many people with ADD are above average in intelligence and can have a variety of interests and activities that they can bring to the workplace. Many of these people are quite good at the computer and knowledgeable about the Internet, for example. Also, they like to "multitask," or do several things at the same time. The key to working effectively with these individuals is often to let them do things their own way and not try to pigeonhole them into some arbitrary standard. They march to the tune of a different drummer. In fact, many researchers of the disorder suggest that ADD is not a disorder at all, but rather a distinctive style of doing things.

How the Organization Can Cope with or Avoid Toxic Coworkers

What all of the toxic workers in this chapter have in common is that their disorders, are treatable. Naturally, not all will go to or respond to treatment. However, when compared to treating personality disorders, which is a long-term and arduous task, these disorders are more responsive to treatment. Everyone probably knows an alcoholic or addict who has been through many rehab programs, only to find that they drank or used drugs hours or days after discharge. Yet, we also know many people who did get clean and sober. It does happen, but no one knows when it will happen. The same holds true for some of the anxiety and mood disorders. Some people will respond well to one treatment and not another, one therapist and not another, Prozac but not Paxil, Lithium but not Eskalith. Sometimes treatment can involve a degree of trial and error before the right combination of treatment and/or medications is found. We wish we could say that this was an exact science, but from years of clinical practice we know it's not. With personality disorders, precise treatment regimens are even more elusive, although some personality disorders are more amenable to treatment than others. In the event, that you do find yourself in an intolerable situation with a toxic boss or coworker, and there is no visible means to deal with this person, it may be better to cut your losses and seek other employment. It is always best to do this in a non-disgruntled way, without burning bridges. Brandon Toropov (1997), in a book entitled, *The Art & Skill of Dealing With People: How to Make Human Motivation Work for You on the Job,* suggests several ways to leave an employer on good terms. For example, rather than verbally attacking your toxic boss, Toropov suggests that the employee show appreciation for those past occasions where this boss had helped you to work more efficiently. Or perhaps to compliment them on any help they've given you. Also, and most importantly, get a letter of recommendation from this boss or manager *before* you move on to your next job.

But what can corporations or small companies do in order to avoid bringing toxic workers into the fold? Is there a way to avoid hiring people who will only end up costing the company in the long run? Couldn't psychological tests, such as personality tests, be used to screen out potentially toxic workers? In order to answer this question, we will briefly explore the issue of psychological testing, because it is an area where there is tremendous controversy. This controversy began shortly after the passage of the Civil Rights Act of 1964, when judges began to make distinctions between intentional discrimination (called "disparate treatment") and unintentional discrimination (called "disparate impact"). In a landmark case, *Griggs v. Duke Power Company*, the plaintiff claimed that African American males who applied to work at the Duke Power Company in North Carolina were being discriminated against because all applicants were required to have a high school diploma and pass two intelligence tests. The court concluded that this resulted in disparate impact on African American applicants (McWhirter 1994). Since that time, it was determined that psychological tests could only be given if the test was reliable (it would produce the same or similar results if repeated), valid (the test was true to its purpose), and the test was job-related. In other words, you could not give a typing test to someone who would be working in food service. Therefore, any employer who uses a personality test (such as the Minnesota Multiphasic Personality Inventory) or the Millon Clinical Multiaxial Inventory must prove that it is job related. The other caveat to testing is that the Americans with Disabilities Act (ADA) bars the use of any medical test or asking about alcohol, drug use, or past psychiatric problems until after a job offer has been made (DeAngelis 1996). We know of two situations where personality testing is used as a screening device. This would exist in the case of police officer candidates and in the case of daycare workers. The rationale is that personality testing is "job-related," because being psychologically healthy is an essential component of being able to care for children and is also essential for anyone entrusted with protecting the safety of others. Usually, these tests are administered only after a job offer has been made, and would therefore not be considered a violation of the ADA standards. In other words, a person with a mental disorder would, ostensibly, not be restricted from taking the job. Under the ADA, they would need to be afforded "reasonable accommodation," so that their psychological disability would not preclude them from employment. Personality testing remains quite controversial and, if used in settings other than daycare or police work, the company administering the test would have the burden of proof in justifying that the testing is job-related. It may be dubious whether psychological testing, and particularly personality testing, could be justified in other settings. How then might employers be able to screen for toxic workers?

The job interview and references are the most obvious source of information. In the past, there were few restrictions that existed for what could be asked in an interview and what could be said or written in a reference letter. The restrictions that do exist in interviewing usually revolve around discrimination or disparate treatment issues. This is why human-resource professionals cannot ask an applicant about their marital status, whether they have children or want children, child-care arrangements, whether they are an illegal alien, whether they have been arrested, their height or weight, their religious preference, or whether or not they have any physical or psychological disabilities. These are all areas that could be read as discrimination if the person is refused a job offer. McWhirter suggests that it is best to stick to the job description and to ask the applicant questions specifically pertaining to the job. So, instead of asking whether a person has a disability, the applicant can be asked if they can perform the specific functions of the job. It's okay to ask about prior work experience, personal strengths and weaknesses, and what the applicant's goals are. While it is not permissible to ask about alcohol or drug use, it is okay to ask about how the applicant manages stress, given that most jobs involve some degree of stress. It's also permissible to ask about the person's résumé, which may provide you with some insights into their character. Astute interviewers will look at body language, such as any signs of discomfort, any mannerisms or unusual habits, eye contact, and the like. The applicant's approach to the interview and their overall attitude is also important. Does the person seem likable and accessible? Do they seem like someone who is a good team player? You may ask for situations where they've worked on group projects and instances of solitary work and what functions they performed. These types of questions are permissible especially if they pertain to the job the person is applying for, e.g., if the job involves solitary work or cooperative work. Basically, the goal here is to get a sense of interpersonal style and a sense of whether the applicant can work with others effectively. Having done several psychological screenings of police officer candidates, we've found it helpful to come up with various scenarios that a police officer might deal with on the job and have the candidate respond with how they would deal with such situations. You might try the same, keeping in mind the characteristics of the disorders you've learned about here.

Naturally, no letter of reference will tell you about an employee's personality disorders. Often, a reference will only give you the dates of the applicant's employment with their former employer and whether or not the former employer would hire this person back. Not much information, is it? These restrictions protect the employer from getting sued for bias and also protect the employee, by preventing a disgruntled employer who might have treated the applicant abusively from seeking retribution because the applicant left their employ. But are the letters of reference even worth checking? Sometimes they are. There may be instances where a former employer may tip off a prospective employer to a problem employee. Remember the old adage, "If you don't have something nice to say about a person, don't say anything at all"? Usually, if the employee was a good worker and got along well with everyone at their former job, then the former employer will happily volunteer information and accolades. However, if the employee was problematic the former employer may give only the required information (e.g., date of hire, last day of employment, job title, etc.), or they may simply refer the prospective employer to human resources, thereby avoiding liability for any negative comments that might be made. Therefore, the lack of information becomes the "tip off" in many instances. The only time when this may not hold true is where the employee was nonproblematic but their former boss resented their leaving. A narcissistic or paranoid administrator, for example, may feel slighted or offended when a well-liked, hardworking employee moves on. However, a good prospective employee will usually be able to supply other references from within the company to verify their prior work without denigrating their former boss. So, as a rule, you should get letters of reference and/or verbal recommendations and figure them into the information you gather as a part of your employee-selection process.

In a book entitled *Workplace Hostility: Myth and Reality* by Gerald Lewis and Nancy Zare (1999), the problem of how to avoid hiring toxic, disruptive coworkers is considered. The authors recommend that employers contract with outside job-screening agencies who will conduct a preemployment screening. At one time, these preemployment screening agencies were only utilized in hiring upper-management personnel. Today, however, they can be utilized to screen workers at any level. These agencies will often utilize psychologists who are able to conduct more in-depth interviews and who will also administer psychological tests, as part of the screening. They can conduct more detailed depth background checks of the applicant, which would include driving, military, credit, work, and criminal records. Another strategy suggested by Lewis and Zare is to utilize other employees in the screening process. Here, interviews are set up not only with the brass, but also with those employees with whom the person will be hired to work. These employees are often adept at telling whether the applicant will be a "good fit" with their team. They can also help the new employee adjust once they're hired. For this reason, some companies will also involve employees in the orientation process of the new employee.

What about situations where a potentially violent, destructive, or abusive worker has passed through the screening process and now is wreaking havoc in your company? How can corporations or organizations deal with or manage these toxic workers effectively? We all know of horror stories where school boards have spent hundreds of thousands of dollars to buy an ineffective or caustic school superintendent out of their contract. Or where boards of directors have paid huge sums in order to buy out a CEO or some other executive-level administrator. Unfortunately, this is sometimes considered to be "the cost of doing business," but could these situations have been avoided? It is sometimes just as costly to deal with a toxic coworker, such as the kind we have discussed throughout this book. Take, for example, the following case scenario. Mark is a police officer with a local municipality who is caught using drugs on the job. It later comes out that he was selling drugs as well. This is a clear-cut case where dismissal is warranted, right? Well, prior to being fired, Mark goes to rehab and seeks help. He challenges his dismissal on the grounds of "wrongful termination." Under the Americans with Disabilities Act (ADA), Mark would be considered to be suffering from a substance-use disorder and the job must provide reasonable accommodation. However, Mark also violated the rules of conduct of his job as a police officer. What is the right solution to this dilemma? Prior to passage of the ADA, the answer was clearer. Then, even if you had a mental-health or substance-use disability, you still were required to live up to the rules of conduct of your job. Today, this issue is less clear. For example, let's say that Marie is working as an administrative assistant to a corporate VP. Marie begins to have a rather torrid love affair with Mr. Jones in accounting. When Mr. Jones breaks up with Marie, she goes into a tirade at work and then goes to his home and boils his kid's pet rabbit. (Sound familiar?) Marie's boss can no longer take her screaming at Mr. Jones, coming in late for work, and her threats to harm herself. He decides to do the humane thing and refers Marie to the employee-assistance counselor. At this point, if Marie's conduct on the job continues to be unacceptable, her boss could not fire her on the basis of this conduct under the ADA. Firing her would be tantamount to firing her for having a psychological disability. If she is unfit for duty, she could be put out on disability, but she could not be fired. When she does return to work, her boss would also need to make reasonable accommodation because of her disability, if possible. This is where things get sticky, because in situations like this, what constitutes "reasonable accommodation"? What if Marie were to turn violent and start threatening to boil Mr. Jones? Again, she would need to be referred for a psychiatric evaluation immediately. If she were found to be a danger to herself or others, in most states she would be hospitalized. However, again under ADA, she could not be fired from her job. Instead, she most likely would remain out on disability until she would be considered (usually by psychiatric evaluation) safe to return to the workplace. If Marie refuses to take the medication her doctor prescribes to her or she refuses psycho-therapy, then she most likely would not be cleared to return to work or would not been deemed "fit to return to duty." But let's say that Marie were deemed "fit for duty"and her psychiatrist says she can safely return to work. Under ADA, her job would be open for her and her company would be forced into providing her with reason-able accommodations. In the event that she could not perform par-ticular job duties, then, again, "reasonable accommodation" would need to be made which could mean that she would be working dif-ferent hours or that she would be given cooling-off time if she got upset. Reasonable accommodation does not mean that a new job would be created for Marie; rather, accommodations would be made so that she could function within the context of her current job. What seems to be happening in the real world, however, is that supervi-sors and managers are hesitant to refer these toxic coworkers to employee assistance because it presupposes that the person may be suffering from some form of emotional disability or psychiatric prob-lem and, in making the referral, the employer ensures that the employee will be covered under the ADA. Instead, some supervisors or managers are being told "off the record" *not* to refer to employee assistance and, instead, to let the progressive disciplinary processes take place. In other words, if the employee is breaking company pol-icy or rules of conduct, then they are treated as any other employee who breaks rules of conduct. What other companies are providing in their contract with employees is a "rehabilitative opportunity." In other words, if a worker requires psychiatric or substance-abuse treatment, then they would be provided with the chance to go to treatment. However, once they are back on the job, the employee is expected to meet the code of conduct for the workplace. So, if the employee does not follow treatment recommendations, if they relapse or continue using drugs or alcohol, then the employer is not responsible for maintaining their employment.

Another area that corporations need to look at in dealing with the whole issue of toxic coworkers is what type of corporate climate they have created. Is it any surprise that a highly aggressive, cut-throat corporate culture will hire cut-throat, sociopathic managers or will somehow reinforce this type of behavior? After all, not all of

Hitler's Gestapo and SS commanders were psychopaths before the war started. We know that corporate climate can influence or shape behavior in the workplace. Lewis and Zare take the approach that workplace violence is a combination of both the personality of the potentially violent worker in combination with a "toxic workplace," which becomes the breeding ground for violence. They describe the toxic workplace as being characterized by several factors: limited opportunities (i.e., few opportunities for promotion or advancement, poor benefit packages, low wages); poor conditions (i.e., no say in decisions, inadequate resources, substandard facilities, and heavy workloads); ineffective management (i.e., management that is withholding, authoritarian, inflexible, or inconsistent); favoritism (i.e., certain employees are given preferential treatment or are not recognized for their hard work, rewards are given or taken from employees haphazardly); mistrust (i.e., companies that promote suspicion and mistrust among workers, managers, and owners); micromanagement (i.e., managers or administrators are constantly telling employees what to do and are constantly checking to see that the work is done the way they want it done); theory "X" management (i.e., the theory based on the presumption that employees are disinclined to work and must be forced to do so). Basically, toxic workplaces often embody a combination of the aforementioned characteristics. Now combine the effects of a toxic workplace with a toxic administrator, such as a narcissistic boss or manager, and you have a powder keg just waiting to be ignited.

In Conclusion

While there are many different types of toxic coworkers, bosses, and employees who inhabit the workplaces of America, there is also hope. There are ways to manage the stress they create and ways to cope with their idiosyncrasies and antics. In some instances it will be best to take an active, directive approach, while in others, it may be best to keep a low profile while you seek employment in a saner environment. Probably the worst thing to do is to give up hope or become overwhelmed by a sense of helplessness. For most Americans, choices for better working conditions do exist. Yet, the stresses of the American workplace have changed dramatically, as we have discussed throughout this book. Although technological advances have made our work easier in many ways, workers often find themselves battling stressors that arrive from many different sources, most notably from interpersonal interactions. Hopefully, we have touched upon some ideas and suggestions in this book that may help people caught up in the throes of workplace stress created not by the work itself but by the people one works with. We will leave you with this quote by Maxim Gorky from *Lower Depths* (1903): "When work is a pleasure, life is a joy. When work is duty, life is slavery."

References

Agho, A. O., J. L. Price, and C. W. Mueller. 1992. Discriminant validity of measure of job satisfaction, positive affectivity and negative
affectivity. *Journal of Occupational and Organizational Psychology*
185-196.

American Psychiatric Association. 1994. *Diagnostic and Statistical Manual of Mental Disorders*, Fourth Edition. Washington, DC:American
Psychiatric Association.

Babiak, P. 1995. When psychopaths go to work: A case study of an
industrial psychopath. *Applied Psychology: An International Review*
44:171-188.

Beck, A. T., A. Freeman, and Associates. 1990. *Cognitive Therapy of
Personality Disorders*. New York: Guilford Press.

Brown, J. A. C. 1961. *Freud and the Post-Freudians*. Middlesex, England: Penguin Books Ltd.

Cavaiola, A. A. and M. Schiff. 1988. Behavioral sequallae of physically and/or sexually abused chemically dependent adolescents.
Child Abuse & Neglect 12:181-188.

Cavaiola, A. and N. Lavender. 1999. *Personality disorders in the workplace*. Paper presented at the conference The American Psychological Association and the National Institute for Safety and Health.
Work, Stress and Health: Organization of Work in a Global Econ-
omy. Baltimore, MD. March.

Dauer, C. 1989. Stress hits 25 percent of workforce. *National Under-
writer*. 32:49-50.

DeAngelis, T. 1996. ADA confounds use of psychological testing.
APA Monitor, March, 24.

Dykeman, J. B. 1995. Handling violence in the white-collar workplace. *Managing Office Technology* 40-45.

Easer, R. and S. Lesser. 1965. Hysterical personality: A re-evaluation.
Psychoanalytic Review 34:390–402.

Eisenman, R. 1980. Effective manipulation by psychopaths. *Corrective and Social Psychiatry and Journal of Behavior Technology, Methods & Therapy* 26:116-118.

Ellis, A. 1962. *Reason and Emotion in Psychotherapy.* New York: Lyle Stuart.

Freud, S. 1908. Character and anal eroticism. In *The Standard, Edition of the Complete Psychological Works,* edited by J. Strachey.London, England: Hogarth Press

Fromm, E. 1947. *Man for Himself.* New York: Holt, Rinehart & Winston.

Goleman, D. 1998. *Working with Emotional Intelligence.* New York Bantam Books.

Gorky, M. 1903. *Lower Depths.* New York: Branden Publishers.

Greenwald, J. 1995. Is your 401(k) at risk? *Time* 146:24.

Gustafson, S. B., and D. R. Ritzer, 1995. The dark side of normal: A psychopathy-linked pattern called aberrant self-promotion. *European Journal of Pesonality.* 9:147-183.

Hare, R. D., A. E., Forth, and S. D. Hart. 1989. The psychopath as prototype for pathological lying and deception. In *Credibility Assessment,* edited by J.C. Yuille. Boston, MA: Kluwer Academic Publishers.

Hare, R. D. 1993. *Without Conscience: The Disturbing World of the Psychopaths Among Us.* New York: Simon & Schuster.

Haspur, T. J., and R. D. Hare. 1990. Psychopathy and attention. In *The Development of Attention: Research and Theory,* edited by J. T. Enns. North Holland: Elsevier Science.

Horney, K. 1950. *Neurosis and Human Growth.* New York: W. W. Norton.

Janis, I. L. 1972. *Victims of Groupthink: A Psychological Study of Foreign Policy Decisions.* Boston: Houghton Mifflin.

Johnson, S. 1994. *Character Styles.* New York: W. W. Norton.

Kelly, G. 1955. *The Psychology of Personal Constructs.* New York: Norton.

Kessler, R. C., K. A. McGonagle, S. Zhao, C. B. Nelson, M. Hughes, S. Eshleman, H. U. Wittchen, and K. S. Kendler. 1994. Lifetime and 12-month prevalence of DSM-IIIR psychiatric disorders in the United States. *Archives of General Psychiatry* 51:8-19

Lewey, L.A., and B. L. Davis. 1987. When techies manage. *Training and Occupational Journal* (October): 66-68.

Lewis, G. W., and N. C. Zare, 1999. *Workplace Hostility: Myth and Reality.* Philadelphia, PA: Taylor and Francis Group.

McDonald, J. J., and P. Lees-Haley. 1996. Personality disorders in the workplace: how they may contribute to claims of employment law violations. *Employee Relations* 22:57-80.

McWhirter, D. 1994. *The Personnel Policy Handbook for Growing Companies: How to Create Comprehensive Guidelines, Procedures, and Checklists.* Holbrook, MA: Bob Adams.

Meyer, R. 1999 *Case Studies in Abnormal Behavior.* Needham Heights, MA:Allyn-Bacon.

Miles, J. B. 1985. How to help troubled workers. *Computer Decisions.* 66-73.

Millon, T., and R. Davis 1996. *Disorders of Personality DSM IV and Beyond.* New York: John Wiley.

———— 2000. *Personality Disorders in Modern Life.* New York: John Wiley.

Moffie, R. P., D. J. Moffie, and R. B. Tower. 1985. Auditing the troubled employee. *The Internal Auditor* 30-36.

Oldham, J. M., and L. B. Morris. 1995. *New Personality Self- Portrait: Why You Think, Work, Love and Act the Way You Do.* New York: Bantam Books.

Robins, L. N., J. E., Helzer, T. R. Pryzbeck, and D.A. Regier. 1988. Alcohol disorders in the community: A report from the Epidemiologic Catchment Area. In *Alcoholism: Origins & Outcome,* edited by R. M. Ross and J. Barret. Nw York: Raven Press.

Toropov, B. 1997. *The Art & Skill of Dealing with People: How to Make Human Motivation Work for You on the Job.* New York: MJF Books.

Weiss, L. 1996. *A.D.D. on the Job: Making Your A.D.D. Work for You.* Dallas: Taylor Publishing.

Widom, C. S. 1977. A methodology for studying non-institutionalized psychopaths. *Journal of Counseling and Clinical Psychology* 45:674-683.

————. 1989. The cycle of violence. *Science.* 244:160-166.

Wouk, H. 1951. *The Caine Mutiny.* New York: Simon & Schuster.

More New Harbinger Titles

DANCING NAKED

Imaginative exercises help you embrace the uncertainties of today's job market and manage your career with confidence and maximum effectiveness.
Item DNCE $14.95

WORKING ANGER

A step-by-step program designed to help anyone who has had trouble dealing with their own anger or other people's anger at work.
Item WA $12.95

UNDER HER WING

In-depth interviews with dozens of women whose lives have been shaped by a mentor-protégé relationship share insights about developing mentoring relationships, avoiding common pitfalls, and benefiting from these unique and valuable alliances.
Item WING $13.95

MAKING THE BIG MOVE

An innovative collection of exercises and practical suggestions help you come to terms with the anxiety of a major relocation and make the transition an opportunity for personal growth.
Item MOVE $13.95

LIVING WITHOUT PROCRASTINATION

Provides effective techniques for unlearning counter-productive habits, changing paralyzing beliefs and attitudes, developing task-directed thinking, and attaining a new sense of purposefulness.
Item LWP $12.95

DON'T TAKE IT PERSONALLY

Shows you how to depersonalize your responses to rejection, establish boundaries that protect you from hurt, and develop a new sense of self-acceptance and self-confidence.
Item DOTA $15.95

Call toll-free 1-800-748-6273 to order. Have your Visa or Mastercard number ready. Or send a check for the titles you want to New Harbinger Publications, 5674 Shattuck Avenue, Oakland, CA 94609. Include $4.50 for the first book and 75¢ for each additional book to cover shipping and handling. (California residents please include appropriate sales tax.) Allow four to six weeks for delivery.

Prices subject to change without notice.

Some Other
New Harbinger Titles

Freeing the Angry Mind, Item 4380 $14.95

Living Beyond Your Pain, Item 4097 $19.95

Transforming Anxiety, Item 4445 $12.95

Integrative Treatment for Borderline Personality Disorder, Item 4461 $24.95

Depressed and Anxious, Item 3635 $19.95

Is He Depressed or What?, Item 4240 $15.95

Cognitive Therapy for Obsessive-Compulsive Disorder, Item 4291 $39.95

Child and Adolescent Psychopharmacology Made Simple, Item 4356 $14.95

ACT* on Life Not on Anger, Item 4402 $14.95

Overcoming Medical Phobias, Item 3872 $14.95

Acceptance & Commitment Therapy for Anxiety Disorders, Item 4275 $58.95

The OCD Workbook, Item 4224 $19.95

Neural Path Therapy, Item 4267 $14.95

Overcoming Obsessive Thoughts, Item 3813 $14.95

The Interpersonal Solution to Depression, Item 4186 $19.95

Get Out of Your Mind & Into Your Life, Item 4259 $19.95

Dialectical Behavior Therapy in Private Practice, Item 4208 $54.95

The Anxiety & Phobia Workbook, 4th edition, Item 4135 $19.95

Loving Someone with OCD, Item 3295 $15.95

Overcoming Animal & Insect Phobias, Item 3880 $12.95

Overcoming Compulsive Washing, Item 4054 $14.95

Angry All the Time, Item 3929 $13.95

Handbook of Clinical Psychopharmacology for Therapists, 4th edition,
    Item 3996 $55.95

Writing For Emotional Balance, Item 3821 $14.95

Surviving Your Borderline Parent, Item 3287 $14.95

When Anger Hurts, 2nd edition, Item 3449 $16.95

Calming Your Anxious Mind, Item 3384 $12.95

Ending the Depression Cycle, Item 3333 $17.95